Pathway to Peace
A 365 Day Devotional

Cara Poe

Poehouse Publishing—Abilene, TX
ISBN: 979-8-218-26022-4
Library of Congress Control Number: 2023915927
Title: *Pathway to Peace: A 365 Day Devotional*
Author: Cara Poe
Digital distribution | 2023
Paperback | 2023

Dedication

To my sister who went to hell with me.
To my children who forgave me.
To my parents who never gave up on me.
To my boss who took a chance on me.
and
To my husband who always believes in me.

I was a drug addict and an alcoholic. I was losing my mind and dying. I had not been able to look at myself in a very long time. On Tuesday, December 9, 2014, I caught a glimpse in the mirror as I was getting out of the shower. I was covered in track marks and bruises and my skin was gray. As I got closer to the mirror, I realized that what I was looking at was my corpse. In the mirror I could also see a man standing behind me. The brightest light that penetrated the darkest moment of my life. I very clearly heard the voice of Jesus that day. As He stood with me looking at my own death, He gave me the first true choice I had in 25 years. He told me that I could stop, follow Him, and I would live, or I could continue in the life I had, I would die very soon, and I would go to hell.

I died in that bathroom that day. Not in the physical sense of death. However, the creature that I had become met its demise in the arms of Christ. What happened after that was nothing short of a miracle. He transformed me by the renewing of my mind through the Word (Romans 12:2).

About 4 months later I watched a movie about Mother Teresa. In the movie she spoke with a reporter, and he asked her about her work. She took the pencil out of his hand and said, "the work is God's, like this pencil, I am only His tool." I immediately prayed, "God, make me your pencil!" Shortly after verses started to be highlighted as I read the Word and I began to write. These writings are the product of the overflow of that prayer.

My life has completely changed since that Tuesday. In repentance, I turned from the old and truly began to live as the new creation He promised I would become in 2 Corinthians 5:17. I developed a hunger that could only be satisfied by a feast created by God in His Word. I have a need to praise and an unquenchable desire to spend my life in worship. You will read several times that I have searched the bible over to find where it says that because I am a follower of Christ, now I get to have an easy life. That verse is not in the Word nor in any personal promise of the Lord. What I have learned is that life on this side of the resurrection is just as hard. However, because of Holy Spirit dwelling in me, I am able to rely on the strength of the Great I AM. Life continues to happen, the difference is as I walk through it with God, nothing is impossible (Luke1:37).

The pages in this book cover a number of years. Please keep in mind this is not a book of interpretation of the Word but of subjective application. I pray as you read it you find inspiration and edification through my personal experience with the verses herein. It is my hope that you relate to the darkness and find your own hope in the Light and your pathway to peace.

For by grace you have been saved through faith, and that not of yourselves; it is the gift of God, not of works, lest anyone should boast.

Ephesians 2:8-9

December 9, 2014 was the day that changed my life. I will recount and tell it as often as I can because it is the glory of God in my life. It was not the day either of my children were born. It had nothing to do with a man. It was not even the day I got sober. It was a Tuesday. Like every Tuesday before that, I was high. In this one, though, I was closer to death than I had ever been. Not just physically. I wanted death. Being alive was not working out for me. I was angry at God. I was so mad about the tree being in the garden. I would not stay in a room where His name was spoken. I wanted no part of the Creator because I just knew He wanted no part of me. The only work I was doing was in trying to get away from Him and the life I thought He had cursed me with. That did not matter to God though. He chose this day to offer me a choice. I had not had a choice in years. This day, 7 years ago, Jesus walked into my bathroom and changed that. I am a pretty matter of fact chick; I want the point quickly. That is what Jesus gave me. He simply said, "you can follow me and live, or you can keep going, die and you will go to hell." I had never experienced such clarity of decision. Regardless of the fact that moments before I only wanted to die and wanted nothing to do with the Almighty, my choice was clear and quick. I chose Christ. I did not get what I deserved that day. I deserved immediate hell. I broke every commandment and cursed God. Yet He showed me grace and mercy. Jesus took my dusty, buried mustard seed of faith and completely altered the course of my life in 5 minutes. I do not deserve to walk hand in hand with the Lover of my soul. Thankfully, walking with Christ has nothing to do with what I deserve. It has nothing to do with earning His favor. I never did that. I was a drug addict who broke every commandment and cursed the church. I was not looking for God and I was working for His enemy. Christ found me angry and dying. There was no action in my life that merited the grace and mercy of God. He saved me because He loves me. I am alive, not because of anything that I have done, but because of everything that He is. Think about your salvation today. That moment when Christ kissed your spirit and saved your soul. Remember the amazing power of the grace and mercy of God on that day. You do not need to remember the time or the day, only the unrelenting pursuit of Christ for your life, knowing you did not work to get Him, and you cannot work to keep Him. But it is by His grace that you have been saved.

Jesus wept.

John 11:35

I love the pure love of my God. He was standing with the family of a deceased man crying with them. Imagine the things He knew in this moment. He knew Lazarus was dead before He got there. Jesus knew in just a few moments He would call Lazarus from the grave and he would live again. Jesus knew the spirit of Lazarus was already with the Father according to Jewish tradition. He knew the impact raising Lazarus in that moment would be felt for not only generations, but for centuries to come. Yet, Jesus wept with the family because He felt the magnitude of the loss. However, Jesus also knew what was in the raising. I have been in that tomb. As my parents watched from the outside, Jesus was there with them. He comforted my family in ways I pray I never need to understand. I was in a darkness that I was helpless to escape, wrapped in the death cloths of insanity. I can vividly relate to Lazarus. I can close my eyes and feel the breath of God as Jesus called me to come out. I could sense the tears my Savior shed over my decaying life. He knew I was dead, but He knew I was also still alive. He wept, not out of sadness over the loss of my life. Jesus wept for joy because He knew I was walking out of that tomb and into His arms. With the family outside He wept in comfort and agony. Inside the tomb He wept with joy for the new beginning that He knew was coming. Stepping out of that tomb and into the arms of Jesus altered everything in my life. I can only imagine that Lazarus felt the same. The family standing on the outside of my tomb were just as surprised and amazed as the family standing outside of Lazarus's tomb. Jesus does the same thing for you. If you are part of the family on the outside, know Jesus is weeping with you. Jesus is with you in the grief. I pray you find comfort with Him today. If you are in the darkness of the tomb, I pray you hear His sweet voice calling you to live. Jesus is there and it can be different. You do not have to live in the darkness forever. I pray you step out of the tomb and into life.

This book of the law shall not depart out of your mouth, but you should meditate on it day and night …

Joshua 1:8a

Do you know the meaning of the words in this verse? The first time I read it, I thought I knew them all. Then I heard a sermon once that completely shook this verse up for me and I had to study the words myself. I believed I knew that meditation meant a time of silent aloneness focused on the thing at hand. I thought Joshua was supposed to sit in quiet contemplation of the Word, that he was supposed to hold it in his spirit. After studying though, I found that is only a half right interpretation. One of the meanings of meditate, as it is used here, is to roar. To roar does not mean to sit in silence. Strong's defines it as to raise a loud cry either of grief or of joy. Joshua was told to hold the Word in his spirit, but not in quiet contemplation. He was to boldly roar the Word of God into the decisions he made and the lives he touched. Everything he did out loud was to be a reflection of what God gave him in the quiet times. We are encouraged to get alone, get quiet and meditate with God. It is the time when God can speak to you and set His Word in your spirit. What about the rest of the day? Do you leave your quiet time and remain silent? Do you quietly contemplate the Word without ever allowing it to reflect in your daily life? Do you roar the meditations of your heart into the decisions of your day? Imagine how things could change if you did that. I encourage you today to get alone with God in quiet meditation. Let Him set His Word in your spirit. Then go and reflect that time throughout your day. Roar the meditations of His Word into your life.

And I sought for a man among them who should build up the wall and stand in the breach before me for the land, that I should not destroy it, but I found none.

Ezekiel 22:30

We are called to intercede. This verse calls us to stand in the gap in protection of the land. Can you imagine living in a place overrun by sin? Where the inhabitants care only about living for themselves and have no love for God? Now imagine God can find none to step up and stand in the gap. He can find none willing to pray for the land. God gave warning. The people were not ignorant as to why God destroyed the land. They also were not ignorant of His pleas. Yet still, God could not find one man to pray. Look around you today. We live in a land that is divided by an aisle with very definite views on each side. There has come a time where there is no acceptance of a middle ground and that has left open a lot of gaps. We fight about things, that while they matter, leave no desire to pray for the other side or for the land. What seems to be happening, instead of praying for God to heal the land and put the people in control who can do that, we pray for our party, dead set that the other side is completely wrong about everything. That is not truly standing in the gap. That is picking a side of the gap to stand on. God is seeking brave and bold inhabitants of our land to be placed firmly in the gap and pray only for Him to heal in the best way that He sees fit, not in the manner that suits our own politics. He needs those prayers to be united in Him instead of divided by opinion. Our country is facing destruction from the inside, by its own people. Our enemies really need only to sit back and watch. But God is calling courageous people who will build up a wall of prayer and who will intercede for the restoration of our land. Are you part of the problem today, or will you choose to reach across the aisle and take the hand of your fellow with an opposing opinion and stand in the gap? Will you truly stand in the breach for God so that He does not destroy the land? Will you step forward?

If I were still trying to please men, I would not be a servant of Christ.

Galatians 1:10c

Paul was not an apologetic man in the things he did. As Saul, this persecutor of Christians killed our ancestors with unrelenting vigor. He acted upon the beliefs of his people and defended them until he was given sufficient evidence by Christ Himself that he was wrong. As Paul, he preached and taught and lived the Truth with unrelenting vigor. He acted upon the Truth of God and was unashamed that though he was once wrong, now he was not. Paul preached Truth knowing he would not please the masses. He knew whom he served, and his purpose was to please God while spreading a message he knew would not please men. It was the way Jesus lived also. Jesus knew that his teachings caused controversy and anger. He knew not everyone agreed with everything that came out of His lessons. That did not stop Him. It did not stop those who followed Him. Jesus and the men and women who came after said the Truth with bravery and boldness. Their purpose was to spread the message and please the Lord by not straying from it. I have heard several preachers say from the pulpit, "what God has put on my heart today will not please you". Yet they spoke with courage and the strength of Christ. There are parts of the bible that feel good. Parts that bring joy and peace. Then there are parts that feel less good. They are usually lessons that bring discipline and conviction and a need for repentance. Those teachings are hard to hear. They are also hard to say. A teacher's purpose is to say the truth and please God, not sugar coat it or twist it to please man. Each of us has the same mission as the Apostles. Spread the Truth and please God. Paul very plainly states if we are attempting to please men, we are not servants of Christ. How do you share His message today? Is it with His courage and strength, knowing whom you serve? Or is your goal today to have people like you? Sometimes you get to please both man and God. Are you ok if you speak the Truth and only please God?

Submit yourselves, therefore, to God. Resist the devil and he will flee from you.

James 4:7

Have you tried to resist the devil without first submitting to God? I sure have. Recently I was in a situation I knew I should not have been in. There was temptation and this raging internal battle. I sometimes forget that there is a very well laid out process for fighting the battles against the enemy. God did not leave me to fight alone. He gave me a full instruction manual so that I can be successful and victorious in the resistance. He did not stop there either. God places in my life people more mature in their walks who know how to submit to Him. They are there as examples of how to fully submit. The awesome thing about submission to God is the power it holds. A disciple who is completely submitted to the Lord can resist the devil and he will flee. The bible says I will stomp on his head. I can put the enemy under my feet and proclaim victory in Jesus' name. The devil will come at you in an attempt to kill, steal, and destroy you. However, if you are in submission, you have the power to resist him. You cannot do it of your own will though. Submission is a process that begins with knowing God. It is not knowing Him like you know your neighbor. It is knowing Him better than your best friend. You have to trust Him and have faith in Him. You have to actively pursue His statutes through His Word and follow them. It's fasting and praying in order to align yourself with Him and His will. True submission makes things on earth as they are in Heaven. Then resistance is possible. It is not hard, and it does not take a long time. It does take dedication and a conscious decision to live with God. Are you submitted to God? Or do you think you can resist the devil without Him?

I can do all things through Christ who strengthens me.

Philippians 4:13

Life has a way of showing up and punching you in the face. If you are anything like me, when that happens you try to roll with the punches, attempting to take care of everything while accomplishing nothing. I remember the first part of this verse and my magnificent magnifying mind finds a way to stop there. I can do all things through Christ becomes I must do all things by self. The outcome is physical, mental, and spiritual exhaustion. It becomes very evident that I can do nothing, and I cry out, "where are you, God". To which He immediately replies, "I am right here". When I take this verse in its fullness, I stop, breathe, and remember where my strength comes from. I can do all things through Christ who strengthens me. I could be a single mom, full-time employee, full-time student, and the other 20 things I have done through Christ. I can roll with the punches and admit I am weak so that Jesus can then offer me His strength to take the next hit. He promises I will be able, through His strength, to do every one of the things. How then do I get the strength of the One who commands the wind? I find it in His Word, which means I have to open my bible. I find it in prayer, which means every day I have to take time to talk to Him. That also means I take the time to listen for His response. I have a nurtured, vital, and growing relationship with the Lover of my soul. His strength is breathed into my life through Holy Spirit who dwells inside of me. Strange to think that I often feel I need to go it alone, even though I am not ever truly alone. Today, I will do all things through Christ. In doing so, I will have the strength to go forward. Are you doing all things through Christ, or are you relying on your own will?

…Choose this day whom you will serve.……

Joshua 24:15b

Choice is presented through the whole Bible. Ever the gentleman, God will let you choose to allow your self will to run riot and He will not interfere. He sets before us, life, and death, blessing and cursing (Deuteronomy 11:26; 30:19). We get a choice. Sometimes, making the right one is hard. There is not one verse in the whole bible that says it will be easy. Believe me, I have looked. Sometimes you look at the decision ahead and you only see the best of two evils. At other times, both choices look like blessings. We do not have to choose alone though. The bible says we are given the Helper (John 14:16). Upon your salvation, you inherited the promise that you never have to make another decision alone. However, therein lies yet another choice. You can choose to accept Holy Spirit's help or not. Some decisions seem so minute that I almost feel as though I do not want to be a bother and ask Holy Spirit. How selfish is that. The bible plainly says I have not because I ask not. If I am choosing to serve God then I should also be choosing to involve Him in the choices in my life. By choosing this day to serve the Lord, you should be choosing to build a relationship with Him. Through prayer, reading the Word, and making time to be with God you begin to know how to choose things. You have to nurture and grow your relationship with the Lover of your soul. In return, He helps to guide you and He never leaves you. It is a choice. You get to choose this day, today, whom you will serve. It is my prayer that today you choose God.

But God shows His love for us in that while we were still sinners, Christ died for us.

Romans 5:8

There is so much love in this verse. I do not know about you, but in the kind of sin this verse refers to, I was a different person than I am now. I was heartless and cruel. I was constantly operating out of my own self-will. Nobody mattered to me except me, and I hated me. When Jesus walked into my life, I was amazed. I did not understand how He could so fully love someone who did not even like herself. I did not need to understand it though. I just needed to get out of the way long enough to know it was true. It did not happen just overnight. I spent 25 years not loving myself and inside of relationships built on dishonesty, no trust, and total lack of anything real. I had to put all of that behind me. Several years later, that process is still on-going and sometimes I have to go back to this verse and be reminded. God loved me at my dirtiest. He loved me when I began to recover. He loves me when I start to stumble. He loves me when I feel lost. He loved me thousands of years ago and still, He loves me today. Not only that, but His love was also so complete that He put on flesh, walked the earth, and died for me. I am constantly amazed at His love. It is completely unconditional, its pure, its raw, and its real. Do you know that love? It is my prayer today, that you not only feel the love of God. I pray you know, better than you know anything else, that Jesus loves you so much. He not only died for you, but He rose for you. So that in this moment, on this day, you can know you are not alone.

…One thing I do know, that though I was blind, now I see.

John 9:25b

We all have varying stages of blindness. Before salvation, my blindness was whole. I did not know I was in darkness because I could not see the light. When Jesus came, I was blinded in a different way. His Light shined so bright in the first moments of my salvation that I could see no darkness at all. I could see nothing but Him. As I adjusted to the light I began to see some things clearer than others. As I immersed myself in the Word, God revealed some things of Him to me. He cleared my blindness on faith and forgiveness. He let me see Truth about Holy Spirit and His love. God cleared the fog on repentance and truly walking with Him. There are a ton of things I am still blind to. I often have to remind myself that in salvation, I am only a 5-year-old. It is sometimes frustrating when things, which seem so clear to others, are still clouded for me. I forget that revelations are of God and in His time. He is opening my eyes in a manner best suited for my 5-year-old intake. I want to rush ahead and have all the knowledge and full understanding now. But what I want is oftentimes not what is best. So, I do the next best thing. I praise God that I am not blind as I once was. Today I can live seeing the revelation of Truth God has blessed me with this far. I pray that He never stops opening my eyes to the things of Him. If you are blind today, it is my prayer that God shine light into your darkness.

And Jesus answered them, "Have faith in God".

Mark 11:22

I was talking with someone this weekend and she said the most astounding thing to me. We were discussing the Word and I commented how odd I find it when people seem to not believe what is written. She said most people do not read their bible. We were not discussing people who do not know Jesus. We were discussing people who are active in their churches, people who talk a lot about God. It astounds me even more that I see the validity in her statement. So very often people go to church, listen to podcast sermons, and attend awesome conferences but they do not take the time to open their own bible. They have faith in what they hear from their pulpit and never search out the truth with God. The bible did not say to have faith in man. It says have faith in God. How can you have faith in Him if you do not know who He is. How can you know who He is if you are not reading His Word, or you are not praying and listening? My pastor tells us not to take his word on anything. He urges us to get out our bibles and study what he is saying. I wonder how many people do that though. Do you? After hearing your pastor or your podcast do you take God's hand and search out His truth in what you have been told? When was the last time you opened your bible? Is your faith truly in God, or is it in the man of God?

Search me, O God, and know my heart! Try me and know my thoughts!

Psalm 139:23

I love to read, and I consider myself pretty intelligent. At least, I generally think I am smart enough to know the meaning of common words. When I started to immerse myself in the bible, it was suggested that I read it with a concordance. It is a good idea to take the advice of those who are wiser than you. I like to look up words I think I know. I once heard a short sermon on this verse, and it got me thinking about the word 'search'. In my mind, search meant to look around. To me, the verse meant, 'look around and know my heart God'. What I found when I studied out the word is much deeper. According to Strong's concordance, the word search means to examine intimately, with deliberation to test thoroughly. Literally, this verse says, 'intimately examine and deliberately test my heart, O God'. I am all for God coming in and looking around. Am I willing for Him to intimately examine me though? If God comes and deliberately tests my heart, what will He find? I would love to say that right now He would find awesome faith, bravery, and joy. If I am honest, I would admit that there is fear, inadequacy, some exhaustion and other less than upright issues. I am not letting that stop me from inviting God in though. I know without His searching of my heart, the things I would rather keep hidden will take root and fester and infect my spirit. If I do not allow God the opportunity to intimately examine my heart, He cannot cleanse it. And if He cannot cleanse it, the desire to fill it with awesome faith, bravery, and joy cannot be met. What would God find upon intimate examination and deliberate testing of your heart today? Are there things you would rather Him not see, or are you willing to ask Him to search you?

I will restore to you the years that the swarming locust has eaten, the hopper, the destroyer, and the cutter, my great army, which I sent among you.

Joel 2:25

I love this promise. I never would have known about it if Mom would not have told me. There were decades of locust in our family. Drug addiction and alcoholism ran rampant for generations. For a very long time it seemed as if there were no end in sight. Mom knew the end would come though. She also had faith that there would be full redemption and reparation. God showed her this verse years ago. Through words written thousands of years before we were flesh, God set the promise of salvation for her children in my mother's spirit. Having the promise and the faith that it would come did not make the waiting easy. She prayed for decades while she watched her children almost die. She stomped her feet and yelled and cried. Finally, she surrendered. In the raising of her hands and giving full trust to God to work it out, she saw this promise bloom to life right before her eyes. When God fulfills His promises, He does it so much better than we could ever imagine. The prayers my momma prayed for so long are still being fulfilled. God gave my mom a promise and set it in her spirit. She stood on that promise, and she had faith that God would keep it. She never stopped praying and today her family knows peace and joy because of it. Are you praying for someone today? Do not stop. It does not matter if you have been praying for one year or for 20. Stand on the promises that God has set in your spirit.

Do your best to present yourself to God as one approved, a worker who has no need to be ashamed, rightly handling the word of truth.

2 Timothy 2:15

I am a lover of knowledge. I enjoy studying and reading and seeing known words in a new light. That is not an enjoyment everyone has though. I know many people who go to service, do not bring a bible, do not take notes, and do not check the words of the pastor against the Truth of the Word. They attend their church because it is what is expected, or its habit. They never open their bible in order for Holy Spirit to guide them through a study of it. This verse says that could cause them to be ashamed before the Lord. It is the lazy way of Christianity to sit on a pew and reflect the old adage, "Teacher, teacher, scratch my ear, tell me what I want to hear". If you simply go to a building and take a man for his word, without dividing it by the Word of Truth, how do you grow? In that practice, how do you understand what God's true intention is? Without studying the Word of God, and talking with God, how do you know God? And if you don't really know God through the relationship formed by walking with Him and allowing Holy Spirit to teach you how to rightly divide the word, how are you able to decipher if the man in the pulpit speaks God's truth? There are so many advantages to opening your bible and studying, learning to rightly divide the Truth. When you invite Holy Spirit to guide you in this endeavor, the bible comes to life. God speaks to you and reveals the deeper things of Him as you dive into a relationship with Him through His Word. Holy Spirit teaches you to decipher truth because you learn to divide the truth by the Truth. I am not saying you do not need human assistance. Ask questions of your elders. Attend a bible study where there are several people with whom you can process what you are learning. Read what you are focusing on in several different translations. It does not matter if you have a book or a computer or a phone. What matters is that you open your bible, pray, and invite Holy Spirit to guide you, and study the Truth. That way, you are a workman who needs not be ashamed before the Lord.

And it shall be, when you hear the sound of marching in the tops of the mulberry trees, then you shall advance quickly. For then the LORD will go out before you to strike the camp of the Philistines.

2 Samuel 5:24 (NKJV)

Wait on the LORD: be of good courage, and He shall strengthen thine heart: wait, I say, on the LORD.

Psalm 27:14. (KJV)

I do not know about you, but I tend to rush ahead and take care of things myself. I have a hard time waiting. In David's day, they were told to take refuge in the trees and to wait on God. They heard an audible sound as the LORD went before them and then they went behind Him to conquer their enemy. David reminds us in the Psalm that waiting on God causes courage and strength for the task ahead. Today the same applies. While we do not hear the audible sound of God going before us, we have Holy Spirit. That still small voice that tingles our belly and says, go right instead of left. Oftentimes we disregard that voice because we have not taken the time in the waiting to get to know Him. Like Elijah (1 Kings 19: 11-14), we want our direction to be loud, earth shaking, and bright as fire. However, it is more like David, standing quietly, that we hear Him. Be still today. Take time to find refuge and listen to the voice that will give you courage and strength. Know that He goes before you. Then make that decision, have that conversation, or conquer that enemy. If you are waiting and going behind God, nothing is impossible.

Unless the Lord builds the house, those who build it labor in vain.

Psalm 127:1a

I labored for a very long time in a huge amount of vain. What I had built for myself sat on a crumbling foundation. The frame was off square. The wires were faulty and there was no completion of anything. Today, I am not doing the building. The house God is building for me is different. The greatest change is foundational. I do find at times that I question the integrity of that foundation. So, I go, with Holy Spirit, and we inspect it. We look for cracks because I cannot afford anything damaging to creep in. Holy Spirit ensures that the foundation is level because everything else being framed on top of it needs to be true square. In this new building of my life, what is in the foundation? The Word and prayer cemented together by a relationship with God. I could not form this foundation totally of myself. I tried that and the collapse of what I had built almost killed me. Since the Lord is Master of this new building though, it is strong. He has started construction on top of His foundation now. The frame has gone up and little by slow I see the completion of some rooms. That does not mean there will never be changes in a completed area of my life. It does mean that the load bearing walls are intact. The frames in my life hold the wires which will shine light into each and every room as God builds them. God helps me to ensure those wires are cared for and protected. There are several different kinds that serve multiple purpose. Some are preachers, some teachers, some friends. All are needed to shed Light into each room of this building. My house the Lord is building is strong. How is yours? Are you allowing God to be the Master Contractor, or are you building it yourself? I truly hope that today you are not building in vain.

No temptation has overtaken you that is not common to man. God is faithful and He will not let you be tempted beyond your ability, but with the temptation He will also provide the way of escape, that you may be able to endure it.

1 Corinthians 10:13

People very often cut this verse apart. Usually what happens is we are left with the assumption that God will not give us more than we can handle. While that sounds awesome. It just is not true. What is true is that we can walk through any temptation with God and be okay. When my daughter told me that she was pregnant for the second time and giving the baby up for adoption, it was not up for discussion; her decision had been very firmly made. Over the next three months my sobriety was tempted over and again. I was not consistently graceful. My heart was being shattered and there was nothing I had control of in the situation. While I did make some decisions outside of my character, I did not give in to the temptation to numb out everything. I did not give in to the temptation to fight and demand to have my way. That was not easy and walking through those very tempting things was not something I could do alone. Through those months I learned the true meaning of praying without ceasing. I did not just crawl into God's lap, I clung to His neck as He helped me see the way through. I dove into His Word and let the comfort of His scripture wash over me. While my temptation was common to man, it was not common to me. God faithfully provided a way of escape that was in and through Him. His way of escape was my ability to overcome. If you are facing something today, lean into God. What you are going through is not a unique situation. While it may be uncommon for you, it is not uncommon for God. Trust the faithfulness of God today and let Him be your escape so that you do not give in to the temptation in your path.

After this many of his disciples turned back and no longer walked with him.

John 6:66

Jesus had a lot of followers. Apparently, He had more than twelve disciples. It says so right here in this verse. When Jesus began to talk of the world eating of His flesh and drinking of His blood, He lost "many disciples". The essence of taking the mark is shown in verse 66 of chapter 6 in John. They walked with Him no more. Can you imagine? These people had Jesus standing in front of them. His Truth got a little hard to hear and they walked away. That sounds like insanity. Is it really any different than what happens today though? We do not have Christ physically walking with us, but we have Holy Spirit living inside of us. Still, there are people who go back. Walking the road with Jesus gets hard, truth is not always easy to hear, so they give in and stop walking with Him. In this passage, Jesus goes on to ask Peter why they stayed. Peter asks, in return, where they would go? He boldly declares that Jesus has the words of eternal life and that they know Him to be the Son of God. In today's world, it would be the equivalent of looking at Jesus and telling Him to not ask ridiculous questions. To Peter, their reason for staying is obvious. How about you? Is it obvious why you continue to walk with God? How are you dealing with the, sometimes, hardness of Jesus Truth? Will you go back and cease from following Him, or will you boldly declare Him Lord and continue to walk with Him?

The second is this, "You shall love your neighbor as yourself" ...

Mark 12:31a

These are really two commandments appearing as though they are one. First you love yourself, then you love your neighbor. I have read this verse in many translations, and they all read the same. We are to love others AS we love ourselves. Essentially, if you cannot love yourself, loving others is difficult, to say the least. There have been times I have not loved myself very well. I, like everyone, endure seasons of change. I become unsure of many things about my identity and some days I am so discombobulated I am not sure I even like myself. I have found through these seasons that when I am unsure of how I feel about me, I am also unsure of how I feel about you. Because God loves me though, He places reminders along my path. I come across a verse, a sermon, or a book that reminds me of my identity. I hear things about being a blessed child of God. I absorb phrases like, "heir to the Kingdom of God". Someone reminds me in those moments that the Great I AM loves me so much that He came to find me in the darkest pit of insanity. The king of Kings went into the darkest kinds of filth and cleansed me simply out of love. He did not do it because He needed something from me, but only because He loves me. Being reminded of my true identity allows me to love myself again. What I know about my identity is today, I am free. I am able to enter the Throne Room and rest in the care of God at any time of the day. For me, in knowing who God says I am, I can truly follow this commandment. Do you know your identity in Christ today? Use that to strengthen the love you have for yourself. Then use that love to truly love your neighbor as yourself.

Yea, though I walk through the valley of the shadow of death, I will fear no evil for You are with me, Your rod and Your staff, they comfort me.

Psalm 23:4 (NKJV)

I thought I would have to be near literal, physical death to walk through this valley. That is not true. I think the valley of the shadow of death is often more mental and emotional than physical. My magnificent magnifying mind begins to run a thread of anger and doubt throughout my thought process. It invades everything. It stinks like Lazarus on the fourth day. But I am breathing. My heart is beating. I am very much alive as I trudged through the valley of the shadow of death. In my time in this valley, I forget I am supposed to be walking through it. I stop and get stuck in the filth of the muck. It also escapes me that I could be here without fear of evil. That thread of anger and doubt that plays in my mind transforms into fear and condemnation. Generally, in the beginning of the valley, I dwell there in anger and fear. Eventually I realize I have allowed fear to take over and I have allowed myself to become stuck. So very often I like to blame my problems on the enemy. He is an easy target when things go wrong, and life is so very hard. Honestly though, at least most of the time, I am my enemy. Sometimes, getting out of my own way proves to be difficult. Praise God, I have a Shepherd who wants to help. In order to get unstuck and continue my walk through the valley, I only need to call on God. It is often a change of mind and a decision to live in His will and to allow God to light my path. In these times I have to choose to let Him really be my Master. My prayer changes from "Where are You?" to "I need Your help." God pulls me from the mire, He relieves my fear, and He comforts me as I walk. It does not matter that this specific valley of the shadow of death was mostly self-created. What matters is that I refuse to be stuck in it anymore and I begin to walk in faith that God will carry me through it. I will choose to let the rod and staff of God guide me out. I will let Him comfort me today so that I may truly fear no evil. Are you in the valley of the shadow of death today? Are you walking through it, or have you become stuck and fearful? Go to the comfort of God and let Him guide you out?

For I consider that the sufferings of this present time are not worth comparing with the glory that is to be revealed to us.

Romans 8:18

The verses before this one talks about how we are joint heirs with Christ. If that is true, and it is because it is in the bible, then my suffering should not be a surprise. While Jesus suffered physically in ways far beyond anything I could ever imagine, He also suffered mentally, emotionally, and spiritually. I no longer deal with serious issues in my body. I have annoyances, but nothing that would be considered suffering. Today all my sufferings are in the prison of my own mind. I am overwhelmed recently by stress, worry and anxiety. I have cried, yelled, and groaned more in the last month than in the last year. I felt doubt and confusion in totally new ways. Some days I really think I am getting better only to wake up worse than ever. I am suffering in this very present time. But this verse reminds me that my present suffering is nothing in comparison to the glory of the future. I cannot begin to imagine that. All I can see right now is what is right in front of me. The pain I feel so locked-up by today is very much at the forefront of my mind. I could choose to get bogged down in that, like I have done the past few weeks. Or, I can hope. I can have faith that the glory to be revealed in me, far outweighs the yuck I feel right now. This verse does not say "glory revealed to me". It is talking of an event inside of me. This verse, to me, today, says, "stop dwelling on today's trash, have faith, that even though it hurts today, it will mean nothing in a very short time because God's glory will be actively revealed inside of you soon". Are you suffering today? Do not be like me. Do not sit in it, allowing it to eat you alive. Feel it, walk through it, and hope. Have faith today that the glory soon to be revealed in you will diminish any suffering you endured to get there.

Be still and know that I am God.

Psalm 46:10a

My mom taught me this verse when I was a teenager. I was rebellious and crazy. She
wanted me to know the Lord though. Sometimes, well, most times, all the bible stuff was hard for me to hear. I know today, it had nothing to do with the messenger. It was hard to hear the message through my mess, especially since I did not want to. I had scales over my eyes and my ears were plugged. Most of what she told me; I cannot recall today. There are a few things I do remember though. This verse is one of those things Mom taught me that I will never forget. While I do not always rest in the full revelation of this verse, I do go back to it when I just need to rest. I pray this helps you today.

Be still and know that I am God.
Be still and know that I am
Be still and know that I
Be still and know that
Be still and know
Be still and
Be still
Be

Immediately they left their nets and followed him.

Matthew 4:20

Jesus walked into the lives of His disciples and gave them an awesome choice. He only said, in verse 19, "Follow me, and I will make you fishers of men". Immediately they left. These men had lives. They were married, they had businesses and responsibilities, yet they straightway left. The disciples could have chosen to wait until a better time. They could have told Jesus they would catch up with Him after they talked to their wives and kissed their children. They did not though. They heard Jesus, they saw Him, and they immediately dropped everything to follow Him. In doing so, they not only chose to change their own lives, but they became vessels God used to change lives thousands of years later. When Jesus walked into their lives, everything changed. That is exactly how it is supposed to be for us too. In our humanity, it does not always work like that though. We make excuses as to why we cannot immediately follow Him. We mask our responsibilities as reasons to follow later. What would the impact be if you decide to immediately follow Jesus today? What if, just for today, you choose to drop everything and follow fully? Think of the impact God could make in the lives of the people you encounter if you were willing to be His vessel. I encourage you today, follow Jesus. Allow Him to work in and through you. Be a vessel God can use to change someone's life.

For God shows no partiality.

Romans 2:11

I am so grateful that God does not show partiality. He does not look over the face of the earth and choose only those who were well behaved or did exactly what their parents said. He does not pick His children based on how greatly they screwed up or how very desperate their lives had become. I know people who are warriors for God, and they come from all walks of life. I know the materially rich and poor and both live lives of absolute abundance. I know people who never bent a rule and I know hardened criminals; both live inside of pure forgiveness. I know people who were virgins until marriage, and I know those who were whores; both go to bed nightly with the Lover of their soul. I, myself, carried a ton of damning titles, descriptions of my former self that God did not care about. God does not care about the labels caused by the lives we have led. Jesus comes and sees each of us exactly the same. He gives us a choice to follow Him. He does not force us, and He does not pick and choose the circumcised from the uncircumcised. God is looking for the willing. Do you feel less than worthy today? Do you look at your fellows and think they are of more value to the Kingdom than you? It is my prayer today that you believe God sees you in the same manner He sees them. Jesus has given you a choice, you only need to be willing to look away from your past and into His eyes. God is not partial, it is my hope, that today, you are not either.

We rejoice in hope of the glory of God. Not only that but we rejoice in our sufferings, knowing that suffering produces endurance.

Romans 5:2b-3

I like to rejoice. It feels good to show great joy or delight in God. I have confident expectation in God, and it feels awesome to know I can put that hope in my Creator. What in the world does it mean to glory in tribulations though? How am I supposed to feel good about something that feels bad? Well, I am not. Sometimes it is not about what I feel. There are times when I have got to be sure of what I know. Otherwise, the bad that I feel can violate the good I know. If I do not learn to glory in my tribulation, what I feel in the hard times could lead me to make unwise choices. I might begin to doubt God because I am leaning on feelings. To glory in the muck means that I have to ignore how bad it feels and rely on what I know is good. Or, rather, Who I know is good. That is not easy. I have had days that make me want to curl up under my bed with boxes of cookies and wait till it passes. Some days it feels impossible to glory and rejoice in anything, much less the very thing that is making me feel worthless. I have to ignore my feelings and use my logic. In all logical knowing, I know I believe in the love of God. Since I know that, I can glory in my tribulation. In that process, Paul says I will build patience, gain experience, and have a hope in God I am not ashamed of. I can have the confident expectation that God will fulfill the things He has promised in my life. No matter how bad it feels to glory in my tribulation today, I am going to choose to do it anyway. I encourage you to do the same, knowing, in the end you will have a hope in the love of God you will not be ashamed of.

Because, if you confess with your mouth that Jesus is Lord and believe in your heart that God raised him from the dead, you will be saved.

Romans 10:9

It is so very human to complicate things. In our humanity, we can take a very simple and straightforward verse and add concepts that just are not there. Salvation is one of the things that gets twisted. Nowhere in the bible does it say we have to earn our salvation. If it were a thing to be earned, I would be dead and eternally enduring hell right now. Salvation is really very simple. You have to believe in Jesus and His resurrection. Did you know the word believe is a verb? Being such, it requires an action. How do we actively believe Jesus is Lord? Well, the verse tells us. We declare it. Out loud we claim, "Jesus is Lord"!!!! Then how do we actively believe in His resurrection? We become born again. In the act of belief, we allow for change to take place in our lives. Sometimes the change is quick. At other times, its slow. Things do start to change though. It looks differently in each life too. What changes in one person's life may not be the same thing that changes in their neighbor. This is where our traditions start to complicate things. It is easy to see our own change and know that it is right in us. But we can become so convinced of that rightness we think everyone should have the same change. That is not the way it is though. We are to allow everyone to work out their own salvation with fear and trembling. Each man's (or woman's) declaration that Jesus is Lord is the most personal thing they ever do. One man cannot say to the next that his declaration was not right because he did not do it in the same manner. After salvation, we cannot look at anyone and say they are not holy enough. We cannot see their heart, but it is very accessible to God. That is why we do not judge. It is my prayer today that you work out your own salvation with fear and trembling. If you have yet to declare Jesus as Lord over your life, I pray you do that today. I also pray you give your fellows the chance to do the same.

Do all things without grumbling or disputing.

Philippians 2:14

God uses the word 'all' quite a bit. It often pops up in verses like this one. Since God knew we would find it difficult, He reminded us to do all things without grumbling or complaining. Sometimes it is hard to walk through life without murmuring. How often do you find yourself in the heat of the wilderness with life punching you in the throat? Do you sound like the Israelites, groaning and complaining? God had just delivered them from slavery in a spectacular way. Within three days they were disputing the benefit of their freedom. I have been in one of those seasons where it feels as though life hates me. Almost every day, it seems, something goes crazy. I, historically, do not walk through those seasons with much grace. Some days I am completely defeated; on others, I am so angry. Every day during those times, at some point, there are tears. I want to walk through those seasons gracefully. How do I change it? I cannot change the season; I am in control of how I respond to it though. I go to God in prayer when the tension hits. Instead of complaining, I will praise when the stress rises. I remember to remain in gratitude and thanksgiving so that my perception of the situation remains in Christ and His goodness and not the frustrations of the moment. I will go into my closet and crawl into the lap of my Father when I am feeling defeated and overwhelmed and I am going to ask Jesus to help me through it without murmuring. Whatever season you are in, I encourage you to walk through it without murmuring and disputing. I pray you go to God and ask Him to help you get through today with grace and gratitude, without murmuring.

Be strong and courageous. Do not fear or be in dread of them, for it is the Lord your God who goes with you. He will not leave you or forsake you.

Deuteronomy 31:6

I always only hear the last part of this verse. I hear it so often, I forgot there was more before it. There are times I hear the last sentence of this verse over and again. God will not leave you or forsake you. Sometimes it was spoken directly to me. Sometimes it is in a sermon. Other times it is part of general conversation. Seems like God is trying to tell me something. When I looked it up, I was surprised to see that there is so much more to it. Because God does not leave me I can be strong. In not being forsaken, I can find courage. It does not always feel like that. Thank God that is only a feeling. Just because I feel alone does not mean that I am. I have been through a lot of tough seasons. I have felt alone and distant. Feelings are not reality though. Reality and truth lie within the promises of God. Very early in the bible He tells me that He will not leave me alone. I imagine He put that promise so close to the beginning because He knew I would feel alone. Since God cannot lie, I get to decide to believe Him. The ball is in my court. I can choose to walk in the fear and dread of life, or I can choose to be strong and courageous. I get to decide. God only makes the promises. It is up to me to allow Him to fulfill them in my life. I may not be in total control of how I feel, but I am in control of how I choose to believe. Today, I choose to believe in God's promise. I am going to be strong and courageous today. God said He will not leave me or forsake me, and I am putting my faith in His word. I hope that you do the same today. If you feel lost or defeated or left to handle life on your own, I pray today that you take this verse and meditate in it. Be strong because God has not left you. Be courageous because you are not forsaken.

Watch and pray that you may not enter into temptation. The spirit indeed is willing, but the flesh is weak.

Matthew 26:41

The disciples fell asleep after Jesus said this to them. Jesus walked back to the place where He had been praying and they could not fight their flesh, so they slept. They could not have honestly thought much of it. Otherwise they could have gotten up, watched, and walked as they prayed. The weakness of their flesh was allowed to override the willingness of their spirits. That is not such an uncommon thing. Consider the temptations of today's society. It would be a simple thing to disconnect from technology and devote that time to building on a relationship with Christ. I even hear people who talk about doing that. Yet, instead of taking the actions to resist, they rest in the weakness. While that is a societal example, each of us have a personal temptation we should be actively resisting. So often though, instead of being in watchful prayer, strengthening the willingness of our spirit, we rest in the weakness of our flesh and are left wondering why we could not resist the temptation. It does not matter how willing the spirit is, if I am not actively strengthening my defenses, my weak flesh will override that willingness. Jesus gave us direction on how to not walk into temptation. Watch, meaning to be on guard, and pray, remain in communication with God. Resisting our temptation, no matter what it is, requires action. You cannot simply sleep your way through it. God will help us to resist, but the action is ours to take. God will only do for us that we cannot do for ourselves. I encourage you today to watch and pray. Be on guard and in constant communication with God. Build the defenses of the willingness of your spirit so that you do not sleep in the weakness of your flesh.

I will restore to you the years that the swarming locust has eaten.

Joel 2:25a

Restoration often looks different than I imagine. In my finite mind I see big things. That may be because in the beginning of this journey everything was big. God began the process through sobriety. Simply being clean and sober restored huge pieces of my life. Most of my family was able to heal in places we had been shattered. God did not just fit the pieces back together though, He has helped us to build new, solid, and strong relationships. My once broken family has developed bonds that shine God's light. Not everything was put back though. I imagine those parts were not yet shattered in a way God was ready to repair. Last night I saw pieces coming back together right in front of me. It is funny that God used a broken truck to begin to repair a part of my family I thought may never fit back together. That relationship has nothing to do with me, really. This restoration is not directly for me. It is not coming together in huge ways right now either. There will be, from a finite standpoint, fights and disagreements that will seem to be breaking it down further. God gave me a glimpse at His infinite work though. Nothing shatters without pain and it is a painful process. I get to witness over the next few months the restoration of a relationship very dear to me, though not my own. God has set a new promise of restoration in my spirit. Are there shattered parts of your life, or those you love? God promises to restore the years of destruction. Pray for that relationship and those involved. Restoration may not look how you imagine it should. God will make it better.

Iron sharpens iron, and one man sharpens another.

Proverbs 27:17

I have heard since salvation that I should read 5 Psalms and a Proverb every day. Some people use that method to knock out two books in one month. The advice was given to me though because I needed to know how to live. I had no idea about wisdom or understanding. I did not understand the concept of praise and talking to God the way that David did. At the time I was learning how to take the suggestions of those who had gone before me and because I like to be challenged. I got to this verse, and I instantly understood it. If iron sharpens iron, then it would only make sense that the dulling I had experienced in my previous life was, partly, because of the people I surrounded myself with. Because of that, now I tend to surround myself with people who enjoy learning and questioning. Every person in my circle sharpens my outlook on life. I find that in the toughest seasons, my circle evolved. My church group changed, my intellectual group changed, and my recovery group is in the process of changing. I do not think God intended for me to only sharpen my intelligence or simply focus on my spirit. I also do not think He intended me to only have one group of people to sharpen me. I am in recovery and have a group of women I hang out with who sharpen that aspect of my life. I also love knowledge and I have a group of people who sharpen my intellect. For my spiritual sharpening I have a vast network of people I can question, and who question me. God did not mean for us to sharpen ourselves. He created us to help grow each other. This scripture makes it very clear that we are not to walk through life being dulled by our people. We should be sharpened by the people we choose to keep in our lives. Are you choosing people in your life who give you a more defined edge? Or do your people assist in keeping you dull?

Look carefully then how you walk, not as unwise but as wise.

Ephesians 5:15

I read a lot of books. I listen to several different types of podcasts and sermons. More than anything else, I enjoy learning. However, learning things of finite humanity does not cause wisdom. I can gather all the academic knowledge available and still not have a drop of wisdom. That is a gift that does not come from man. True wisdom is a gift from God. It is not difficult to find. The bible says wisdom is given to any believer who asks for it. A true child of God can find wisdom in the pages of the bible, in prayer, and in listening to God. Looking carefully at how you walk is the application of that God given wisdom. When there are no obstacles in the way, no trial, no temptation, walking in wisdom is simple. However, sometimes, we experience, not only days, but seasons where walking in wisdom is difficult. I have said it before, following Christ was not promised to be an easy adventure. In seasons when life seems to be trying to rip you apart, looking carefully how you walk is exhausting. God knew that would happen. Its why He encourages us to do the hard stuff. God gives you His strength in your weakness. Because of that you are able to walk in His wisdom. God causes you to be wakefully observant of where you are putting your feet. That can only happen if you are diligent to walk inside of His wisdom. If you lack wisdom, ask God, and open your bible. Being wise does not mean you will not stumble either. It does mean that you will stand back up and not stumble over the same things over and again though. I encourage you to look carefully at your walk today. Are you being wise or unwise? If you are not satisfied, make a plan to change it. Ask God for His wisdom so that you may be wakefully observant.

And we know that for those who love God all things work together for good, for those who are called according to his purpose.

Romans 8:28

I love God. I also know that I am called according to His purpose. I know that because I am His child. He came into my deepest darkness and showed me His light. That is the moment my life completely altered. I did not change to show God I could do good things for Him. I changed because of His purpose in my life. That is not so He could give me great blessings. If I live the rest of my life with little, that is fine because my purpose is His presence. Do not get me wrong, I pray to be able to pay all my bills, have groceries and good coffee beans. That is not the goal though. The purpose of God in my life is to shine His light into yours. All things working together for good does not always feel good. There are seasons of great pain. Days when I do not want to get out of bed and times when the hardest thing to do is smile seem to be in abundance lately. There is struggle and grief. Decisions are being made that break my heart. I am stuck smack dab in the middle of the part where all things are working. Not all days are rough, but I would be lying if I said any of them were easy right now. Some awesome things happen in the midst of the chaos. God winks at me through the clouds to let me know He is still with me, working things out. I get to take all these struggles to Him in prayer and He does not leave me to walk through His workings alone. God is guarding me in these times it does not feel good so that He can guide me to the good He has prepared. Are you called according to God's purpose? Is your life in the midst of chaotic working together? Do not lose hope, good will come, even if it does not feel good in this moment. Continue to love God, believe and act inside of His purpose for you. Trust He is working all things for good.

Therefore, if anyone is in Christ, he is a new creation. The old has passed away, behold, the new has come.

2 Corinthians 5:17

This verse was the foundation of my new life. There is such freedom for me in these words. Today it holds new meaning. The new creation in me is different today than it was when I was first saved. Back then every single thing about me absolutely passed away. The person I was died. The people who knew me then were amazed at the way my life totally turned around. Everything about me was new. Now, in the middle of my chaos, my relationship with God is changing and evolving. In the process, I am seeing that there are still parts of me that are becoming new. I am learning, sometimes slowly, how to better function inside of relationships. I do not do it well, but in being willing to learn to stay, I am running less. I am being taught to walk by faith, not by sight. It is a rough lesson. My flesh wants to choose what it sees as the best path while my spirit wants to fully wait on God. I understand how the spirit can be willing, but the flesh stands in the way of progress. I have been thinking that I am stuck or going around in circles lately. It occurred to me that I have not begun to go backwards. If I were going in circles, at some point I would be facing south instead of north. That just is not true. My momentum may have slowed, but I continue to move forward. These are signs in my life that it takes time for some new things to bloom. There are parts of me I did not realize were still being made new. It gives me peace to know, whether I have been on this walk with God for 4 years or 34 years, there are still things to be made new. If God fixed everything in 5 minutes that Tuesday, how could I possible continue to grow and mature with Him? Today I am grateful for the growing pains I have been experiencing. It means there is newness being birthed in me by Jesus. Are you in Christ? Have you become completely new, or is He still working in you too?

For we walk by faith, not by sight.

2 Corinthians 5:7

I am a logical person. I like focus and direction. If I know where I am going, or someone shows me what to do, I can accomplish almost any task thrown at me. I can just as easily change my oil as I can change a diaper. Once I learn how to do a task, I am generally able to do it again with little assistance. When I learn something new, I like instruction manuals or a step-by-step conversation and I take notes. I even like glovebox maps you can never fold right. They give perfect direction. So, for me, learning to let go of logic and walk by faith is often challenging. One of the decisions I am in the process of making right now is causing me to step out in full faith. I have prayed about, cried over, and fought the answer, but I continue to get the same response from God. He is moving me out of my comfort zone. God is showing me how to trust Him instead of myself. The great part is though, God does not mind if I ask questions. He knows I am a logical thinker because it is how He created me. Questioning does not mean I am not walking by faith. Being scared does not mean I am trying to walk by sight. At the end of the day, I know God only has good in store for me. In my logical brain, I know that taking this step-in full faith, not knowing what absolute direction I am going, is the most logical thing to do. There are people who will not agree with me. There are those who will think I have made a huge mistake. That cannot matter though. Walking by faith means I have talked to God, and I have done so in a manner that allowed me to hear His answer. The product of that conversation is action. Walking by faith essentially requires us to put down our natural instinct, be it logic or emotion. It means we have conversations with God, and we listen to His direction. We walk towards the purpose He has laid out for us, even if we cannot see where our feet will land. Walking by faith fosters the bravery and boldness God created inside of us. Are you walking by faith towards the purpose God sees, or are you directing your own path by your own sight?

…Walk in a manner worthy of the call to which you have been called to.

Ephesians 4:1b

I have not recently been walking in a worthy manner. I have been in a negative pity party. Because of that, I have forgotten the position I have been called to. This past week, my mother had a hand in reminding me. She sent me a text with this verse and reminded me. It said, "As Sister Marcia told me…"walk in the authority of the position God called you to!!!" You have the authority - you are seated with Him in heavenly places - at the right hand of God - a place of honor and majesty, a place where your enemies are your footstool; a place where angels, principalities and powers are subject to you!!!" Along the line, somewhere in the last four years, I had forgotten my position. I have stopped walking in the authority of Christ and began crawling in submission to my finite humanity. My perception has become negative and enslaved to the idea that I am inadequate and faulty and without any authority. That is a false perception. In the last few days so many things have changed. I have begun to remember the position God called me to. I am a daughter of the King. I am co-heir of Jesus Christ. The exact same power that raised Him from the dead and allowed Him to step out of the tomb, that power lives inside of me. When this becomes the perception of reality I walk in, I begin to walk in a worthy manner of my calling. It is not about what I feel, and I have allowed feelings to seriously fog up my view lately. It is about what I know. I know the truth given to me by God, through His Word. God did not call me to walk alone or to be a slave. He called me, He filled me, and His power lives inside of me. God called you to walk in a worthy manner today also. Do you know what you have been called to? Are you walking in His authority?

Now faith is the assurance of things hoped for, the conviction of things not seen.

Hebrews 11:1

Literally, faith is the tangible evidence of confident expectation. People refer to faith being blind or a leap. In those contexts, someone would have to be mad to live by faith. It would be like a bunch of people leaping with their eyes closed. That is wishing, not having faith. True faith is trust. It is taking steps you know are in the right direction, even though you cannot see the destination. When I started school, I was walking in faith. I knew it was the direction God wanted me to go, but I could not see the end result. I can, though, look back and see how taking that step of faith has allowed God to put me in an amazing position this week. When I started school, I had confident expectation and trusting God in it produced tangible evidence. The bible says faith comes by hearing and hearing by the word of God (Romans 10:17). Faith in God's direction is not a product of choosing it. Faith is built through hearing God's promises and knowing His character and believing His truth. It is in His Word. Through the Word of God, trust is developed. As in any relationship, the more you know your counterpart, the more faith you have in your trust of them. How do you develop unshakable faith in God if you do not know Him? I encourage you to hear the Word of God. Build a relationship with Him so that He can build faith in you. Then you can have the tangible evidence of your confident expectations, you can trust He will bless you with the things not yet seen.

If God is for us, who can be against us?

Romans 8:31b

Not long ago, I told someone that life hates me. Things had gotten so hard that every single day something was coming against me. It has been one of the hardest seasons of my life. Sometimes it is difficult to see God's promises when it is pouring. Today I see it differently. When it seems as though everything is against me I can rest knowing that because God is for me, nothing that is coming against me will prosper. What makes me so sure that God is for me though? I believe Him. God saved my life when what I deserved was death and hell. Since then, He has shown me His promises. The biggest promise is that I am His child. I have my own children. As their mother, I am for them unconditionally. I may not always agree with them. However, I am always in their corner, always prepared to protect them, always for them. If that is how I am in my finite motherhood, why would God be less in His infinite fatherhood? He is not. He is more. Since I believe He is more and He is for me in ways I cannot even imagine, I know that when life seems to hate me, it is only shooting blanks. Today I stand in victory. I know that nothing can be against me because I know, more than I know anything else, that God is for me. Do you know that in your life today? Do you believe that the things coming your way cannot stand against you because God is for you? If you are in a season like the one I have been in, I want to encourage you today. If you believe in God's promises, rest knowing you have the victory in this situation. God is for you.

For I know the plans I have for you, declares the Lord, plans for welfare and not for evil, to give you a future and a hope.

Jeremiah 29:11

I was never much of a planner. I was more the fly-by-the-seat-of-your-pants-girl. Since I have gotten a bit older, that has changed. While I do not need a check-box-to-do-list, I do appreciate knowing what is coming. The last year has brought a ton of changes and routine to my life. In just a few short months, I will be able to look back and nothing about my life now will resemble it a year ago. As this book in the series of my life closes and the next one starts, this is the promise I am holding onto through the fear. It is not the type of fear that paralyzes. It is fear that propels. It is an excitement for what is to come, but a tremble in the face of the unknown. I am walking forward, out of this season, with hope in my future. That is not of my own making. I have hope because God says He has a plan. I pray and He hears me (v. 12). I seek Him and He becomes evident (v. 13). These are the promises I am resting in today. I do not always find this rest easy. In those times, God places people in my life who speak words of encouragement. He whispers His strength into my day through Holy Spirit. He stills my trepidation in the sweet moments that are just me and Him in the Throne Room. Do you know your promise today? If not, make some time to find it. Let God plant it in your spirit so that, by faith, you can fully believe it. Listen for Him in the breath of Holy Spirit and the words of the people He puts in your path. Meet Him in the Throne Room and let Him soothe your fears while He fulfills the promises He has made to you.

He leads out the prisoners to prosperity.

Psalm 68:6b

This chapter of the Psalm is about God scattering His enemies. It talks about how He rose above them, and they fled. We are told as the righteous to be glad, exult before the Lord and to praise Him for the release from bondage. Then it goes on to say that He will bring the prisoners out and prosper them. I had been a complete prisoner. This was not in the bondage of addiction in a life before Christ. It was in the last few months. I was not a prisoner to any outside source, but to my own mind and my own negativity. I had trapped myself inside of such magnificent magnifying that I could only see the weight of the world and not the world itself. I had sentenced myself to a very parched land. God did not leave me in it though. Throughout this whole time, He has been directing me through it. He placed red flags and warnings along my path that steered me away from deeper bondage and towards freedom. He reminded me of my inheritance as His child through people He has placed in my life. God began to refresh my zeal and vigor for living life for and by Him. In the last couple of days, the storm has started to come to its end, and I have seen the SONshine. Prosperity instantly came with a change in perception. It came in gratitude and switching from extreme negativity to positivity. The freedom from my prison came from the guidance of God. The prosperity He promised was always here because it is in His presence in my life. Have you been imprisoned? Let God set you free. Live in the prosperity of His presence.

For everyone who calls on the name of the Lord will be saved.

Romans 10:13

I have done a lot of searching in my spirit. I have searched the scripture with fear and trembling working out the essence of my salvation. When I started questioning, I was going to people. While it is good to get advice from others, I had to realize they are only humans. I would get a variety of answers and was becoming confused. The bible, though, says my God is not a God of confusion. So, I stopped asking people and started asking God. I spent a lot of time in the Word and in prayer. What I was ultimately doing was trying to get back to a place where it was just me and God, back to His beginning truth. When I was first saved, it was not in a church. It was not after hearing a sermon that made me feel good. I was at home. It was just me and God. He came to me, and I was able to cry out to Him in a way I never had before. I was not begging Him to get me out of a mess then offering Him an empty promise that I would do and be better. I was asking Him into my life. I was inviting Him to teach me about Him and His character. God is so faithful. He led me into His Word, and I was sure of who it said He is and who it said I am. I was confident in our relationship and there was no confusion. At some point that changed. I stopped feeling confident in who I was and began to feel as though I was not measuring up. Through the searching of scripture, by the guidance of God, the confusion ceased. I set out in fear and trembling to work out my salvation. In the process I became very confused. However, in calling on the Lord, I have again become confident, not only in my salvation, but in what that means. Have you been confused in your walk with God? Are you relying more on the answers of God or man to settle that confusion? When was the last time you really took the time to call on the name of the Lord? I pray today is that day.

…Choose this day whom you will serve…

Joshua 24:15b

This day, today. Every time I wake up I am given a fresh opportunity to choose. I choose God. There was a time when I was burdened with what this means. I began to measure myself against the Word. There is nothing wrong with that in theory. However, in practice it caused some issues. Mostly because I was using the entire Bible to compare my life to what I thought God wanted. I fell very short in comparison with women like Rahab and Ruth. I thought, if I cannot compare to a whore and an idolater, I have no chance if I try to stand next to Abraham, David, or Moses. That is not how God intended me to be though. I am not supposed to measure myself against the Old Testament heroes. For one, I am not a Jew. For two, that is not the covenant I am in. So, with the help of Holy Spirit, I switched gears. I learned that God does not require me to measure up. He asks me to believe His Gospel. More than anything, I believe in the death, burial, and resurrection of Jesus Christ. I believe, in His death on the cross my sins were taken. I know, in His burial I was washed. I walk in the salvation of His resurrection. Because of those very firm beliefs, I know I am choosing correctly when I choose each day to serve the Lord. I also know I am only capable of choosing to serve because Holy Spirit lives inside of me. In choosing to serve the Lord fully, I am choosing to walk by faith in the direction He is leading me, no matter what anyone else thinks. It has not been easy, but I am not promised an easy life, only an abundant one. This morning I woke up and I chose to serve the Lord, in choosing to do that, I commit to walking in the path He directs me in, not comparing myself to anyone along the way. You get the same choice. Whom do you choose to serve today?

For by grace you have been saved through faith. And this is not your own doing; it is the gift of God

Ephesians 2:8

I have done a lot of praying and searching lately. I had become stuck in a rut of works. I was trapped in thinking that if I could just do enough God would see I was trying, and He would then offer me His grace in some very trying areas of life. It was in the searching that I realized I was not living in faith of God's grace. I stopped walking in the knowledge that the things of God are gifts. They are freely given and there is nothing I can do that will buy God's grace. If I could do that, what would be the need for Jesus? When Christ died, was buried, and resurrected, He paid for every single thing. God does not need me to work for my inheritance. I had come to a level of pride I did not realize existed. How could I possibly be able to do enough to earn blessings from the King? He needs nothing from me. At the same time, He wants to give me everything. When I first met Jesus, I was blown away. In the beginning though, I came to Him as a child. I knew I had no knowledge so I spent every moment of time I could with Him, and I believed every word He showed me. I knew then that the works produced by faith were an outward showing of an inward change. They were not spiritual currency. My faith in God's grace allowed Him to save me and His gifts produced a gratitude that allowed me to alter things about myself that were unbecoming. I have now gone back to the foundation He built within our relationship. Today I am not working for God's grace in any aspect of my life. I am choosing to have faith that because He started this work in me, He will finish it. I have decided to walk by faith in His grace that is freely given. That does not mean I will rest on my laurels in service, or any other aspect of the work produced by my faith. It means I know those works cannot buy me anything. Are you walking by faith in God's grace, or are you trying to work for it?

Behold, now is the favorable time; behold, now is the day of salvation.

2 Corinthians 6:2c

In 2014, I had an experience that forever altered the course of my life. I was dying. I was out of hope and out of time. But God. He came into my life. I was not looking for Him. Truth be told, any time someone mentioned God or the Bible I would leave the room. I was angry and full of fear. He did not care about that though. On a random Tuesday He walked into my bathroom and held me in His arms. He offered me a choice and I chose Him. I thought that was the day of salvation. Do not misunderstand, I was saved on that day. That was years ago and I cannot live today off that one experience. I am human. In my humanity I forget things. So, the way God works in my life is that He offers me spiritual awakenings along the way. As I endeavor to build and grow a fully intimate relationship with Him, He opens His Truths to me. If God had given me everything that day in my bathroom, I would have been overloaded. That is why He nurtured me like an infant, feeding me slowly. As time passes and I mature in our relationship I understand things differently. I know that the "now" in this verse never changes though. Now, right now, this moment is the appointed time for me to choose to walk in the grace of my salvation. By being in the now of salvation, my spirit remains hot, not lukewarm, and rarely cold. In choosing to value the now, right now, my life is better than it has ever been. Right now, this moment, I am saved unto God by Jesus Christ my Lord. Now is your appointed time also. What are you doing in the now of your salvation?

In speaking of the new covenant, he makes the first one obsolete. And what is becoming obsolete and growing old is ready to vanish away.

Hebrews 8:13

When I read this verse yesterday during my bible study I thought of computers. The first ones created were huge. They were meant for only a select few people to operate. They undoubtedly served the purpose they were created for, but they have become obsolete and have really vanished. The old covenant is the same way. It was huge. There were 613 laws given to a select people. While the old covenant served a definite purpose, the people it was given to could not operate inside of it and they could not continue in it. Through Jesus Christ God created a new covenant. The writer of Hebrews says because God called this covenant new, it caused the old to be obsolete. When a thing becomes obsolete, it is generally replaced by something better. That is what we experience in the new covenant. Under Christ we are given grace. God does not hold our transgressions against us because through Christ those were forgiven. So much so, God says He has forgotten them once and for all. Does that mean we continue in sin because we have been forgiven once and for all? No, of course not. That is not the point of living in grace. Grace provides freedom from sin. Where the old covenant pointed out sin, made it visible and caused wrath from God, grace in the new covenant covers sin with the blood of Christ, allowing the forgiveness of God. I see people who constantly speak of the grace of God, saying they believe in the new covenant, but they live in the bondage of the old. God says the old is ready to vanish though and through His Word teaches us to live in the new. Which covenant are you in today? Do you profess the grace of God, but live in bondage of the law? Or do you walk in the grace of the new covenant, understanding your freedom as a new creation?

For God has not given us a spirit of fear, but of power and of love and of a sound mind.

2 Timothy 1:7 (NKJV)

I was up to my neck in fear over this last season of my life. I could feel everything beginning to change and change terrifies me. School was ending, my son was starting Senior year, I needed to get a new job, and I was only financially hanging on by a thread. On top of that, God was showing me new things in His Word and through prayer that caused me to reevaluate my faith and my place of worship. Some days I really felt like I just could not go on. I was paralyzed by the spirit of fear that had permeated every facet of my life. I told someone that I had not at all walked through the season with grace. I forgot I had power. I failed to love others before myself. There for a bit, while I have a sound mind, it did not always feel that way. The biggest problem was that I was acting by feeling and not by knowing. I know this verse. I understand the promises of God. I let my feelings override my logic. It was a completely out of character way to spend three full months of my life. When I truly came to my senses and I was put into remembrance of these things, God displaced the fear and filled the space where it had been with Himself. Then everything began to change. Because I was no longer operating out of fear, but walking in the power of God, I was able to show real love to others. I was again capable of maintaining the soundness of mind that has allowed me to make huge God directed decisions. By expelling the spirit of fear, I regained the active promises of God in my life. Do you have a spirit of fear today? I pray you ask God to remove it. I pray you change the fearful perceptions into ones of power and love. Today, do not act in fear, but in the soundness of mind God has given you.

And by this we know that we have come to know him if we keep his commandments.

1 John 2:3

I am a Gentile. As such, I was not given the laws of Moses. I was not brought up reading the Torah and memorizing all the law that God gave to the Israelites. Because of that, I am not under obligation to those laws. If I were, I would start by breaking them each week. I do not keep the Sabbath. I also do not offer sacrifice or keep to the feasts, and I mix my cottons with my linens. There are quite a few, most, of those commandments that I would fail at consistently. So, I praise God that I am Gentile and under the commandments of the new covenant. Under grace, the command is to love as Christ does. Do not get me wrong, I still fail. I find it considerably difficult to love some people. That does not stop me from trying too though. What I have learned is that love allows me to follow the law God writes on my heart. If I am endeavoring to love my neighbors, I do not want to cause them any harm. Through love, I am able to honor my mother and father, not lie, not covet, not kill. I do not always love fully. I can tell because I can become a gossip or hateful. I stop looking at others where they are and get irritated because they are not where I think they should be. I form unrealistic expectations and that makes it difficult to love. When I am actively keeping the commandments laid before me in the new covenant of God's Word, people around me can see the difference. I am kind and deliberate with my patience. I am able to display the fruit of the Spirit because the love of Jesus is flowing through me. What commandments are you attempting to follow today? Are you stuck in the law of the old, or are you walking in the loving grace of the new?

But as for me and my house, we will serve the Lord.

Joshua 24:15c

I am the head of my house. I was not always. Only in the last almost 5 years have I been the one to make the decisions and take care of things. Before then I was not in the church either and we did not serve the Lord. Now though, I do make that decision. I get to wake up every morning and set the standard for my house. When I get up and choose to serve the Lord, my kids see that. Not only them, but my neighbors see it and those I work with and even complete strangers. Serving the Lord is not something I can do quietly and discreetly. I suppose that some people can. That is not my character though. Living out loud is a fundamental trait for me. I am an extreme personality; I am not good at hiding the things that are defining my life. In my addiction, everyone knew what I served. Why would that change now? I choose to serve the Lord today. Since I started making that choice, God has helped me to do some awesome things. In the beginning of salvation God came in and made huge changes. Those were examples of Him doing for me what I could not do for myself. God would not, however, do the things I could. In choosing to serve Him out loud and fully though, He gives me strength. He also guides me into circumstances and seasons that make me so uncomfortable the only thing I can do is change. God challenges me to be a better leader and that produces growth. By choosing this day to lead my house in serving the Lord, God is doing things for my house I never believed were possible. It is not easy, and not everyone agrees with some of the decisions I make (read that again). As head of my house, I seek God's guidance in all things and I, to the best of my ability, follow his lead. Nothing in my life can ever compare with the peace and joy that comes from it. You get to choose this day what or whom to serve. Your choice could set the example for your house and the people who cross your path. As Joshua so famously said, "choose this day whom you will serve…as for me and my house, we will serve the Lord".

But no human being can tame the tongue.

James 3:8a

I pray for the ability to be able to better control my tongue. There are times, generally when I am angry with myself, when I say things I probably should not. Through the last several years I have gotten better at not speaking out of turn. There are times when I am good at having restraint of tongue and pen. Generally, I can think before I speak and before I act. But, like with everyone, there are moments when I seem to lose control of my mouth. Occasionally those are times when life is coming at me from every angle, and I feel trapped. Generally, though, in the situations I fail to control my tongue, I have backed myself into a corner and caused a situation to occur that puts me in a bad head space. It usually has nothing to do with anyone else, and I overreact like a child. I know that if I bite my tongue and pray the situation will generally work out in a manner that is suitable for everyone involved. It is a lesson I am still trying to learn. What God has taught me is that not everything needs to be said. Not every person needs to know if I am in a bad mood or offended or even if my feelings are hurt. There are things I simply do not say to people anymore. There are opinions I keep to myself. I could not stay quiet without the help of God. This verse says no human can tame the tongue, but if I go to God, He is able to help me do that. As I said, I do not always do it well. But if I ask God to help me, I do it better. How is your restraint of tongue and pen today? Are you attempting to tame your tongue today? If so, ask God for help. You may not do it well alone, but with Him, you can do it better.

Be still and know that I am God.

Psalm 46:10a

I am so glad that I do not need to be still and feel God. I am a logical being. Feelings often irritate me. Not that I do not appreciate them, I just know that they are fleeting. I read a study once that stated feelings generally change within 15 minutes. While there are feelings that last longer, eventually they do change. There are even stages of feelings, such as grief. That shows that if I wait long enough, that thing I am feeling will naturally change into something else. I would never want that to happen with God. That is why He tells me to be still and know. God tells me in His word what I need to know about Him. He is the same, yesterday, today, and forever (Hebrews 13:8). He will never leave me nor forsake me (Hebrews 13:5). God wants me to be strong and courageous (Joshua 1). God wants me to know he loves me so much (John 3:16). By knowing these things, it helps me to be still. He does not want me to be still simply because He is God, and He says so. God wants me to be still, not worry, and not rush to take care of things myself. In faith God wants me to rest in the promises He has given me and be still, knowing that He will take care of today just like He did yesterday. When I am fully still, knowing that He is God, my anxiety calms, my peace increases, and His joy fills my spirit. Are you still today in feeling or in knowing? Is your stillness fleeting because it is based in feeling God? Or is it unwavering, based in a knowing that does not change?

And He said to her, "Daughter, Thy faith hath made thee whole..."

Mark 5:34a (KJV)

I love the story of this woman. She was a social outcast because of a disease that was deemed unclean. It was an issue of blood that she had no control over. She had spent years with the problem. Some say she saw doctor upon doctor and spent all her money and nothing could help. I have been through that exact same thing. My disease was a different one. But the result was the same. I was a social outcast because of it. I had lost all control over, not only the disease, but myself. I was sick for a quarter of a century. There were many attempts to help me, but there was no relief. But God. When He came into my life, it was not by demand. He gave me a choice. Boy did I ever reach out for the hem of His garment. I did not even know what faith was. In a moment though, it was the only way I knew how to be free. It was the first thing I had truly known in a very long time. I was filled with an unwavering certainty that I was really suffering from a very embedded spiritual malady. Within a very short time I was presented with a solution. It came in the form of 12 steps that walked me directly into the arms of God. In the program they say you get to choose a God of your understanding. I do not come anywhere near understanding God though. He is so vast and so great and so gracefully merciful. He has shown me in the last few years that He is full of love and kept promises and goodness. I will never understand how He looked at what I had become and still wanted to show me who I could be. In reaching for the hem of His garment with faith that was barely there, I became whole. Everything changed and most of the time my wholeness does not look like what my humanity perceived it would. It is so much better. I know today that I will die with my disease. I have faith in God that I no longer have to die from it. That is a beautiful reality. Do you have the faith to reach for the hem of the garment of Jesus today? I pray you do. He promises your faith will make you whole.

…Love your neighbor as yourself…

Mark 12:31b

It is sometimes easier to like my neighbors. Some days I get stuck in myself. I think about my old habits, my old life, the dead me. I know what I was once capable of. I have no idea what my neighbor is capable of so that makes it much easier, on some days, to like my neighbor more than myself. Most days though, I can love myself. I am only capable of loving myself because of God. Upon salvation God took every horrible thing I had done and covered it with the blood of the greatest sacrifice ever made. He took my heart of stone and replaced it with His heart of flesh. God breathed life into my very dead spirit. He offered me an inheritance and authority directly connected to the Kingdom of the Great I AM. Today I am a child of the King of kings bold enough to approach the Throne of my Creator. When I look at myself and see what God sees, I can then honestly love my neighbor because I can truly love myself. When I consistently see myself through the eyes of my very loving God, I cannot help but see you in that light too. God's love is contagious, because He loves me, I can love me and that makes it possible for me to love you. How do you see yourself today? Are you seeing the love of God, allowing Him to let you love yourself so you can love your neighbor? Or are you looking through your own view, diminishing that love to a like?

Seek first the kingdom of God and His righteousness, and all these things will be added to you.

Matthew 6:33

This verse comes at the end of a passage that talks about God being our Provider. He tells us to not be anxious for the things He will provide. God says there is not a reason to feel anxious about food or drink, your body or what you will wear. God Himself says He knows that His children are in need of these things and that He will provide them. God does not want us to go without. I do not very often pray for a full fridge, though I often need one. I have asked for clothes; they always seem to appear through other people. I do think it is amazing that we are told to seek what is inside of us. Jesus tells us that when we accept His desire to come into our lives Holy Spirit comes and dwells inside of us. The very Spirit of the Great I AM lives inside of us. Because of that absolute truth the kingdom of God is here every single day. Holy Spirit is the nature of God. His goodness, His mercy, God's grace dwells within. Usually when we think about the Kingdom we think of Heaven. However, the true Kingdom is not trapped as a place paved in gold with feasts and mansions. That is only the best destination. The Kingdom of God is where He dwells. Since He dwells inside of us, how do we seek that? By learning about Him. In developing a relationship with God, I learn His nature. In learning His nature, I take on His traits. In taking on His traits I am able to worry less and trust more. Are you seeking first the Kingdom of God? Do you have things you feel anxious about that He has very plainly said He will provide if you are seeking Him?

So also, faith by itself if it does not have works, is dead.

James 2:17

I used to think this verse meant now that I had faith I have to work for everything after salvation. I have even heard sermons say while salvation is free, now the work begins. I just could not reconcile in my spirit how God, who is the King of kings, has His own Kingdom, and owns the cattle on a thousand hills needed me to earn my inheritance. I could not reconcile it to my understanding because those things are not true. What is true, however, is that without faith, there are works I simply could not do. If I did not have an active faith, I would not be sober. I would not be able to help others in the ways I very much love to do. Without faith, I would not be able to write these words. I could not understand the Bible and I could not be transformed by it. If I did not have faith, I could not walk through the fires of trial knowing that God is refining me in it. There are things that I do that show the people around me that faith is a live and active thing. If I only had faith and then sat around and did nothing with it, what good would it be to even have it. God sees faith. People I encounter in my everyday walk also see faith. Perhaps some of them have never seen it before. If I am not living and working in faith, maybe they never will. While it is very true that I can never work to earn anything from God, it is equally true that without faith I could not do the things that show He is very much inside of my life. Are you trying to work for your inheritance today? Or are you letting your faith allow you to do the things that show God is in your life?

For as yet they did not understand the Scripture, that He must rise from the dead.

John 20:9

I do not know about you, but I find it easy to get stuck at the cross. I get to places where I feel like that is the goal. I camp out in sacrifice. I feel like I have to nail this sin and that sin to the cross and get them all taken care of before I can go on. The cross is only part of the Gospel though. I am not supposed to nail myself to it and live there. I get to fully know what happened on that wood. Jesus made the sacrifice that I never can. He nailed each of my sins there and covered them in His blood. Then He came off the cross. For three days His body laid in a tomb. But then, Jesus rose. He came out of the grave. The Great I AM Himself died, was buried, then He walked out of the grave. I am supposed to follow the example of Jesus. He did not stop at the cross. I do not need to either. When I got saved I died. When I was baptized, it represented the burial. Now I am supposed to live the resurrection. I did not get saved to sit at the foot of the cross or inside of the tomb. Jesus saved my life so that I could go forward. He has a purpose in me to share Him and to serve others and to produce His fruits. Jesus never went back to the cross. He did not re-nail Himself to the blood-stained wood. He said already, "It is finished". He rose to live. Today I get to do the same. Where are you today? Have you stopped at the cross, remaking a sacrifice that has already been made? Or are you walking forward into the resurrected life?

And this commandment we have from Him: whoever loves God must love his brother also.

1 John 4:21

Love is not always easy. Sometimes it seems completely impossible. People are flawed. They can be crass and difficult. It is easy to get so engulfed with my own self that I do not always see how I touch my fellows. I also have to remember to take the time to remember who my brother really is. It is not just my fellow believer. My brother is everyone who takes a breath today. The Word does not say I get to pick and choose who my brother is. It also does not say I do not love who I do not like. That is another line that often gets blurry. I do not like everyone. People who are terminally unique get on my nerves. Those who sit in judgement of anyone not like them do not sit well with me. There are a ton of other defects I can point out that leave a bad taste in my mouth. The bible does not one time tell me to like my brothers though. It says, if I love God, I must love them. That means I do not have to like you, but I get to love you. It takes some pressure off when I look at it like that. Your flawed humanity does not need to interfere with my love for you. Better than that, my flawed humanity does not need to interfere with it either. I get to love my family, the person sharing my pew, the recovering alcoholic and addict, and those who are still dying in that disease. I get to love my enemy and those I do not want to have a simple conversation with. When I walk through my day loving everyone I see, no matter where they are in life, it fills my spirit. I love God; therefore, I love you. It is just that simple. Do you love everyone today because you love God? Or do you choose to love only those you like?

Be sober, be vigilant, because your adversary, the devil, as a roaring lion, walketh about seeing whom he can devour.

1 Peter 5:8

For most people being sober is not a difficult thing. Most simply wake up and are that. I am not one of those people. There was a time when I would wake up and have to not be sober. That made being vigilant very difficult. I could not be cautious if I could not be sober. So, I was devoured by my adversary. My devil was not some little red guy with horns and a pitchfork. It was not even a fallen angel. My enemy was myself. I became victim of a disease that attacked me in my own voice. It tells me I am not good enough, I do not matter, I have already gone this far down, may as well keep sinking. Being on guard against that enemy, for most of my life, proved to be impossible. But God. In my absolute darkest moment, He came into my life, recreated my spirit to reflect His, and became my defense. God gave me a spiritual experience with Him that altered my disease and allowed me the chance to be sober. He also gave me 12 steps that showed me that what I actually suffer from is a spiritual malady to which He is the solution. With Jesus I was, at last, capable of being vigilant and standing against the adversary in my mind. As my relationship with Jesus grows so do my defenses. Now, I get to be one of the many people who wake up and just be sober. Being sober allows me to be vigilant. Being vigilant allows me to not be devoured by my adversary today. Without God though, none of that could happen. Are you sober today? Stand in vigilance with God. Let Him be the defense you have against your enemy today.

And by that we will have been sanctified through the offering of the body of Jesus Christ once for all.

Hebrews 10:10

I have learned that if I sit under a teaching it comes to be what I think is right, regardless of what the bible says. I had been taught that sanctification is a process I have to work towards for the rest of my life. So, I came to think that was right. That is odd because I have read the bible for myself, and I knew what this verse very plainly states. Because of the sacrifice of Jesus, I have been sanctified. Since I fully believe in the Gospel of the new covenant, Jesus lives inside of me. That means I am sanctified. It is a work I can never accomplish simply because it has already been done. There is not a redo here. If I really want a redo, just to ensure that I have been fully set apart by God, I have to have Jesus here in the flesh. I have to redo the beatings and the bloodshed. I have to again crucify Christ and bury Him. All of that would have to be done again because I cannot rest in the truth of the Word of God. Can you imagine? I cannot. Recently I have left the teachings of men and gone back to the Word. It is in the things God says that I find truth. Through the finished work of Jesus, I am sanctified, righteous, and holy. No work that I can do makes any of that truer. Today, because I know that, I act differently, talk differently, and live differently. Just because I do those things does not mean I am working for what has already been done. They are a product of the finished work of Christ. No do overs needed. When God says it was once for all, I get to take Him at His word. I trust that through His grace and sacrifice I am what He says I am and today I am sanctified. Are you working today, trying to redo what has already been done? Or can you rest knowing that through Jesus you are sanctified once for all?

You are severed from Christ, you who would be justified by the law; you have fallen away from grace.

Galatians 5:4

The law was completely based in works. From resting on the Sabbath, correctly pairing your fabrics, and making the proper sacrifice on the appropriate day, everything was about how to earn the way to God. Then that all ended. When Jesus died and then rose a brand-new covenant began. God even tells us, several times, in Hebrews that the old covenant passed away. It was obsolete and replaced by the new. Through the sacrifice of Jesus and the indwelling of Holy Spirit, grace became the better way. He fulfilled the law to the point that it is finished. Now, I am supposed to rest in His grace. That message gets misconstrued though. It is thought that grace is dangerous. What if people will take it as permission to keep sinning? The full grace message is bypassed and clouded with the law. You do not have to sacrifice animals, but be sure you follow the commandments, except the Sabbath, that one does not count anymore. And you do not need to keep all 613 laws but follow some so that there is balance between grace and works. People are taught that they are justified by their actions. Justification by action is the law. Paul says that severs us from Christ. I lived in that works mindset for the last several years. It was a standard I could not meet and somewhere along the way, I lost the knowing of grace that enveloped me in the beginning of salvation. There is no part of my inheritance in God's Kingdom that I can work hard enough to earn. But in trying to I can sever my relationship with Christ. I did not want to live like that anymore. So, I stopped. In going back to the Word of the new covenant, Holy Spirit reawakened inside of my spirit the knowing of grace. I no longer feel distant from Christ. I have remembered who I am because of who is in me and I have begun again to walk in that knowing. Do you seek to be justified by law, distancing yourself from Jesus? Or are you relaxing in the grace given through His finished work?

If we confess our sins, He is faithful and just and will forgive us our sins and purify us from all unrighteousness.

1 John 1:9

When Jesus found me there was no way I could remember all my sins. Every moment of my existence had been in sin. Praise Jesus I did not need to sit and recount every single moment. I do not for a minute believe that Jesus wants to hear us say everything we have ever done. I know that everyone is different, but the way confession and repentance worked in my life was astounding. I simply said, something like, "I have not led the kind of life that I should have. I was a soldier for your enemy and my life has been consumed by sin. I ask that you forgive me of that life and teach me how to live a new way." While there were things I was specific about, that was pretty much the extent of my confession. There was no shame. There was no guilt. I was truly and honestly ready to repent (completely change my mind and my ways) and Jesus met me there. The result was even more amazing. Jesus forgave me. He even forgot the things I had done before that moment. It did not matter that I could not name off every sin. It did not matter that in that moment I did not go to another human and spill my guts. What mattered is that I was willing to say that I had sinned, I did not want to continue to live that way and I needed help to do it differently. Today, what that looks like is interesting. When I am doing something, even something I have done for a long time, if it is something I need to repent of, I get a feeling in my spirit. Some people call it a conviction to repent. (The word repent means to turn around and go the other way.) I then have a conversation with God. I confess that I have been in sin and ask Him to help me to stop that action. It is one of the ways God is molding me to be more like Him. I have other women that I talk to. They hold me accountable to the things I am doing in my life. It is not like going to a confessional. Not one of them singularly knows everything I have done, however, collectively, they all do. I have people I trust to tell my stuff to. These people do not judge, and they do not condemn. I never leave them feeling guilty or ashamed. If that happens, it is not biblically what confession is supposed to be. The bible says we have all sinned and fallen short. God is not surprised by anything that you have done, and His desire is to forgive, not to condemn you. Go to Him with your sins, repent and ask Him to help you do it differently. Find women you can be honest about your life with. Confession is not a time for guilt, but a time of freedom and forgiveness. Seek for that and do not be ashamed.

You do not have, because you do not ask God.

James 4:2c

I am a member of an amazing organization; part of what they believe is that you ask things of God only if the request is for the express purpose of helping others. It is a means to keep us from being selfish. While it sounds noble and humble, it is the exact opposite of what the bible tells me to do. Then there is the religious camp that says you can ask absolutely anything you want of God. Do not get me wrong, I can. But I do not think He is going to give me a Jaguar when He knows I can afford a Nissan. When I go to God in supplication, in order for Him to be able to give, my request needs to be logical. When I started my journey, I had no material possessions. I lived in the same house as my ex-husband, drove his car, ate his food, you get the idea. Several years later, I have my own mortgage. I have a tremendous job that I love. While I was gifted the car I drive now, I have been able to purchase two in between. These were things that I needed and when I asked, God provided. However, He always provides on His time and not on my own. God does not just answer the big material requests either. There have been times when I was completely lost emotionally and spiritually. In these times, when I went to God and requested the things I needed, He consistently provided. When I ask for peace or strength, for help persevering or not worrying, He provides those things from Himself. It is very comforting that He does not just conjure up peace for my chaos. He brings it from His Spirit and plants it into mine. Sometimes I do ask for things that I want. I find that, for me, when I begin longing for something and asking God to provide it, that is because He has set that desire on my heart. You should never be afraid to ask God for anything. Do keep in mind that He will provide everything you need right on time, though not always on your time. Also remember, when asking for material things, what He may give you first is the way for you to provide them. And when you ask for the important things, those things that fortify your spirit and build your character, know that those requests are answered with precious pieces of God's own Spirit.

Enter His gates with thanksgiving.

Psalm 100:4

The word "enter" means to begin to be involved in. I have to wonder; at what part of my day do I begin to be involved with God? Personally, it is before I even get out of bed, most days. Usually it is a request about facing my day. This verse suggests that I change my words though. I wonder how the day would go if I began, before my eyes fully open, to express my gratitude to God instead of requesting something. Even if that something is His presence in my day. In the other fellowship I am a part of, we encourage daily gratitude lists. There is something about gratitude that sets the day off in a positive and content mood. Perhaps that is why God suggests that in thanksgiving, with gratitude, we begin to enter into communion with Him. If I am starting my time with Him before my feet even hit the floor, and I am entering with thanksgiving, that sets a whole different tempo for, not only my day, but in my relationship with Him. Can you imagine if all of your relationships were filled only with requests and lacked gratitude for the enrichment brought to each other's lives? That does not make for fruitful, fulfilling, or desired relationships. What kind of gratitude though? God is good. It is His essence and His character. There are more things than I can say that I can express gratitude to God for. Enough to fill my morning prayer for the rest of my life. And God does not care if I repeat myself. It is a high form of praise to recall the things God has done for my life. In my opinion, it is an even higher form of praise to recall who He is in my life. Letting praiseful gratitude be the first prayer out of my heart in the morning, I can see, is the best way to begin to be involved with God. How do you start your time with God? Is it with requests and petitions, with small talk, or do you go in with an attitude of gratitude for who God is in your life? Enter with thanksgiving today and enrich your relationship with Him.

You will know the truth and the truth will make you free.

John 8:32

I love my freedom. For a quarter of a century I lived in complete bondage to self. In the end, I was locked in a prison of my own making inside my own mind. There was no peace, joy, or happiness. I could feel nothing except physical pain and there was plenty of that inflicted. When Jesus found me, I was dying inside of that prison. He came in and opened the doors. When I allowed salvation to permeate my life, freedom was the natural outcome. God showed me His truth not only through His Word, but through the miracles He was causing in my life. They were not small things, and they were not things I could cause myself. Jesus showed me who I am in Him and the authority of the inheritance I now possessed. He showed me how to walk in that authority through faith and by grace. The truth of the love and goodness that defines God set me truly free. The truth of the salvation given by grace gave me boldness to be able to approach the throne of the Great I AM at any time with every praise and every trial. Daily the truth sets me free. Each day I get to walk in the grace of the goodness and love of my Father. The truth not only set me free, but it also completely changed my life. It is my sincere prayer that today, it does the same for you.

By the grace of God, I am what I am, and His grace towards me was not in vain.

1 Corinthians 15:10a

Sometimes I forget how important it is to share our stories. When people see me today they see the victory of the grace of God in my life. A lot of the time when I tell my story people tend to be surprised. Today I do not look like a drug addict or an alcoholic who died in order to live. When other people tell me their stories on the victory side of grace, I often have a hard time imagining them in their own pit of darkness. It is because today we live in the light and where the true light is, darkness cannot overcome. It is only by the grace of God that I am even alive today. It is through His grace that my mind has been transformed and I have been given a sanity I never dreamed of. How could I let that be in vain? I cannot work for the grace of God. But I can live in a way that shines the light of His grace. I get to share my story and help other women to walk out of their own darkness. By living in the victory of God's grace and not being ashamed of the past He saved me from, I get to not waste the life God has given me. Before God, there was no grace, and everything was in vain. Today, because of His grace, I am able to walk in His victory, not regretting my past and cherishing my present. I get to shine His light and give His grace so that the life I live is not in vain. Are you walking in the victory of God's grace or are you living in vain?

For God gave us a spirit not of fear but of power and love and sound mind.

2 Timothy 1:7

I love when scripture is given to me in a different interpretation then the one I have always considered. It is one of the reasons I enjoy discussing it and hearing how other people experience the Word. Yesterday this verse was pointed out and I was able to experience this scripture in a new way. The spirit of power I have comes from Holy Spirit living inside. That power includes the ability to heal others from the oppression of the devil (Acts 10:38). In this aspect, it is not as though I can heal people in their bodies. However, through the power of Holy Spirit in my life, others can be encouraged to pursue having that same power in their lives. The spirit of love in my life is perfect. John says that perfect love casts out all fear (1 John 4:18). If I am saturated in the love of God I can be free of the fear that is corrupting, that compromises and distorts my thinking about who I am and what I am worth to God. I always think of the soundness of mind in reference to the sanity that has been restored to me in recent years. What I had not considered is that Jesus came in and caused my mind to be level. He causes the hills to be dropped and the valleys to be filled. When that happens, the rollercoaster feeling of mental ups and down cease and my mind becomes sound. In being able to sit and listen to another person's experience with the Word, I was also given a new experience with Scripture. Do you take the time to let the experiences others have with scripture take you on a new adventure within the Word? Or do you get stuck in your own interpretation, not able to see anything new?

By grace you are saved…not of works lest any man should boast.

Ephesians 2:8a & 9

When I first met Jesus, I was so very confident in His grace. I knew my worth and my position. For the first time in my life I knew peace. I did not just feel peace, I had knowledge of the effect of peace in my life. I also knew the difference between your issues and my own and I did not let yours cause difficulty in my spirit. Then works invaded my life. I began to think about how I could better please God. I changed the way I dressed and talked and made those things a law for my life. Prayer went from an easy conversation to a chore that I eventually did not want to do anymore because it was now hard. Church attendance became a discipline instead of a desire. Even reading the Word became a thing I had to do instead of the thing I most looked forward to. I set standard and law over my life and that produced a look-at-me pride. I was as a Pharisee. I thought if I worked harder to please God He would love me more. I was so wrong. I had more or less trapped myself in a box I could never be good enough to reach the top of in order to get out. So, I stopped trying to. My family reminded me of God's grace. As I have begun to again relax in the grace of God's immeasurable love and stopped trying to work for it, the box has broken. I again know peace today. Not only that, but because I am walking in God's grace and not my works, I know His freedom and His love. I know today that He gives me my worth and position. The salvation, freedom and peace in my life today is by God's grace, not of my works, lest I become prideful in my boasting. Are you relaxing in the grace of God? Or do you attempt to work it out on your own?

For through Him we both have access by one Spirit unto the Father.

Ephesians 2:18

In the old days there was the veil. The purpose of that huge divider was that it kept a wall between us and God. Only one man once a year went through the veil on order to make atonement for the sins of the people. Each year he had to go back and do it again because there was not the forgiveness that we have today. There was only a covering of the sins. But God. In the sacrifice of Jesus, so many indescribably amazing things happened. His sacrifice marked the beginning of the New Covenant. Since a new covenant was coming into being the old ways had to be replaced. As Jesus died, the veil split. The way to God was open in a way it never had been before. Then it gets even better! Jesus's death, burial and resurrection released Holy Spirit to dwell with us. Through that indwelling is the true access to the Father. Holy spirit gives me never ending, full contact access to the Throne of the Great I AM. I get to be in unceasing prayer with God. I used to think that was a strange concept. Considering though, that the Spirit of God lives in me, how could I not be in constant prayer? Does that mean I do not take the time to consciously pray? Of course, I do. But I am always in contact with God because He is with me always. By the sacrifice of Jesus Christ, I have continued access through Holy Spirit to God. There is no veil. There is no law. There is grace and mercy, peace, and freedom. One of my favorite preachers says, "When talking with God, I no longer have to make a long-distance phone call. He dwells within". In this moment I have access to my Father through Holy Spirit, and I praise God for that every day. I encourage you today to think about your access to God. Consider what Holy Spirit truly gives you free access to. Then walk in the freedom of that unity.

Jesus said, "Father, forgive them, for they do not know what they are doing."

Luke 23:34a

I had such a hard time praying for my enemies when I started walking with God. I found also that I needed to pray for people who, while they loved me, still did things to hurt me. Some of that pain was not intentional. Some of it was them acting out in their own pain at the damage I had caused in my addiction. Either way, I was still hurt and needed a way to not be anymore. Since I knew the Bible told me to pray for my enemies, I thought, surely, it would also teach me how to. This is where I found it. Jesus had just spent the worst day in human history. He was betrayed by a man who walked with Him for three years. Then he was arrested and most of those He loved fled, one even denied Him three times. He was put to trial and told He would be crucified. The crowd yelled for His crucifixion. They beat Him beyond recognition. They taunted Him and mocked Him. He carried His own instrument of death as He walked to His execution. Jesus was nailed through His flesh to the cross and His bloody body jarred as it was put in place. As the clouds darkened, the worst part was taking place. The sin of the entire world for all of time was laid upon Him. Everything from Adam to the very last man, Jesus took into Himself. Even as God forsook Him in that moment, He still had a breath of prayer in His spirit. He did not beg for mercy. He asked forgiveness. Not for those He loved, but for those who hurt Him intentionally, and unintentionally. He prayed forgiveness even over me. That is when my prayer changed. The pain I was enduring in my life was nothing in comparison to what Jesus had suffered. So, I prayed His prayer over those things. As I did that, the people, little by slow, did begin to change. However, what happened faster was that I changed. In praying for God to forgive them, I was able to do that too. In forgiving them, the hurt diminished and was replaced with a loving compassion for the hurt they were feeling too. Are there people in your life causing you pain? It does not matter if they recognize it or not. Pray for them the way Jesus prayed. Let God teach you to forgive through Jesus's simple prayer.

You therefore must be perfect, as your heavenly Father is perfect.

Matthew 5:48

In the Sermon on the Mount Jesus said a lot of things. He said if I have mental lust, it is the same as adultery. If I have a hateful thought, I have committed murder. According to the sermon, if I have committed a mental sin it also means I have committed the physical one. Essentially, if I live by the law physically, I must also do so mentally. Well, thank God I am a Gentile, and the law was not given to me. The Israelites show me very plainly that keeping the law physically and mentally was not possible. There is one part of the sermon I am capable of doing. I can be perfect as my Father is. Sounds more impossible than keeping the law, doesn't it? If I take the word 'perfect' to mean flawless, then it is impossible. I am a flawed human. However, in this context, flawless is not the definition. Here, perfect means complete. Jesus tells me to be complete as my Father is complete. Today, I get to do that. For so long I was very incomplete. I was broken and fragmented in ways I thought could never be healed. Because of grace through Jesus Christ today I am complete. There are no holes in my spirit today. I have no laws I have to live up to, I get to rest in the grace that is freely given. Inside of that grace, filled with Holy Spirit, with free access to God, I am fully complete. Today, that makes me perfect as my Father is perfect. Are you complete in your spirit today? Is you prefect as your Father is perfect?

I praise you because I am fearfully and wonderfully made. Wonderful are your works, my soul knows it very well.

Psalm 139:14.

God's creation is amazing. A caterpillar lives a short life before it makes a chrysalis. While in the change, it becomes a new creation. When the process is complete it is a beautiful butterfly. We all know that. But did you know they retain their memories? They remember where they came from, and the process taken before they can fly. The bible often reminds us to remember where we came from. When we change, the memories of our past do not go away. God made us that way so that we do not go back. He causes us to become a new creation, no longer crawling, but flying. This verse reminds us that our soul knows well God's wonderful works. We experience them in the evolution of our lives. When Jesus finds us, we are like the caterpillar, but He grows us into completely different beings. Like the butterfly, He allows us to retain our memories so that we never need to go back to what we were before. Think back today on how God changed you. Search your soul for His wonderful works it knows so well. Praise Him because you have been fearfully and wonderfully made.

Wherefore take unto you the whole armor of God, that ye may be able to withstand in the evil day, and having done all, to stand. Stand, therefore.

Ephesians 6:13-14a

Some days I want to crumble. There are times when I can feel my knees buckle right before I hit the floor. I give into temptation. I allow fear to steal my peace. The worry replaces my joy. Some days those things happen, and I have to get up, brush myself off, start again. But I can tell the difference when I choose to fight. When, being attacked by the spiritual wickedness in high places, instead of giving in, I stand, there is freedom when the attack is done. I do not have to stand up and try again, because I have not fallen. The difference is the preparation. Making sure I am full of my Daily Bread and Living Water and putting on each significant piece of armor ensures that I am able to withstand. If I go to battle the principalities prepared, covered in truth, righteousness, peace, faith, salvation, and the Word I am strong enough to stand and walk forward. Sometimes, as a dear friend said, I need to take time through the day and readjust my armor. Am I walking in the things of the Spirit or the things of the flesh? If I am in the Spirit, I am prepared to stand. If I am in the flesh, I will surely fall. Are you geared up today? Are you standing, ready for battle? Will you still be standing when the attack is done?

You do not have because you do not ask God.

James 4:2c

The hardest thing I have had to learn is how to do is ask. I got stuck in the mindset that I was supposed to be able to take care of everything. After all, I am fairly newly sober and a single mom. I have only fairly recently begun to know how to hold down a full-time job. So, I thought I would add full time school to that schedule. At one point I had an extra job. I convinced myself if I worked hard enough I could carry my whole world on my shoulders, and I did not need to ask for help because I was not weak. The bible says pride comes before the fall. Thinking that I was supposed to be able to do everything by myself is such pride. It is not thinking that I am too good for help but centered in pride just the same. For me, that pride is centered in fear. In Alcoholics Anonymous the book says we are driven by 1,000 forms of fear. That fear, in turn, manifests itself in selfishness and anger and irritability. But it also causes a stagnation in the ability to stop and ask for help. So, for a long time, I did not ask for help. I suffered under the weight of fear covered by pride. I had not because I would not humble myself and ask God to help me. Oh, but when I did just that, God changed my world. It is not always because He puts material possession in my hands. God does, though, put people I my life who help me carry the burden. He gives me His strength in my weakness. Sometimes, God does meet my need with a very tangible answer but that is not always the only thing I need met. When I take the time to get out of myself, lay down my pride and all God for what I need, He consistently provides far above what I ever expected. Are you in need today? Have you asked, or have you let your pride get in the way?

Before I formed you in the womb I knew you.

Jeremiah 1:5(a)

I was so angry with God. In the months leading up to my salvation and sobriety I could not even be in the same room if someone mentioned God, Jesus, or the bible. I was not just angry that I was dying. I was mad because God knew. Before He created the garden and put the tree in it, He knew the decisions I would make. In my mind, had God not put the tree in the garden, Eve could not have been tempted. If that could not have happened, there would be no sin. With no sin, no dope. If there was no dope, I would not have been dying. I was angry and hurt that God knew I would not be able to stop, and He put the tree there anyway. He also knew something else. God knew on December 9, 2014, He was going to get to talk to me. He knew I was going to be so broken and so sick I would finally be able to hear Him. God knew exactly when I would look into the mirror. And He was there. God let me see my corpse. As I stared my own death in the face, I heard the voice of my Creator. He gave me a choice. Him or dope, life or death, heaven, or hell. In that moment, I understood why God created the tree. It was not to kill but to give choice. He knew before He created me that in that moment I would choose Him, and I would live. He loves me so much He wanted me to choose Him in the same way He chose me. God knew you too. He knew your answer before the question was asked. He created you, even though He knew your pain, so that you could choose but for the grace His healing. Have you heard His voice? Have you made your choice?

But by the grace of God I am what I am.

1 Corinthians 15:10

In the program this verse is quoted a little differently. We say, but for the grace of God there go I. I have known people who overdosed or who drank themself to death. I saw a naked woman get arrested in the middle of a very busy street at 8 in the morning. I have seen people who got to stop drinking and using go back to doing those things. It is only by God's grace that any of those instances were not me. I do not only apply this verse to recovery today. There are a lot of things the grace of God has saved me from. I see people every day who chase the law. Without the grace of God, I would be doing the same thing. For a long time, I woke up every morning and wondered how I could do better. What could I change about myself to make God like me more? What could I wear or not wear that would cause God to smile? How could I pray louder and longer to ensure God heard me? What standard could I chase that would get me a greater inheritance? The insanity of chasing the law, for me, differs little from the insanity of chasing the next high. Either way I become trapped inside of a chase I could never win. Today, because of the grace of God I get to rest in sobriety, and I get to relax in Him. I do not have to wake up every day trying to meet a self-imposed standard, I get to know today that God loves me in the exact way that He had recreated me. Does that mean I continue in conscious sin? As Paul said, "By no means." Today I get to live a life of freedom because by the grace of God, I am free no matter where I am. It is only by the grace of God I am here. By the grace of God, you are who you are. What does that look like for you today?

Brethren, I count not myself to have apprehended: but this one thing I do, forgetting those things which are behind and reaching forth unto those things which are before. I press toward the mark for the prize of the high calling of God in Jesus Christ.

Philippians 3:13-14

I had forgotten to forget what I left behind. At one point, I was better at that. I knew that my testimony of overcoming hell was a tool. At some point along the way I had again allowed what is behind me to define who I am today. I stopped being a recovered new creation and had fallen back into the isms of the disease. I got stuck in allowing my past to dictate my present. I stopped reaching forward and pressing toward the high calling because I could not go forward while looking backwards. Today, I am remembering to forget what is behind. I am choosing today to reach forward. I am not what I was. Who I am today is a blessed and highly favored child of the Living God? By grace I have been saved and recreated. I am not my past. I am not my future. Today, in this moment, I am covered by the high calling of Jesus Christ. I am choosing today to turn from what is behind and press towards the prize. That does not mean I am cured. It does not mean I will not fall down. For me, it means my falling down is not what causes my testimony to benefit. It is what happens after I get up. I walk in Christ. I pray. I read His Word. I try to live my life in service and love. Sometimes, I fail. But my true testimony is that I press forward. I choose today to forget what is behind, not using my past as a crutch but as a tool, to walk forward into the high calling of God. What choice are you making today? Are you forgetting what is behind? Are you reaching to the things that are before? Are you pressing toward Jesus? I encourage you today to remember to forget.

..... Love is patient and kind......

1 Corinthians 13:4a

In his letter to the Corinthians Paul speaks of gifts that are spectacular. In chapter 13 he plainly states that without love they are only muted shadows of what they could be. He talks about the diminishing and adverse effect of our gifts if utilized without love. Paul even goes so far to say in verse 3 that we can give up everything and become martyrs but without love, there is no gain in it. Verses 4-7 are a well laid out guideline of things unconditional love does and does not encompass. How often do we truly follow the guide? Are you patient and kind? Are you jealous, boastful, arrogant, or rude? Do you insist on having things your way? Are you irritable and resentful? Do you take pleasure in 'I told you so moments' after a wrong? How do you accept truth? What about bearing ALL things, believing, and hoping? How is your endurance of ALL things? What about the people you are to treat with such tenderness? In Matthew 5:44 Jesus tells us to love our enemies. Do you treat them with the patience and kindness you show to the people you share a pew with? What about your kids, do you hold their past mistakes over their heads or become irritable when things do not quite go your way? The neighbor who insists on mowing at 6 a.m. on your only day to sleep in, do you resent that? What about people in the church, those in leadership, who say they love but attempt to pull the muck from the lives of others without ever looking in the mirror at their own, do you love them anyway? Paul never once in the chapter says to love only the lovable. We are to be Christlike and that requires us to love as He loved. Completely, unreserved, and unbiased. Does that mean we put on blinders and accept everything? No, of course not. It means that we strive to obey the commands and behave in a manner that is laid out so plainly in these verses. Then, as we use the gifts so graciously bestowed on us by God, the world around us changes.

Be still and know.....

Psalm 46:10a

I do not always want to be still. Being a single mom in a single income household is hard. My bills are paid. My mortgage is paid. Food is provided. The vehicles are not perfect, but they run. On top of that, the relationships inside of my house are full of trust and love and respect. We want for things, but we need for nothing. Knowing those things though and fully believing that God is in the business of taking care of His children does not make being still easy. I am not promised easy though. I have said it over and again that I have looked all over the bible to find where I get to have it easy. Nowhere does it say that being still is easy. However, even when I am having a hard time being still, I get to know. What I know is that God is so good. In the midst of the stress of being a single mom and being an adult, I have the privilege of knowing God. In knowing that He is God, I get to know peace and joy. I am able to know grace and mercy because I know the Creator of those things. I do not always feel those things. Inside of sometimes consuming chaos though, what I feel does not matter. My feelings will change. What I know and what I believe is that God is good at being God. Knowing that makes it not so difficult to be still. When I can stop inside the feeling of the chaos and stress and know what I know, then I am capable of being still. When the knowing of God allows me to be still, I get to see things I could have missed. The verse says be still and know, but sometimes I need to remember to know so that I can be still. Where are you today? Are you inside of the being still or the knowing?

The thief comes only so that he can steal and kill and destroy; I have come so that they may have life and have it abundantly.

John 10:10

I spent many years fighting the thief. After a while, the fight got to be too much, and I stopped. I gave in to him and became his soldier. As the thief in my life slowly destroyed everything, he also used me to cast destruction in the lives of others. The only thing I had in abundance was misery and I was willing to share it. When I was in rehab last time though, there was one day, a Sunday, I kept hearing this verse over and again. It was in a letter from my mom, it was in a morning church service and the evening bible study. That day I knew I could have abundant life instead of abundant misery. I thought I could get back all of what I had lost. As time went on, that thought changed. What if abundant life meant I could have back more important aspects of what I had lost. Still more time passed, and the vision of abundance started to manifest into something I could not have imagined. Life in abundance was Jesus as director of my spirit. True abundance had nothing to do with regaining what I had lost. It was the filling of my life with someone I never knew I needed. When I embraced my identity through the filling of the Spirit some of the most awesome things in my life began to happen. When my relationship with Jesus began to consume my life, He added things I thought I would never have. He provides life for me in ways that would be impossible without Him. I did not get my old relationships back, they are better. He did not leave me in my old house, He gave me a home. My family now consists of those by birth, those by choice, and those of His Body. In my abundant life, given only by Christ, I may sometimes want for things, but I truly need for nothing. The thief has no power here anymore. I am no longer a soldier of my enemy. Through the abundance of Christ, I get to be a warrior for God's Kingdom. My life is full today because my spirit is full of Jesus. Life is abundant. Are you fighting the thief today? Or does the abundance of Jesus fill your spirit?

For God so loved the world, that He gave His only begotten Son, that whosoever believes in Him should not perish, but have everlasting life.

John 3:16

I love the word 'believe'. It is one of the words I thought I knew the meaning of. I assumed it was just a thing that reflected an idea. I am so glad I was wrong! Believe is a verb. I can say all day long that I believe in Jesus. However, unless there is a corresponding action, I do not really believe. The best way, for me, to look at it is to imagine that I believe my house is on fire. Once I truly believe that, I do not simply sit in my chair or carry-on making dinner. I have a reaction to that belief. The same is true for belief in Christ. I used to think, of course I believe in Jesus, I am an American. But that thought did nothing to produce any action. That changed when I really believed in Him. True belief in my life produced astounding action. Things began to happen that caused my life to be unrecognizable, especially to those closest to me. My belief caused the action of repentance. I also misunderstood that word. I thought it was saying 'I'm sorry'. What it actually is, is a turning around. For all my life I travelled in one destructive direction. Upon belief, though, I changed direction and began to live in resurrection. God loved me so much, even though I had made such terrible decisions, that He sacrificed His Son in order that I could act upon my belief. He promised that because of my belief, I will not perish. Because my belief is a the most active verb in my life, I will have everlasting life. No work gets me there. Active belief in Jesus Christ, faith in His grace, and rest in the promise of God allow me to not perish but have everlasting life. Is your belief today an idea? Or is your belief seen in action?

And we really are his children.

1 John 3:1b

I am a child of God. I am blessed and highly favored. I am heir to the Kingdom of the Great I AM. God loves me so very much. Is it prideful to say those things? Absolutely not. Is it false understanding to claim the authority given to me by my belief in Jesus? No. How often people assume it is not humble though. For me, it is bordering on disrespectful to deny my place. After everything Jesus did for me, how dare I deny what that gift entails? My earthly parents sacrificed plenty so that I could be where I am today. I do not shy away from saying I am the loved and cared for child of Tommy and Shelby Clayton. Why should it be different with God? The bible tells me to be bold and courageous and secure with the identity given to me through Jesus. That identity is this, I am Cara, blessed child of God who loves me. I am forgiven and clean. I walk in the boldness of that identity. I do not tarnish it by pretending through false humility that I am anything less. I get to be exactly who I am without fear. If God wanted my identity to be different, He would have created me differently. I screw up and I do not do life perfectly. However, that does not make my mom and dad love or think of me less. Why would it cause God, who loves me more than I can imagine to stop His love? To think that it would put limits on the limitless love of God. I will not do that today. Do you know your identity today? Do you see yourself through the mirror of your own eyes, or that of God who loves you?

For God so loved....

John 3:16a

The love of God is a powerful force. Imagine being on the brink of a miserable death. You have exhausted everything in you to the point that you no longer emotionally feel anything. There is no pleasure, happiness left so long ago, you do not even know when the last time you smiled was. The anger has dried up. Fear has been so consuming that it is no longer a feeling but a part of your being. Pain is all you know, and it has to be physically felt, so you torture your own body to just feel something. Your heart is truly stone. Everything is the darkest of darkness. You know death is coming very soon and you know you are helpless to stop it. You welcome it. That is what my life was. In the end, I wanted it to just end. I am so grateful that it did. I did not die that physical death I so very much longed for. But what I had become died. Through the powerful love of God, I died spiritually, emotionally, and mentally. Because of the resurrection of Jesus, I was able to be born again. Like Lazarus, I was raised from the dark tomb of death. For God so loved me I am alive today. I do not live a miserable existence of despair and numbness. I know peace and joy where there was once nothing at all. It is not always perfect. I struggle with things and life is sometimes hard. But God so loves me that He never leaves me alone. He renews my mind, He breathes life into my spirit, and He walks with me through emotions that feel good and often carries me through the ones that feel bad. For God so loved me, long before He physically created me, He gave me His light and I am no longer in my darkness. Do you see His light in the dark? Have you died so that in Him you can live? For God so loves you too.

Whoever confesses that Jesus is the Son of God, God abides in him and he in God.

1 John 4:15

I get to be in a continuously intimate relationship with the people I live with. Living life with people in close proximity requires conversation and understanding. It is an environment where I learn most about someone. With my kids, I know their patterns, their habits, and what is going on in their lives. With my parents, I knew their love and patience and discipline. With my ex-husband I knew his desires and needs and how to comfort him. I knew the most intimate things about those people because we lived together. It works the same with God. Except that God lives in me and I live in Him. That causes a completely different level of constant intimacy. God knows every single thing about me. That is only partly because He created me. The other part is because I share myself with Him. I tell him the most intimate parts of my life. He knows exactly what I need in my life because He knows me. I know that He will provide His joy and peace and grace and love and mercy because His presence inside of me ensures me of those things. Do you live in God today? Do you know His presence in you?

If you love me, you will keep my commandments.

John 14:15

When I first started reading the bible I was not totally sure which commandments this verse referred to. I thought surely Jesus was referencing back to the Old Testament. That was the time that He lived in. They were still under the law. Those commandments involved 613 rules and regulations on every single aspect of their lives. I could not do that! But I love Jesus. I then thought He was talking about the Ten Commandments. Surely I could keep those. I could not though. I am a single working mom, keeping a Sabbath is not possible. I also covet things. So that one is out. Sometimes I do not honor my parents. It started to seem as though I could not even do ten things. Jesus knew I could not do those things, so what was He talking about? This chapter, in context, shows that even as He was living under the law, Jesus was talking about the new commandments under the new covenant. Love the Lord your God and love others. That is, it. I love Jesus, I love God, I love you. How simple is that!! Through that love I am capable of giving grace and forgiveness. I get to serve others and give of myself. Since I love I get to be honest and intimate. Without God I could not love because He is where the love comes from. I love Jesus, so today I keep His commandments. Do you keep the commandments of love? Or do you bypass them and try to keep the commands that others have proven are unkeepable?

There is no fear in love, but perfect love casts out fear.

1 John 4:18a

I have fear today. It is in not knowing and anticipation of what I will know. There is so much that has happened in life that has allowed for security in the knowledge that God loves me completely. I have been healed from a lifetime of damage I caused. The things I tore apart have been pieced back together, only better. I am made whole through the pure uncontainable love of God. Today's fear comes from something outside of my control. This is a thing I did not cause, and I could not stop. In the program, I am promised that I will be able to cease fighting anyone and anything. Today those things I am attempting to cease fighting are within myself. I find if I fight the fear, it only gets bigger. However, I am searching for peace I cannot give answers I have yet to know. So, I do what I know to do. I rest in the love of God. I know that fear and faith are a part of this time in my life. I also know that my faith means I trust God's love, especially in times of fear. Today, He shows His love in the comfort and support of my people. He offers their arms to hold me, God puts His words in their mouths to comfort me. He is present in this fear with me, allowing me to boldly walk through this fire with Him in a very tangible way. In my humanity, things happen in life that cause me fear. But God's perfect love intervenes so that the fear is diminished. When I have trouble walking through the fear by myself, God places people in my life who walk with me, bringing His presence with them. Is there something truly fearful in your life today? Are you waiting for answers that could change your life? I encourage you to be aware of how God is placing His love in your life in order to cast out that fear. If you know someone in a fearful time of life, I encourage you to walk with them. Allow God to be present in their life through you.

And not only so, but we glory in tribulations.

Romans 5:3a

A tribulation is a great trial or suffering. The word great means considerably above average. To glory means to take pleasure in. So, essentially, this verse says I will take pleasure in above average suffering. Taken by itself, this verse makes absolutely no sense! However, when I look at it in full context of the passage, I get a different understanding. By dealing calmly with trials, I develop patience. That helps me to relay my experience to help others. That, in turn, produces hope. It is a hope that is not only meant for me, but those who travel with me. This is not an easy process. Dealing with even small struggles can often be hard. When faced with trials that threaten my finances, those tend to be of above average difficulty for me. When it comes to my health I have a bit of an easier time. Because of how God works in my life, I am able to glory in the trials and develop patience. I now have an experiences I can share that can produce hope. I can choose to not glory in the trials, without God, His word, and His promises. However, He has shown me that He hears me, He does not leave me, and that through Him all things are possible. I cannot handle the tribulations of life on my own. God promises that with Him, I can walk through higher-than-average struggles with peace. He also promises that when that happens, I am more patient and filled with hope. Are you walking through a trial? Glory in it, develop patience and share hope through the experience.

Greater love has no man than this, that a man lay down his life for his friends.

John 15:13

For most of my life I was selfish. I would stand between anyone and my family for a long time. Eventually, that changed. I let people wedge themselves between me and those I should have protected. In the end, I would not have even sacrificed my life for myself. I loved no one and nothing. When I gained full understanding of what Jesus sacrificed for me, that changed. The life that was given in order to save mine was given out of love. I did not know Jesus when He called me friend and sacrificed Himself. He knew me though. From the foundation of creation, Jesus knew me. God knew every single bad thought, horrible decision, and tragic action I would take. Yet still, He loved me so much that He sent Jesus to take my sin and make the ultimate sacrifice for me. He knew there would be a time when I could not love, and He knew that was the moment I would accept His. In doing that, He was able to teach me how to truly love others as He loves me. Today I am a different person. I love people today. Not only my family, but everyone. That does not mean I like all people I encounter. However, in loving others as Jesus loves me, it means I would lay down my life. That does not necessarily mean I have to die. But the way Jesus taught me to love means that I sacrifice for people. For my family and my fellows, I give of myself because I am able to love people today. Jesus loves me more than He loved His life. He told me to love you as He loves me. That means today I get to give of myself to walk with you. Do you love others as Jesus loves you? Do you lay down your life for anyone today?

....and His name shall be called Wonderful, Counselor, the Mighty God, the Everlasting Father, the Prince of Peace.

Isaiah 9:6b

God embodies so many different attributes. Provider. Refuge. Rescuer. Redeemer. Savior. Creator. Father. Friend. Comforter. Strong Tower. Protector. Peace. Healer. Counselor. Grace. Mercy. Lover of my soul. Forgiver. Lion and Lamb. Shepherd. Guide. Joy. Strength. Companion. Love. Master. Teacher. The Great I AM can be everything you need Him to be today. Spend time with Him. Meditate and reflect on the way He shows His presence in your life. Let God reveal Himself to you in the ways He knows you need. I challenge you today to take the time to listen for the revelation of Him in your life.

For we have not a high priest which cannot be touched with the feeling of our infirmities: but was in all points tempted like as we are yet without sin. Let us therefore come boldly into the throne of grace, that we may obtain mercy, and find grace to help in time of need.

Hebrews 4:15-16.

I find great solace in the fact that Jesus was not only tempted, but He overcame. Now, He sits at the right hand of God so that during my times of temptation I can come to the throne for grace that helps me to overcome. There is a privilege here, also. I get to come BOLDLY. Boldly means without hesitating, without fear, courageously. I am a child of God. In my humanity, when I need something, I go and ask my folks or my friends for help. I do that because I am certain of their love and their desire to help. It is no different with God. I ask God for different things though. When I boldly go to Him it is not only for an escape from temptation. I get to go to God for matters of health and weakness, for provision and peace. I go to Him in sadness and when I am filed with hope. I go boldly to His throne just because I want to be near Him, wanting nothing but closeness. Not for a moment do I need to think that my need is too small or too great for my Father. When I need mercy and grace, I am able to courageously go to the throne and lay everything down at the feet of God. Through the sacrifice of Jesus Christ, we have the privilege of being beloved children of God. Your Father wants you to come boldly, courageously to Him with each of your problems. Take your temptations before Him without fear of shame. Go to Him just because you have the desire for nearness without a want for help. He wants you there.

And I am convinced that nothing can ever separate us from God's love.

Romans 8:38a

What if the things I do and the choices I make surprised God? I am constantly surprised by the choices people make and sometimes those choices separate me from them. God though, He is never surprised. He knows my heart and He understands my humanity better than I ever could. I strive today to make good decisions. I do not always do that right. When I get it wrong God is not shocked. He does not obsess about the what if scenarios that could have made the outcome different. What happens when I screw up is that God beckons me nearer to Him. Because I love Him and I live under His grace, nothing can separate me from His love. I did not always believe that was true. For a long time, I figured I had already separated myself so I may as well keep going. Looking back though, I can see God throughout my life. He was there when I refused to acknowledge not only His presence, but also His existence. Now that I truly believe in Him, there is nothing that can separate us. Not even me. God dwells inside of me. He is here fully, faithfully, and eternally. Think about this verse today. Do not take it as a free reign, but as a blessing. Go and be exactly who God created you to be, a flawed human who makes mistakes as you live. But in your humanity, relax knowing that nothing can separate you from His love. When the mistakes happen, hear the beckoning of God calling you closer to Him, let Him help you brush yourself off and try again. Know today that nothing can separate you from God's love.

Blessed are those who wash their robes, so that they may have the right to the tree of life and that they may enter the city by the gate.

Revelation 22:14

We are blessed. Being the children of God, while it means obedience, and chastisement if we do not obey, it means so much more. While we receive blessing on earth, we are promised so much more. Because of Jesus and our commitment to Him and by being set apart unto righteousness and holiness, we are heirs. We will be partakers of the tree of life in eternal paradise. We will forever be in the presence of God. No tears, no pain, no fear. No illness, no addiction, no rejection. Each of our eternal moments will be filled with praise, peace, and joy. Our Savior is preparing for us to come Home. And He is coming to get us. We will enter through the front gates of the Kingdom of the Great I AM with thanksgiving and praise. So, what happens if we do not obey and remain outside the gates? Well, even the demons Jesus expelled from the madman requested to be cast into the pigs rather than be sent back to hell (Luke 8:31). Are your robes clean today? If the twinkling happens today and Jesus comes right now, what would He say about the condition of you? No man knows the moment. If that moment is now, will you enter the gate and partake of the tree, or will you be like the demons, begging to be cast into the pigs, trying to avoid hell?

Let everything that has breath praise the LORD.

Psalm 150:6.

When I am happy, when I am full of joy and life is smooth sailing it is easy to praise. When I am fully focused on the beauty of life, blue birds appear and remind me to joyfully sing. Some days it is easy to turn on worship music and dance around the house in prayerful praise. What about when there is a roadblock? Is praise still the first thing on my lips when life slams headfirst into a brick wall and I am trying to pick up the pieces? I am to enter His courts with thanksgiving and enter His gates with praise. (Psalm 100:4). The stipulation of being in a "good" spot in life is not tagged on to these verses. Do you know why we praise? Psalm 22:3 says God inhabits the praise of His people. Praise is a means of getting into His presence. Once I am there, it is easier to have a conversation with God. His presence is a more intimate place to petition Him, to just chat with Him, or simply be with Him. The Bible also says that if the people do not praise God, the rocks will (Luke 19:40). Can you imagine? I do not want my chance to be in the Presence of the Great I AM to be taken by a stone. I have breath. Whether that breath is taken in a time of chaos and crisis, or in times of still peace, does not matter. Circumstance should not dictate the desire and hunger I have to praise the Lord. Are you sitting in a season of unimaginable joy and peace beyond understanding? Or are you in a time where you just need today to end so tomorrow can go ahead and be over also? Either way, are you praising God?

But God shows his love for us in that while we were still sinners, Christ died for us.

Romans 5:8

He loved me at my darkest. Not only that, God knew my darkness even better than I did. He knew the path I would choose, and He had the perfect plan in place, from the creation of time, to save me from my sin. My sin is no worse and no better than anyone else's. Every sin was hung equally on the cross in Christ. There was no darkness in all of eternity that missed the crucifixion. For me, my darkest was brutal and terrifying and destructive. The cause of it is irrelevant to the fact that God loved me despite it. God knew, when He planted the tree with the fruit Eve would eat, that darkness would enter lives. Since God is love, He created a way out of it. God loved me before it. God loved me in it. He loved me through it. He loves me on this side of it. My darkest times now do not compare to what it was. Today, because I know how very much He loved me then, His light comes into my dark times, and I know His love will get me through it. God loved you at your darkest. He knew how dark it would be before you got there. Through His love, He has provided a way out. Before you even committed the sin, Christ died for it so that you do not have to. God loves you in the dark times. Go to Him. Find comfort that He is there, offering you the way out.

One Lord, one faith, one baptism.

Ephesians 4:5

I wrestled with this verse for a long time. I was attempting to forcibly pull meaning out so I could make it mean what fit my thought. What I have learned is that I was wrong, and God is right. He very plainly tells me there is One. Most people believe there is one God. However, most do not believe in one faith. People ask the time, "what faith are you?". They are wondering about denomination. When the bible was penned, there was only one. In the humanity of translation and disagreement, we have taken one faith and created many ways to understand it. What I have learned though, there is still only one faith in one God. We have done the same thing with baptism. Is the proper way to sprinkle or immerse? What are the proper words to say in order to get the recipe correct? Does it apply completely before choice, or is baptism in the age of innocence complete? No matter how it is done, who am I to disregard someone's faith in the cleansing of their own baptism? God says there is one Lord, there is one faith, there is one baptism. As a believer, I trust those things to be absolute truth. If, as a believer in Christ, you trust that this verse is absolute truth, then we have the same Lord, the same faith, and the same baptism in Him. I encourage you to look past the lines of denomination and human translation today. Accept your fellow believer as the first church did. No matter what building they walk into on Sunday.

No weapon formed against thee shall prosper.

Isaiah 54:17a

I am fond of this promise. The enemy comes in all manner of things, and he uses a variety of weapons. He attempts to strike at what he assumes is an off guard or weak moment. However, if I have built up my storehouse of prayer and have nurtured my faith, I use the attack to press in closer to God. I can begin to praise and pray under attack making an opportunity for God to destroy the weapons the enemy formed against me. It is easy to cower down and shy away from an attack, but why? Jesus Christ already gave me the victory. My Father plainly states that no weapon shall prosper. He causes me to be victorious. God plans hope for me and a future. This is the heritage of the children of God (Isaiah 54:17c). Are there weapons formed against you today? Take them to God. He has promised that they will not prosper. Trust in His plan and your heritage as His child. I encourage you today to spend time building up your relationship with the One who fights for you. Be prepared for the attack before it comes. Then, when the weapons are formed, you do not lose your peace because you know that they can never prosper.

And Jesus answering, said to them, "Have faith in God".

Mark 11:22

I love a straightforward command. There is no thought process of interpretation, you can simply take what is said and choose to follow it. Of course, you can also choose to not follow it. I have gone with both choices. On the days that I choose to not follow this command, I choose to rely on myself. Those are hard days. I am a fallible human, and because of that, relying on myself causes pain and loss of peace and an inability to fully complete my purpose. On days I choose to have faith in God, life is totally different. The choice to place my life fully in the hands of my Creator instantly leads to peace. The choice to walk in faith does not mean that the steps will be easy to take. It means I know I am not taking them alone. Following this command does not stop all pain, but it strengthens me to bear the pain. Having faith in God always allows me to fulfill my purpose in Him. How do I follow this command though? How do I have faith? It comes through the Word of God (Romans 10:17). I daily fill myself with God's Word. I allow Him to breathe life into me through an active relationship with Him. I talk to Him, and I listen when God talks to me. I walk in His steps and live in His love. I encourage you today to look at where your faith truly lies. Are you choosing to have faith in God?

My grace is sufficient; for my strength is made perfect in weakness.

2 Corinthians 12:9b

Life does not always feel good. I have days I would rather not have. I feel feelings I would rather not feel. There are thoughts I would rather not think. I have this great toolbox and support system that helps me deal with these days. However, tools and people only help me so far. At the end of these days, I still tend to feel drained, empty, and lacking. Like Paul I cry out to God for help. I do not always do it when I feel the bad day begin. What I know though, is the sooner I go to God, the better I am. It is not that God makes me feel better, less drained, less weak. The way it happens is that God reminds me of His strength. Then I become more capable of not trying to control things and allow God to take over. That makes my day better. I heard a speaker once who said, if I am truly allowing God to be in control, my life is none of my business. Looking at it that way, it becomes easier for me to relax in God's grace, comfortable in my weakness, because He is strong. If I am walking in faith, relying on God's strength, the feelings, and thoughts I do not enjoy may still be there, but they stay for a shorter amount of time. Are you in a time that does not feel good? Do your feelings hurt, or your thoughts scream at you? Learn from Paul. Relax in the grace of God. Knowing that in this time of weakness God is so very strong.

In the beginning God created.

Genesis 1:1

From the beginning the plan for everything was in place. God knew exactly what would happen when He declared time to begin. He was not surprised by the snake in the garden or the choice that Eve made. He was not confused when His people wandered the desert for 40 years. He knew what He would need to sacrifice when He breathed life into humanity. God loved us so much He sent His son. The sending of Christ was the sign of the end of a very old covenant. Jesus's birth was the sign of grace to come. God knew the birth of Christ would usher in His death. Without the first birth, there could be no resurrection into the second. This week, as Christmas is celebrated, I encourage you to think of what this season ultimately means. We celebrate the birth of Christ so that we are able to be saved by His death and recreated in His resurrection. This celebration marks the beginning of the end. It is my prayer today that you know the truth of the birth of our Savior. He was born so that He could die making it possible for Jesus to rise. All of that in order that we may live. What better gift could you receive?

He had no form or majesty that we should look at Him.

Isaiah 53:2b

God came, clothed in flesh, born as a baby. It does not matter the exact day that it happened. What matters is that when I celebrate His birth I am doing it for the right reasons. This year Christmas is different for my family. We celebrated on a different day, and we did very little in the way of gifts. It was simple. However, I know more of the purpose and the gift that has been given to me this year. I am grateful beyond words for the grace of God. I see His work everywhere. I see His mercy in the rooms of AA. I see His overflowing generosity in my boss. I experience His unconditional forgiveness with my family. I know His goodness in the women He has placed to walk through the fires with me. I understand His love through the new creation I see in the mirror. Because the Great I AM stepped into humanity I get to witness His work every day. I celebrate the birth of Jesus with a gratefulness this year that brings such joy and peace. The party this year was not for the presents, but for the Presence that is priceless. I pray you know the presence of God today. Reflect on the gift He brought through His birth. Celebrate that Christ is born. Though He may not have been much to look at in His humanity, know the majesty of having Him in your life today.

I bring you good news of great joy that will be for all people.

Luke 2:10b

He came for all people. Jesus was born to shed His cleansing blood for the rule followers and the rule breakers. His joy is the salvation of not only the generally good decision makers, but also for those whose decisions have also been mostly bad. He was born for the alcoholic, the preacher, the addict, and the avid churchgoer. Jesus came for the murderer, the adulterer, the ones who covet. The good news is that His birth would lead to forgiveness in His death and the salvation of His resurrection. The joy is that Jesus is for all. Every single person is included in all. We like to think it is just for those who think like we do or hear things in the manner that we do. But Jesus was sent for the world, not only a select few. He came for the sinners who need so desperately to be loved. He did not ignore the whore. He did not shun the thief. He did not walk past the blind. He even shared the truth with those educated and thought they knew it. Jesus's birth ushered in a grace that is for all. The joy of the birth of Christ is not exclusive but is the most intimately inclusive gift ever given. Celebrate the birth of Jesus every day. I encourage you to hear His good news and share His great joy that is the gift for all.

To redeem those under the law, so that we might receive adoption as sons.

Galatians 4:5

I love adoption. In my family we have the blessing of not only experiencing spiritual adoption but also physical. This weekend I was able to gain a better understanding of God's meaning of adoption. Two years ago, the process was the most painful thing I have ever been through. Watching my child do the bravest thing in giving her child a better life was like having my heart torn out. To see a beautiful and loving couple drive off with my grandchild all but killed me emotionally. At that time, we thought our little given gift would not be in our arms again until she was an adult. However, that time came way sooner than anyone thought. I got to watch the woman raising my granddaughter embrace my daughter in pure love. We got to unite and grow as a full family in just a few hours. It reminded me of how we are taken into the family of God. Just like adoptive parents bring a child home and love them fully and completely like their own, God does the same thing. He chose the Israelites as His children in the beginning. He sent Christ to adopt those outside of the family to come in. Not just to come as a Gentile. We are taken into Christ and made heirs. We become fully and completely His own. Through Jesus, God pulls us into His arms and becomes the Eternal Father in our lives. I am so blessed to have seen this in the flesh in my family. I am even more blessed to be seeing it spiritually in those around me. Can you see the full love of adoption in your life and in those who walk with you?

And we know that in all things God works for the good of those who love him, who have been called according to his purpose.

Romans 8:28

This verse has been hitting home for me lately. It reminds me of the great vastness of God's love for me. This is a time of year for reflection. As I do that, I can see where God has been in my life. This year I have decided to look further back. I can see how God had orchestrated my life till this point. I can see how He placed people in my path so that they could be there in the moment I needed them to be. From the woman I called when I needed to get sober, to the lady I work steps with today. They were both placed in my life long before they filled the role they have today. The same thing happened with my boss. When we met it was on a completely different situation, but God put us together for this circumstance. God does not do this only with people though. The verse says all things work together. That includes circumstances. I have spent several years as a single woman. Some days it was so difficult to understand how that could possibly work for my good. Today though, I can see God's hand in it. All things in my life work together for good because I love God and am called according to His purpose. I cannot see it while it is happening, but as I look back, I can clearly see how it is good. As you reflect over your year today, look for the path in which God had worked all things to be good for you.

Who against hope believed in hope?

Romans 4:18a

Sometimes it seems like everything is caving in. Circumstance after circumstance can make it feel as though life itself is conspiring against me. Though I do not feel like this personally, I know people in the midst of one struggle or another today. I know what it is like to come to the end of the money. I understand having an empty fridge with hungry kids in the house. There is such agony in the loss of loved ones. I have been on the humiliating end of just not feeling like I am enough. When it feels as though time has betrayed me, ran out, and taken all my options with it, I have felt that sense of defeat. However, what I know today is the promise of God. Nothing is impossible with Him. He will not give me anything I cannot walk through if I am walking with Him. God works all things together for my good because I love Him. In these promises I find hope. Hope is confident expectation. I can confidently expect God to fulfill His promises in my life because I am His child. He does not do it because I act perfectly, make every right decision, or do some awesome work for it. He fulfills His promises because He loves me. I have faith in His grace and hope in His promises. On the days when it seems bleak and as though all hope is gone, I can still, against all of that, rest in confident expectation that God has His hand in my life. When I rest in that hope, it builds my faith that He is working all things together for my good. Life is not always easy or fun. If you are in a time of stress or grief or confusion, I encourage you to rest in confident expectation today. When all seems hopeless, place your hope in God's promises. He will fulfill them and in greater ways than you ever imagined.

Choose this day whom you will serve.

Joshua 24:15b

At some point, we are all faced with the choice that not only alters our life, but also our eternity. For me, December 9, 2014 was the day. Jesus came and gave me a choice of whom I would serve. Would I continue to serve myself, die an ugly death, and spend eternity in hell? Or would I choose Him? He did not force my choice. He only laid out the options I had. God is always a gentleman. Since He is a gentleman, He did not use sugar-coated words or come to me through someone else's experience. Jesus came and told me the truth I needed to hear in an experience with Him I will never forget. That day, I chose to serve Him. That was 5 years ago though. What about today? I could make a different choice today because each day I have the same options. I have to actively choose THIS day whom I will serve. Yesterday's choice does not dictate this day. Some days, honestly, I choose myself. When I do that, I experience irritation, anxiety, chaos in my magnificent magnifying mind. When I choose God though, life is different. It is not easier. The bible never once says that choosing God causes life to be easy. It does, however, promise a Refuge, a Counselor, and a Lover of my soul. Choosing God has given me life so much more abundantly than I could have imagined. I start today with a choice. Same as you. Choose THIS day whom you will serve. I pray you choose the Lord.

Prove me, O Lord, and try me; test my heart and my mind.

Psalm 26:2

How brave David was at the writing of this psalm. He desired that God search the most hidden places of his humanity. Most people I have known in life have a secret. Even one they would prefer to keep from God. In our humanity we like to think that if it is not discussed then our favorite little secret sin can stay just that. In reality, we all know nothing, no matter how small, is hidden from God. How often do you invite Him in completely to test that though? Sure, we let Him come into our hearts and our lives, but do we really open every messy closet and junk drawer for Him to wander through? Do we ask Him to truly help us clean the mess under the bed? Or do we keep that one door locked, hoping He will not want to test that part of our heart or mind? The purpose of inviting God in to test each area of our humanity is not a means to shame or tempt or for failure. It is a chance for God to be involved, for Him to assist in cleaning up where we are still a mess, for Him to show us discipline. Asking God into every place of life allows for self-awareness and growth. It offers a chance for us to become who He truly created us to be. I encourage you today, be as bold as David and ask God to come in to prove, try, and test you. Then be bold and make the changes he puts before you.

On hearing this, Jesus said to them, "It is not the healthy who need a doctor, but the sick. I have not come to call the righteous, but sinners."

Mark 2:17

Sometimes I cannot stand to scroll Facebook and Instagram. There are days when my feed is full of people damning others for their choices. Posts about how one person's choice of church does not measure up to the next persons. Memes trying to scare people to God, almost using the coming of Christ as a threat instead of a celebration. Folks condemning others because of their life choices. Jesus never did that. Not one time did God Himself ever yell at a whore or ridicule the sick. He did not force Himself on anyone. Jesus came peacefully. He spoke words of love and grace and forgiveness. He did not shun the sinners but ate with them. Does that mean He approved of their lives? Obviously not. But scripture states over and again how the lives changed when He left. I like to imagine what it would have been like to break bread with the Bread of Life. In my mind, I am usually at the height of my disease, sitting across from the kindest eyes ever created. I feel loved, whole, clear headed, and forgiven. I take that image with me into life. I spend a lot of time with people who are sick, with people who have been whores, men who have been evil. I do not allow their choices to hinder the kindness Christ showed me. As St. Francis said, "I daily share the Gospel. Sometimes, I use words". For me, Christians who brought fear tactics, intolerance, and cruelness in their actions could never get me to hear their kind words. It was not in their eyes. That is what I see so much of in society today. I know my life cannot make the impact God created me to make if I walk in intolerance and cruelty. I also know I can sit down to eat with sinners and leave knowing that while they may not have heard the Gospel, they saw it. My purpose is like Christ's. Offer Him to people, never with force, always with grace. I pray you get the chance to dine with the dirty. I hope that when you do, your kind eyes match with the loving words and graceful actions of Christ.

Be kind one to another, tenderhearted, forgiving one another, even as God for Christ's sake has forgiven you.

Ephesians 4:32

I have known this verse my whole life. I learned it as a melody in Sunday School. Now I am singing it in my head. Interesting that it has come back all these years later. Kindness has been on my heart a lot lately. I have a friend who tells me that relationships would be so much better if those involved were just kind to each other. An act of kindness can accomplish so much. One of my favorite things to do is tell random strangers how beautiful they are. It brightens their day and I love to see the reaction. I find that when I am consistently kind, my heart grows in tenderness. With a tender heart, I am more likely to notice the moods of people. That puts me in a mindset of prayer for strangers. Sometimes the prayers are silent. Sometimes I pray with people. When I am living persistently with a tender heart, I find that I want to forgive people. It is not that they see how they rubbed me wrong and come ask forgiveness. It is more a desire to not be filled with anything negative. So, I choose to forgive, even if the one I am forgiving is not aware of it. I have not thought about this verse in years, but today I can see how all the parts interact with each other. I am able to forgive because my heart is not hard and that is because I have been living a life of kindness. I do not always operate like that. Kindness does not always look the way we think it should. Things done for the Kingdom rarely look like that. Sometimes the kindness is in allowing people to be on the path they are supposed to be and supporting, but not trying to fix or shield them from what I know is coming. Other times kindness looks like a bouquet of lilies. Often, it is just a sweet word or caring gesture. I love that I get to walk out this verse I forgot I knew. Be kind today. Look at the people you encounter with a tender heart. Forgive without it being known. Do as God does.

Jesus saw their faith.

Mark 2:5a

I love this passage. Jesus was in a packed house. Four men had a friend who was lame, and they just could not get to Jesus. So, naturally, they tore the roof off the house. They then proceeded to lower their friend so he could be close enough to the Healer to be healed. And Jesus saw their faith. He did not just sense it. He looked at the friends of this man, saw their faith and healed him. Can you imagine having faith so great that it is visible? I know people with that kind of faith. I see it in my mom and brother and sister-in-law. I see it in my sponsor and in my sponsor sister. I can see it grow in people as the seed is planted and watered and nurtured. It is not just people I am close to. Faith is visible in strangers I see in public interacting with other strangers. Faith does not always look like a saint praying in the alter or one shouting the Gospel. So often it looks like grace, mercy, and kindness. It looks like trust and hope and raw dedication to God. Faith looks like Mother Theresa taking care of the sick. It looks like an alcoholic and addict walking into a meeting. Faith looks like a cancer patient who believes she wins if she lives, and she wins if she dies. Faith in God through Jesus Christ manifests in people of all denominations and classes. Look for it through your day today. Be aware of the people around you. I wonder if you can see in others what Jesus saw in four faithful men.

At dusk, dawn, and noon I sigh deep sighs—he hears, he rescues.

Psalm 55:17 (MSG)

I heard a wonderful lady say that God hears the meanings of our sighs. The first time she said it, it stuck, and I think about it often. The second time I heard her say it, she put this scripture with it. I looked it up in various translations. Some use the word moan, others say cry. Either way, the verse talks about being in a time when you have no words. I do not know about you, but there are times when I pray, and I have no words left. I am worn out spiritually, emotionally, and mentally. Life is a tough opponent sometimes. I have searched the whole Bible to find a scripture that will promise life gets to be easy now. It is not there. Deep in the midst of life changes, frustration, and aloneness, I have had no words left. It is all I can do to lay at the foot of God's Throne with nothing left to say. All I have left are deep sighs and tears. The Bible says God hears those too. Not only does He hear them, He understands them better than I do, and He is going to rescue me. God knows the prayer of your sighs too. Do not give up. Remember, when you only have deep sighs, He hears, and He rescues.

They received the word with all eagerness, examining the Scriptures daily to see if these things were so.

Acts 17:11b

When I met Jesus I only remembered some of the things I had learned at church as a kid. What I freshly knew of God, after an amazing encounter with Him, did not quite measure up to my memories. That imbalance and a raw hunger to really know Him propelled me into an amazing journey. I absolutely devoured scripture. I would listen to sermons online and everything I heard I cross-referenced with scripture. I prayed for discernment and guidance from Holy Spirit. I read with 4 bibles open and a dictionary so that I knew I understood the words fully and completely. I took nothing at face value, and I stayed away from commentary. I knew all the answers were in God's Word, not man's and God is who I was, and am, hungry for. I knew that if I studied God's Word, He would reveal Himself to me. I was eager and willing to examine scripture. Now, I am so grateful I study for myself. I know what I believe, and I know why I believe it. In taking time to learn about God from God and not man, I have a deep security in my relationship with Him. God consistently reveals Himself to me in new ways every time I open my bible. He breathes life into me through His Word. I eagerly search for the Truth of Christ in scripture, and I never fail to see how absolute that Truth is. I encourage you today to read the scripture for yourself. Commentary and man's opinion is great, but it should not replace the direct teaching of Christ. Let Him breathe into your life through His Words.

Therefore, endure hardness, as a good soldier of Christ.

2 Timothy 2:3

The next verse says no good soldier bothers himself with things of the world in order to please the one who made him a soldier. I was a soldier for the wrong side for a long time. I did bother myself with the things of the world. I was drunk on sin and unable to endure anything at all. But God. Life is, by no means, easier on this side of resurrection. I have months where the ends just do not meet. I have issues with my kids. I sometimes feel as though I am locked in a battle and am constantly fighting to just keep my head above water. As a soldier though, I have been trained. Jesus taught me how to breathe as I strategically look at a situation. He showed me how to go to Him and lay out the circumstance. I learned to listen to His direction, and I learned how to follow His command. In my old life I knew retreat. Today, I know how to endure the hard because I am confident that I am no longer alone in it. I get to be a good soldier of Christ today because I let Him teach me how to be. I fight my battles and endure the hard times through prayer and scripture, I walk with other soldiers. Sometimes we get to fight together, often we support each other through things we need to endure for ourselves. Always we have Christ in the midst of us. Is your life hard today? Go to God, let Him teach you how to endure. Be the soldier He created you to be.

As for me and my house, we will serve the Lord.

Joshua 24:15d

I have always read this part of the verse as a declarative statement. Sometimes I read it and my spirit aches. I have two wonderful children who believe in God, but do not serve Him. Since my children were not raised, in their formative years, by parents who served the Lord, they never truly learned the difference. My life changed though and now they see what it really means to serve. They witnessed the death of the person I was, and they see the sacrifice of the person I am now. They see open and read bibles and they see worship. They see me pray and walk with God. For me, this verse sits as a promise that I can declare. My house will serve the Lord. This day, I will serve God. I will share Him; I will serve others as He did in His flesh. I will walk with Him and talk with Him. I will give an example today that not only my kids, but those around me can see. I will have faith that my whole house will serve the Lord. I encourage you today, set an example of service for those in your life. Make this promise a declaration. I pray that you and your house will serve the Lord.

You do not have because you do not ask God.

James 4:2c

I know people on both sides of prayer. One group believes in very specific prayer. The other believes you should only pray for yourself if it is beneficial for others. I personally believe in specific prayer. I was discussing this with a friend, and I told her I like to put this verse in terms of flesh. My parents know I have a hard time. However, if I do not tell them I need groceries or help with my car, then they do not help me with those things. It is natural in a relationship to tell the other person what it is you need. It is no different with God. I am in an active relationship with God. So, I am able to ask Him, very specifically for the things I need. Sometimes I do need groceries, there has been a time I needed a job and that included making a specific amount of money, on occasion I have needed a help with bills, a couple of times I needed a vehicle, I even pray for my life-long companion. While God knows each and everything I need before I tell Him, He still wants me to have the confidence in our relationship to ask Him. It is humbler to admit my needs than it is to assume either He knows, or it does not matter. When I pray specifically I do not ask for more than I need, and I do not ask for things that venture far into the realm of wants. God wants to hear my needs from my mouth, so I ask. I may not have the things I want, but I have everything I need. Do you have a need or desire today? Talk to God about it. Chances are you do not have it because you have not specifically asked for it.

Then Jesus said to his disciples: "Therefore I tell you, do not worry about your life..."

Luke 12:22a

My sponsor is very fond of reminding me that right now, in this moment, everything is exactly as it should be. I know that if I am in worry then I am assuming the future. However, when I listen to God, and the reminders He places in my life, and I stay in the present moment I have been given, I find peace. In The Screwtape Letters, CS Lewis says, the present moment is the time when human reality is fully connected with Eternity (paraphrase). In this moment, I am able to completely connect with God. I cannot rely on my past connection because it is gone. I cannot rely on the connection even 5 minutes from now because it may not even come. Right now, in this very present time, His breath fills my lungs. His Spirit resides in me. I am fully in His Presence. There is no worry about my life, what I will eat, or what I will wear. It is when I get out of this moment of Presence and begin to assume the future that worry can consume me. Simple, but not easy. Prayer, reading scripture, and writing help me to facilitate remaining in this moment and out of worry for my life. Are you in worry? Or in this present moment is your reality fully connected with the Presence of God?

And he answered, Fear not: for those that be with us are more than they that be with them.

2 Kings 6:16

Elisha's servant was scared. The enemy surrounded them on all sides. I have very often felt the same way. Life happens and sometimes it seems like the enemy has gotten stronger and bolder. It is as though he has sent all his forces to surround me, daring me to come out. Fear can creep in if I do not remember the army that surrounds me. This passage goes on to say that Elisha asked God to open his servant's eyes to the truth of their surroundings. When He did, the man could see the mountain full of horses and chariots of fire. God did not leave them to fight the battle alone. Why did God send His troops on behalf of Elisha? It was not because Elisha prayed ER prayers. It was not because he showed up for service on Sunday and lived the rest of the week with no consideration of God. Elisha served the Lord. He talked to Him and walked in His ways. Elisha allowed God to alter the course of his life and he obeyed Him. Because of the relationship Elisha had with God, he was bold enough to tell his servant to fear not and he knew the army of the Lord was protecting him. How is your relationship with God? When the enemy surrounds your camp, are you fearful like the servant, or are you faithful in your trust like Elisha?

Also, I heard the voice of the Lord, saying, Whom shall I send, and who will go for us? Then said I, here am I, send me.

Isaiah 6:8

Isaiah was full of bravery and boldness. Nothing different than what you and I are called to though. God needed someone to be willing to go, Isaiah stepped up, apparently without giving it a second thought. The disciples reacted the same way to Jesus. He said, come, follow me, and that is just what they did. Sometimes, God will ask me to go, and the flesh of my humanity does not want to. I will even remind God that I am unqualified and unworthy. I mean, look at my life! I was a soldier for the enemy. I bore the labels of some of the most monstrous things you can imagine. Of course, God knew that when He pulled me out of the pit of hell. Today, I pray that whatever God asks me to say or to pray, I will be bold in that speaking. I pray that wherever God asks me to go I will be courageous in the going. I pray that whatever God asks me to do, I will be empowered by His bravery to do. I want to be fully willing to fulfill the purpose God has in my life. So today, when God asks, whom shall I send, I will stand up and boldly say, here am I, send me. I pray boldness for you today too. Do the hard thing God is asking you to do. Say the deep, meaningful things He wants you to say. Go to the places He is leading you to go. When He calls, I pray you are brave enough to say, "send me".

She laughs without fear of the future.

Proverbs 31:25b

I love to laugh. My favorite laughter is with my sister. One of us gets started and its contagious. Pretty soon we are both cracking up. It is usually over something that would seem absurd to anyone else. The cause does not really matter. What happens is inside that moment of laughter, nothing else is happening. Where there was anger or frustration or fear seconds before, when we laugh together, we are in the same present moment. All feelings subside and things look a little different. I did not laugh much yesterday. I barely smiled. I was in fear of the future. It is very difficult to find humor in an assumed future. My magnificent magnifying mind creates scenarios that will probably never happen, but they instill fear and worry, and those things caused my mood and my day to be less than joyful. What I know, however, is that when I get out of the future and remain firmly planted in the present, the fear is gone. If I focus on right now, the future can cause me no harm. It does not mean I will not feel any adverse feelings. It does mean that I am able to feel the emotion, allow it to pass, and move forward. I am not always good at being in the present moment. I do know how to recenter myself here though. Prayer keeps me here. Having a conversation with the One who creates this moment is the best way for me to stay in it. God taps on my heart with scripture and when I think on that, I cannot focus of the fear of the unknown. God places people in my life who are very good at reminding me that right here, right now, everything is good. And I laugh with no fear. Have you laughed lately? Next time you do, notice how it makes everything else disappear and it heightens the present moment that you are in. Then walk the rest of your day moment to moment, without fear of the future.

She dresses herself with strength and makes her arms strong.

Proverbs 31:17

I like to think I am a strong, independent woman. A friend of mine says she is "self-supporting, declining outside contributions". Either way I say it, it means I am in control. That is how it has been for a long time. I controlled almost everything in my marriage. As a single, I control absolutely everything now. That is changing though. I am in the process of learning how to relinquish some of my decisions to other people. I am still a single parent, but my youngest is now grown and I have to learn to let him make his own decisions about his life. My role now is to suggest, not command. It is an odd sensation to go from being the conclusion to being informed of what the decision is. When I get to have a new relationship, I want it to be one of mutual respect and compromise. That would be not like any relationship I have had. I would like to have conversation and mutually agreed upon decisions. Not always, as I am in the very early learning process, and I attempt to control in some moments I do not even realize I am doing it. So, I have had the Proverbs 31 woman on my heart a lot in the process of this change (God's way of tapping on my heart with scripture). As I read about her, I hear God telling me that it is ok to be strong and independent. As long as in doing that I am not attempting to be in control. The balance is in trusting God to have control. It is in being still and knowing that His plan is better than mine. Even if I do not understand it in this moment. In trusting that God has purpose in His placement of the people in my life, I am better able to discuss and compromise. It becomes easier to relinquish the control I hold on to so tightly. I can still be strong and independence if my dependence is on God and I let Him be in control. It is simple. Not an easy lesson to learn though. Do you like to be in control? Do you take care of everything, make all the decisions? Just for today, let your grip loosen. Allow God to have control. Be strong in your dependence on Him.

She speaks with wisdom.

Proverbs 31:26a

Surely she does not always speak with wisdom. I wonder what she was like when she was mad, or her feelings were hurt. Maybe when she argued with her husband her words were not always wise. Perhaps, though, I am looking for excuses for my own tongue. Or, it could be this verse is not about her reactions to normal human irritation. I imagine she speaks with wisdom as she is helping to guide another woman in how to be better today. Or maybe it is when she is teaching younger women in the community how to be a good wife. Possibly when she is simply helping a friend through a tough situation. I have a lot of women in my life. None of us sound consistently wise when we are talking about our own struggles. However, if you need one of them to listen and give you feedback, it is clothed in wisdom. I associate with women who pray and walk with God. We sharpen each other. We think about self-improvement and strive for that every day. I seek wisdom through the Word and relationship with God. That allows me to be for the people in my life what I need them to be in mine. I want people in my life who are wise and challenge me to do better and be better. I think that is the kind of wisdom the Proverbs 31 woman has. Do you speak with wisdom today? Do you know where it comes from? Do you desire it from others in your life? I pray you have people in your life with wisdom that sharpens you.

Neither pray I for these alone, but for them also which shall believe on me through their word.

John 17:20

In my Bible, those letters are red. That means Jesus said them. During His prayer on the night He was arrested, hours before hanging on the cross, Jesus prayed for me. He also prayed for you. He knew that His words would be recorded and thousands of years later you would need to see them. He knew you would need to know He was thinking of you. We hear all the time that He was. It is not just something people say to make you feel better. Jesus was thinking of you at the same time He knew the end was coming. His thought was not of Himself. In verse 23 Jesus prayed that we would be one with Him so that we would know He loves us. Close your eyes and feel the love that was there before the foundation of creation. Love that caused God to put on flesh, walk out of heaven and, ultimately, into hell so that we do not have to. Now, open your eyes and walk in that love. Choose to honor His sacrifice and love as He loves. Speak love into people's lives. Not only the likeminded. Pray for the unbeliever, that they may be one with God. Share Jesus that they may believe. Do not let His prayer be in vain.

For we walk by faith not by sight.

2 Corinthians 5:7

This is an easy verse to read. The words are full of hope and encouragement. They hint at confidence and obedience. It is a choice to walk by faith though. Sometimes, you only have 2 dollars left in the bank. One day, the doctor has terrifying words to say. There are nights you sit up, wondering where your kid could be. There are concerns about being a good parent. You may even, right now, be in the midst of marital issues so hard you cannot see a way out. In these moments, sometimes it is hard to be still and not try to fix things on your own. Life makes it difficult to daily decide to walk by faith. It is possible though. We are told in Mark 11:22 to have faith in God. It is not just a suggestion. Having faith is knowing, beyond every doubt, that God is working, and He already knows the answer before you ask. It is by that knowing you trust Him, and you learn to be still and walk in faith. Some days, what I know must dictate what I see, or what I see will violate what I know. The knowing of faith does not just happen. Romans 10:17 tells us faith comes by hearing and hearing by the Word of God. Immerse yourself in the Word. Walk with God and let Him strengthen your faith. Then it will not matter what the bank, the doctor, or life throws at you. Walk by faith today, so that your sight does not deceive you.

Peace I leave with you; my peace I give you.

John 14:27a

Some verses I can read over and again. I am consistently amazed at the deep meaning in just a few words. Peace defined is freedom from disturbance and from oppressive thought and emotion. Before the cross, more than 2,000 years ago, Jesus Christ knew I would need to know He left me peace. I think He has left peace in a special place for each of us. Some find it in beautiful locations. Others find it in the darkness that has become their prison. I was 36 when I found peace in a bathroom. It was months later before I discovered the second promise of this verse. Not only had Jesus left me peace, He was also giving me His peace. The Son of the Great I AM, Savior of the whole world died on a cross was buried in a tomb and rose so that He could give me His peace. But what does that mean?? I no longer know the kind of chaos my life used to hold. That is the peace He left. There is more though. When Jesus died, the bible says He gave up His Spirit. This is the peace He gives. For me, it is the feeling of the peace Jesus left and the knowing of the peace He gave. In knowing peace through Holy Spirit, I believe in the peace I have. Feelings change much quicker and easier than what I know I believe. I will not easily give up things that I know. The peace Jesus gives is in knowing the Spirit of Christ. Have you found the peace Jesus left for you? Do you know the peace He gave to you? I pray today that you do and that your spirit rests in the peace of Holy Spirit.

If I do not go away, the Comforter will not come to you.

John 16:7c

I find it exceedingly sad that the offense of the world was so great that Christ had to die. The circumstances that had to play out in order that prophecy may be fulfilled is equally sad. In my mind, He would have been just as dead had He been poisoned. It would have been much less painful. Isaiah, though, said Jesus had to be rejected and beaten, humiliated, and hung. As sad as the circumstance, I am eternally grateful that He did go away. The only reason I am alive today is because Jesus died. His Spirit that dwells within and comforts me is the reason I have not gotten what I deserve. What I deserve is hell. But God. In Christ's sacrifice and resurrection and the following ascension His Spirit was freed to be poured out not only on Pentecost, but also into me. Praise God!!! His going away did the same for you. You have the Comforter of Jesus Christ in you. Holy Spirit is comforter, counselor, and helper. I encourage you today to find gratitude that Jesus has left you His Comfort, instead of giving you what you deserve.

She wet my feet with her tears and wiped them with her hair.

Luke 7:44c

She was a whore. That is how she lived. It is the way she knew how to eat and pay her bills. But when she met Jesus her entire life changed. I love her story because it is mine. I venture to say it is also yours. Maybe not the whore part. It all amounts to the same thing though. The only difference is society's perception of the god you served before you could hear the love of Christ. Whether it was lust or money, food or starvation, drugs or alcohol, perfection or service an idol is still an idol. This woman's sin happened to be very public, whereas some are much more private. I had an array of both kinds of sin. Most people knew my biggest idols, but there was an abundance of smaller ones that few saw. Like a Pharisee, I imagine, most people seem to have it all together on the outside. However, when truly examined, the sins are of abundance, even if they seem small. This woman understood the gravity of the forgiveness of Jesus. She boldly walked into a place where she was absolutely unwelcome and washed the feet of Jesus in expensive perfume and tears then dried them with her hair. Can you imagine sitting in church and a drug addicted whore walking in and doing that to your pastor? Would you be forgiving like Christ, or appalled like the Pharisee? Would it put you in mind of your first moment with Jesus? Would you remember when, broken and very aware of your sin, you sat at His feet and poured yourself out on Him? Do you still feel the forgiveness of that day? Are you sharing it with others? Do you sit in judgment or compassion? The better question may be, when was the last time you sat at the feet of Jesus? That is my encouragement today. Go to Him. Feel again the forgiveness of Christ. Then take it into your life and let others see how it can change you.

There is one body and one Spirit - just as you were called to the one hope that belongs to your call - one LORD, one faith, one baptism, one God and Father of all, who is over all and through all and in all.

Ephesians 4:4-6

The body is divided. We humans believe we are right individually and then like to group with those who think like us. When the church began there was one, not 50 different types to choose from. In our brilliance we have chosen bits and pieces that make our denomination what is and have decided that the rest of the camps are, mistaken in doctrine, to put it gently. Can you imagine the force of the Army of God if we were truly united as one body? The enemy comes to kill, to steal and to destroy. Division has stolen music and modesty from some of the church. Not being united has killed morals and values in other parts. Separation of the saints has destroyed obedience to the point of hypocrisy in still more. We ceased being one and became many. The Body is the Bride of Christ. Many separate parts believing individually that we have the whole truth and causing discord in what was supposed to be the true church. One day we will be united as one. When Jesus returns He will call to Him all who came to Father through Him. We will celebrate as we sit at the feast and no longer remember the things that divided us. Perhaps we could do that today. Accept those who are God's through Jesus, whether you believe their doctrine or not. Love them in their truth, as Jesus loves you in yours. Then maybe, the one watching who does not believe will see the truth of Jesus in you.

But he said to them.....I will not believe it.

John 20:25 b & e

Because of his initial disbelief Thomas has since been remembered as the doubter. I am often reminded of my own disbelief. Mine lasted a lot longer than Thomas's. I was baptized when I was 11 or 12. However, I was not saved until I was 36. That is a quarter of a century of disbelief. It did not start that way. I wanted to be a regular, well-behaved kid. I just could not muster the capability. Not much later, the enemy had a very firm grip. Before the end, I could not be in the same room where anyone mentioned God, Jesus, or the Bible. I was so very angry with God. What I know today is that the root of anger is fear. I was suffering, not from anger towards God, but from fear that He would never save me. It was by no means a conscious fear. I only believed I was very angry. And I doubted as Thomas doubted. Jesus answered Thomas's doubt with proof. He appeared and Thomas was able to see and touch the wounds. Jesus told him it was well that Thomas now believed but blessed are those who believe without seeing. I do not fall into that category. Like Thomas, I needed proof. Not that Jesus was who He claimed to be. Not even that He walked out of the tomb. I needed proof that I was worth saving. God never fails to give His children exactly what they need. He not only saved me from death, He saved me to life. In a moment, through His Presence, Jesus completely altered the course of my life. I believe He did it again last night, only in a much different way. Are you as Thomas was? Do you doubt? Do you need proof? I pray that you go to God today. Sit in His Presence. Be blessed by your belief in Him you cannot see. Then look around you and see His proof in the life He has given you today.

Jesus took the bread, broke it, blessed it, and gave it to the disciples ... and He took the cup and gave thanks and gave it to them.

Matthew 26:26b, 27a

I love to take part in corporate communion. It is a time for believers to come together and to remember the sacrifice of Jesus and what He offered to us truly means. I think most churches have their own ritual. Some dunk bread into a shared cup. Some use individual cups and wafers. There are churches who do the traditional ceremony every Sunday, others every quarter, and a few who do it very rarely. I sometimes wonder if it has become vain repetition like the Pharisee prayer Jesus spoke of. The New Testament never once mentions corporate communion. The writers do not talk about the traditional ritual communion has become. Do not misunderstand, they still participated. They, however, had a supper. When Jesus said to do this in remembrance of Him, I do not think He was speaking about a future vague symbol of His flesh and blood. He broke bread and had a cup with His fellows. In 1 Corinthians 11 Paul talks about how, when gathered for the Lord's Supper, some get full and drunk, and others are left to go without. Sounds like more than a cracker and half a shot of grape juice. I think Jesus spoke of the fellowship and the supper. It should be understood, in my opinion, more like, when you come together for a meal, break the bread, and bless it, bless the cup, share in these things as Jesus shared His own flesh and blood for us. As you are gathered, remember Him and His sacrifice. I also cannot believe He wanted the time to be somber and quiet. I imagine He would want us to humbly rejoice as we remember He is the reason for the fellowship and the supper. Leave it to humanity to take something meant to be pure and turn it into the vain repetition of tradition and ritual. When was the last time you participated in the Lord's Supper? Was it inside the building we call church? Or was it around the table, being celebrated with the Body of the Church?

Your Kingdom come …

Matthew 6:10

I was going to start by saying "I am embarking on a new journey." While that is a dramatic beginning, it is not true. What is happening is that in my continuing forward, I have found new terrain. In the last months I have been traversing this dry sandy desert. At the top of each dune I could only see more of the same. I finally see something different on the horizon. I expected more land after this wilderness. Perhaps something green, a nice relaxing meadow. However, I think what I will be passing through next is water. I am so excited about it! In the last 4 days I have been rekindled. Last night I was reminded of not only who I am, but Whose. I am the daughter of the Great I AM. Heir to His Kingdom. I was also reminded how far I have to go to get to that Kingdom. Nowhere. Because I am God's child, Holy Spirit dwells within me. With Him comes God's Kingdom. I used to walk in the freedom of that knowledge. I have forgotten how lately. But I have made a choice to learn again. I know what the result will be. If I choose to nurture the Kingdom inside, it will naturally flow out to those around me. When Jesus taught this prayer, He was not speaking of the time when He will come back to reign. He was talking about right now. Jesus meant for us to pray God's Kingdom and will into our lives so that we could share it with those around us. I have been longing for the dunes of my desert time to end. Last night I topped, hopefully, the last one. I am praying the waters God takes me through now are deep and as refining as the fire. I pray it is a time for the Kingdom in me to grow so much that God spills it out into the lives I touch every day. How do you treat the Kingdom in you? Do you allow it to come forth and shine light into the lives of others? Or do you hold the Kingdom back from the purpose it has in you?

Do you not know that your body is a temple of the Holy Spirit?

1 Corinthians 6:19a

Technically a temple is a dwelling place, which is a house. Most houses are built sturdy. They withstand storms and heat and cold. Houses are built to ensure that valuable things are protected. We treat some differently than others. Most people would never dream of smoking inside of a church or hospital. A funeral home is rarely a place for a party. A nursing home would never be treated like a high school. These places are respected and taken care of. Some are even revered. Can I say I treat my body the same way? What is different between my body and a brick-and-mortar church? The brick does not forget its purpose, but I do. I do not always treat my body with the reverence I treat a building. I do not eat right. I rarely exercise. I smoked for decades. I do not think of my body and instinctively think, 'Holy Spirit is inside of this flesh, I should be more careful with it'. Why is it believed that a building, which is truly empty when the Body leaves, is more sacred than a real temple of Holy Spirit? I feel conviction over the state of the body I have today. While I have stopped allowing it to be a den of carnality in some ways, in other ways I still allow damage to be done. I have not been a good steward of this house. Today my goal is to treat my body as a sacred temple of Holy Spirit. How do you treat yours? Are you a good steward of the temple God has entrusted to your care? Or could you use a good cleaning? I challenge you to really think of yourself as a temple of Holy Spirit. He lives inside of you, are you taking care of His house today?

His mother said to the servants, whatever He says to you, do it.

John 2:5

I tell my kids all the time if they would listen to mother life would go smoother. That is what this verse made me think of today. It is the advice my mom has given me. She did not use the exact words, but close. I did not listen for a long time. When I finally did and I started to do whatever God told me, my entire life changed. Since I am an extremist, I took every word to heart. God told me to repent of the only lifestyle I had known for 25 years, so I did. I did a 180 and went the opposite direction. He told me to change the way I dressed and spoke and who I associated with. So, I did. God told me to walk by faith. That one was tough. At first it felt like walking a high tight rope with no net. Now, though, I know when I step out in faith, I am stepping from my own will into God's by way of His hand. God told me to love, even my enemies. I learned to pray over them, "Forgive them Father, they know not what they do". He told me to be kind. When I have an issue with that, I take the advice of my dear friend and say the sick man's prayer, "God, show me how I can be of service to this person". God has told me to do a lot of things. At first I did whatever He told me, and the results were amazingly life changing. Then I changed. I got complacent and stopped doing some things He told me to do. When I stopped really doing whatever He said, I got grouchy. I stopped saying the sick man's prayer and I lapsed on loving my enemies. Soon, stepping out in faith became something I sometimes did instead of the way I daily walked through life. I find I much prefer to live like mother says, doing whatever it is God says for me to do. Do you listen to mother? Do you do whatever He says? Or do you like to do things your way? If so, how is that working out for you today?

For as a man thinketh in his heart, so is he…

Proverbs 23:7a

Have you ever considered that your heart thinks differently about you than your mind? I think, in my head, that I am an overcomer. A lot of obstacles I do overcome. Smoking has been a big one for me. Like the rest of my addictions, I had decided that I was just a smoker. It has been the way I deal with stress, sadness, happiness, everything. I had also convinced myself that it is too hard to quit. My mind had control of the problem. About 4 weeks ago I started to stop smoking. My heart changed about what my mind could accomplish. That did not just happen by my own will though. Jesus came in and He changed my heart. I read about healing in His Word and talk to Him about it. I find out what Jesus thinks, and I allow His thoughts to penetrate my heart. Jesus causes the way my heart thinks to change the way my mind thinks. Sometimes, what I think in my head, does not truly reflect my heart. I still experience insecurities brought about by what I used to be. My mind can tell me I can do all things, but if my heart is not thinking the same thoughts, it makes little difference. So how do I rid my heart of invasive insecurity? I go to Jesus. I let Him penetrate my being through His Word and His love. I talk to Him. I tell Jesus all the darkness that I feel and then I listen as He tells me His truth. I allow Jesus to alter the thoughts I think in my heart. By doing so, I become what He thinks I am, and I am able to overcome. Are the thoughts of your heart and mind in conflict today? I encourage you to go to Jesus, let Him change the way your heart thinks so you can truly be who Jesus says you are.

Be therefore perfect, even as your Father which is in heaven is perfect.

Matthew 5:48

When we think about the word perfect, we think of flawless. Thought of that way, this verse implies that we should be flawless as God is flawless. It is not translated literally in that sense though. In this verse, the use of the word perfect speaks of completeness. Until I met Jesus, I had been a lot of things, never complete. Mostly I had been broken. I had this huge void that sat directly in the middle of everything. As I tried to fill the void with things of the world, it got bigger and deeper. I was never complete. But God. When I allowed Jesus to begin to fill in what was missing, for the first time, the void began to shrink. As I read the Word, learned to pray, and grew my relationship with God, I started to become complete. One day, I woke up and fully understood this verse because I felt perfect. I do not feel like that every day. If I am not reading the Word and praying and if I am not actively pursuing my relationship with Jesus, I am not complete. Without the Word and prayer - that consists of mostly listening to the voice of God - I could not be perfect as my Father is perfect. When I am though, my life is more abundant because I am richly filled with the things of God. It is possible for me to become so complete in Jesus I overflow with peace and joy. I stop being as defiant and I walk in faith. I relax in the promises of sonship, boldly enter the Throne Room, and I rest in grace freely given. Are you perfect? Do you know completeness in God? If not, I encourage you to let God fill you through His Word. Let Him fill you with His voice in prayer. Hunger for completeness in Him so that you may be perfect as your Father is perfect.

Therefore, if the Son makes you free, you shall be free indeed.

John 8:36

I treasure my freedom today. Not long ago I was trapped in a prison of my own making. The bars were not made of metal. The walls were not cinder block. My cell was not 8x10. My prison was constructed of a thousand forms of fear and pride, anger, and self-loathing. The only guard was my own warped mind. I kept myself firmly trapped inside my self-constructed cage. I became comfortable in the darkness of sinful self. One day Jesus stepped through a crack in my walls. He came in and shook my prison, opening a door I did not even know was there. He then stood in the open doorway and offered me a way out. God amazes me in the way that He is always a gentleman. In opening my self-made prison, He gave me a choice. Jesus offered me His hand and showed me His way. He made me free, but He did not force me to take the freedom. God only does for me what I cannot do for myself. He taught me how to take the steps that led me to freedom, but I had to choose to move my feet. Remaining free is a choice I get to make every day. Do I talk to God or self? Do I read the Word or scroll on social media? Do I walk in His way or do I forge my own path? Is God everything or is He nothing? Years ago, the Son made me free. Today, through Him, I am free indeed. Have you walked into the freedom Jesus has freely given you? Or are you still choosing to be a prisoner of self?

Not one of the Lord's good promises to the house of Israel failed; everyone was fulfilled.

Joshua 21:45

 I am a Gentile. By birth I am not of the house of Israel. However, by blood I am of the house of God. He loved so very much that God put on flesh in order to shed His own blood so that I could be of His house. God is so very faithful. Through God's own faithfulness I am able to experience His greatest miracle. He is faithful to allow the breath taken inside of the tomb to alter my life more than 2,000 years later. Then He also made promises. He will never leave me. I will have an abundant life. He gives me His peace. He sends me His Comforter. He dwells with me. By leaning on His strength, nothing is impossible. If I live I am healed, if I die, I am healed. No matter how I look at it because God is faithful to fulfill His promises, every situation becomes a win-win. Even in those time I can only see loss at the moment. The bible says, very early on, that God fulfills His promises. I forget that when life seems only like it wants to punch me in the face. Yesterday, the sermons point was to recall God's faithfulness in those times when it is so hard to see it. Remember how He has caused everything to work to the good so far. Then know He will not just suddenly stop doing those things now. I want to encourage you to remember God's faithfulness today. Make a list, visualize the times, or share them with someone else. However, you do it, remember that God fulfills all His promises.

For God gave us not a spirit of fear but of power and of love and of a sound mind.

2 Timothy 1:7.

It is easy to become fearful when faced with the unknown. I am going to go through something next week that, while I have elected to do it, will be one of the most physically painful things I have gone through in a very long time. Because of an allergy, I will not be able to treat the pain by popping a few pills. My humanity wants to be completely full of fear. I would be wrong to say I am not terrified. The inability to control the circumstances surrounding me could send me into a state of panic. I could react in ways that are out of character and irrational. In a state of fear self-control is difficult, to say the least. God tells me, several times, that I am not to be filled with fear. As a matter of fact, 365 times I am told, "Fear not". He wants the opposite for me. If fear leaves me weak, without control and irrational, what is the opposite of that? It is not courage, it is love. Since God is love, He, Himself opposes fear in my life. So, even though my flesh may be terrified, my spirit is calm because I am filled with the love of Christ. Since I am truly His child, God makes His dwelling place inside of me. I have the opposing force of fear already embedded in my spirit. The same is true for you. How awesome is that! When you are faced with the unknown, fear not, God's Spirit dwells inside of you. If you turn to Him instead of self, He will fill you with power and love so that in a sound state of mind you can overcome and defeat the fear you face.

Not only that, but we rejoice in our sufferings, knowing that suffering produces endurance, and endurance produces character, and character produces hope, and hope does not put us to shame, because God's love has been poured into our hearts through the Holy Spirit who has been given to us.

Romans 5:3-5.

It is difficult to glory in tribulations. When I am looking at a mountain that seems insurmountable sometimes I want to know the easy way around. I sometimes want to scream at the unfairness life can be. Facing a fire and knowing the only way out is through it causes me to want to turn around and throw my hands up, screaming, 'why, God!!!' as I run the other way. God wants me to hope, have trustful expectation, that the He is walking through the refining of the fire with me. He wants me to have faith He is giving me ability needed for the perfection of my spirits. But then I can become discouraged when I think that the tribulation I am facing is going to affect me physically, mentally, or emotionally. I sometimes cringe when I consider the changes about to take place if I keep moving forward. I do not mind the hope, but I wonder if I really need the kind of patience this experience will produce. If I never go through the tribulation, how will I develop the patience to hope? To glory in tribulations develops trustful expectation in God. Patience that He is working the experience to His perfect will. Even if the end result is not quite what I expect, it is always what God intends for my good. How are you dealing with the tribulation in your life today? Are you using it to grow or are you getting burned instead of refined?

......I am not ashamed: for I know whom I have believed.....

2 Timothy 1:12b

My life today is not guided by what I believe. My beliefs help to direct my actions. I believe I should not live a life dedicated to self. I believe, as a woman, I should act and dress in a proper and modest way. I believe I should pray earnestly and continuously. I believe I should not do drugs or drink or become involved in a sexual relationship. Those are great beliefs, but they are ideals. I do not live up to all of my ideals 100% every day. While I do not consistently adhere to every one of them perfectly, they help direct my actions and create my character. However, the things I believe in do not wake me up in the morning. Those things, while virtuous, do not breathe life into my dry bones. The things that I believe do not guarantee an eternity with the Almighty. The big things in life, the choice to instill my morals and values, the decision to walk by faith and not by sight, the ability to live in sobriety and not die in filth have nothing to do with what I believe, and everything to do with Whom I believe. It is my belief in Jesus Christ that ensures my path to God. It is the action that the belief produces that helps Him show others the way. Jesus saves my life and shows me glorious and awesome things. I am not ashamed of my God. He is my Creator, my Redeemer, the Lover of my soul. Jesus is my Strength, Refuge, and Peace. He is my Master and Teacher. Jesus breaks me perfectly and recreates me in ways that are beyond my belief. The One in Whom I have believed has altered my life and I will never be ashamed. Are you ashamed of God in your life today? Or do you know Whom you have believed?

From new moon to new moon, and from Sabbath to Sabbath, all flesh shall come to worship before me declares the Lord.

Isaiah 66:23

This verse makes worship sound like it is supposed to be daily. If you go from one thing to another you are in constant motion. The scripture does not say on each new moon. Nor does it say on this Sabbath and then the next. We are told to have continuous worship before the Lord from Sabbath to Sabbath. This verse is not talking about praise either. Praise is the joyful recounting of all God has done for you. Praise is easy and can absolutely be part of worship. True worship though is losing self-adoration and humbling yourself before God. It is becoming one with the Lover of your soul. It is getting lost in Him and adoring God for who He is, not what He has done. Worship comes from a part of your spirit that is surrendered and devoted to God alone. We are to be there daily. It takes time, effort, and a conscious decision to be willing to go before God. This verse makes me think worship is a lifestyle. Worship should be a continuous action that flows through every day of our lives. It does not just happen though. I challenge you to worship before the Lord daily. Get in the same room with the Great I AM and surrender yourself to His glory. Be with Him for who He is, not for what He can do for you.

And without controversy great is the mystery of godliness: God was manifest in the flesh....

1 Timothy 3:16a

How amazing is God's sacrifice for man? He created us when He did not need to. Then, in true human form, we seriously messed up. He could have just left us, but in true love He chose to give us a way out of the mess. He chose to step out of Heaven. Can you imagine? God, by the grace of His mercy, left His glory and put on flesh. He knew it was the only way. The Great I AM had to walk in our world. He came and was tempted on all points. He felt our pain. He cried with us. He showed us pure love in a human body. He taught us, by showing us, how to live abundantly. Then in the ultimate act of gracious mercy He died for us. The flesh God put on to save us was ripped to shreds by us. With every stripe He took, He healed us. He was mocked and spit on and judged so that we would never have to endure those things alone. He refused the vinegar and gall on the cross so we would never need to be numb to our own pain. He bore every sin while he hung on the cross. All those centuries ago, he bore their sins, my sins, and yours. As Jesus hung, dying in the flesh He did not deserve to be in, His final human sacrifice was one of forgiveness and death. His wonders did not stop in the grave though. Jesus walked through hell and took back the victory of life. Jesus then rose as a new creation, no longer a mortal man able to be overtaken by death. This is the miracle in my life. As I was walking through hell on earth, Jesus came. He met me and scooped up every bit of horrible, deceitful darkness my life was. And the creature I had become died. The person who walks in my flesh now is a new creation. And while my flesh will pass away, I will never truly die again. God chose to step out of heaven, be manifest in the flesh of humanity specifically so He could die for your sins and rise so that you too will have victory over death. How do you honor the death, burial, and resurrection of Jesus Christ in your life? Do you think it is an awesome story? Or do you allow this great mystery to alter the way you live?

Call to me and I will answer you, and I will tell you great and hidden things that you have not known.

Jeremiah 33:3

When I first started reading the Bible, I knew very little. I remembered the children's stories we heard growing up, Daniel in the lion's den, Samson, Jonah, and the whale. I remembered the books of the Bible and how to find them. Other than that, I knew nothing. I found that just reading the Bible through my own human lens produced very little effect. However, when I called on God and asked Him to guide my spirit through His Word, it came to life. I could almost hear David slay Goliath. I stood with Elijah and felt the whisper of God. I cried with John as Jesus was hanging on the cross. I understood the earnestness of the fervent prayer. I worshipped with the elders. I hollered out "Even so, come" from an island I have never seen before. By calling to God, He answers me through the breath of His Word. It is in asking for Holy Spirit to walk with me in His Word that it becomes living, breathing, and life changing. Call on God today. Ask Him your questions. Then let Him answer you through His Word as He shows you the great and hidden things.

I shall not die, but live, and declare the works of the Lord.

Psalm 118:17

I could not say these words a few years ago. I was dying. My physical body was wasting away. My mind was failing. My innate human desire to live was all but gone. Had I remained where I was, I would not be here today. But God. He gave me a choice I could not see or make without Him. It was so complete. I walked into the bathroom at death's door, but when I walked out I had a hope in my heart I never had before and for the first time I understood true faith. In that bathroom God gave me the choice to die. Or I could live for Him. I did not know then that living would include declaring His works. But my purpose is no different than anyone else's. When we take the mantle of Christ, we become missionaries. Every true child of God has the same mission. Declare His works. St. Francis once said, "I spread the Gospel. Sometimes, I use words". We are not all called to teach, or preach, or write. However, each one of us who lives and does not die by the blood of Jesus are called to declare His works. I heard a pastor say, "salt and light do not speak". Yet, they declare the Light and the savory preservation of the Lord. Declaration of the Good News comes in all forms. Some people post, there are those who sing, others write. Those things are great, but there is nothing that beats sitting down and sharing the works of God in my life with someone else. When I take time out of my busy schedule to spend time with someone and talk to them about God's sacrifice for my salvation or the amazing things that have happened because of Him since then, a seed is planted, or perhaps watered. Declaring the works of God is cultivation of the spirit of those around me. It would be exceedingly irresponsible and rude of me to keep such amazing wonders to myself, don't you think? Are you alive today because of Him? Do you sit and talk with people and show them the awesome things in your life because of Christ? Do you declare the works of the Lord?

Then Peter came up and said to him, "Lord, how often will my brother sin against me, and I forgive him? As many as seven times?"

Jesus said to him, "I do not say to you seven times, but seventy-seven times.

Matthew 18:21-22.

In scripture very important things are repeated numerous times. Pending on the version you read, variations of the word forgive are mentioned 119-150 times. Not one of those times are the words 'do not' preceding the command. Nothing is unforgivable, we simply choose to hold onto our grudges. We think somehow that causes the other person harm. I have learned that you do not forgive people to let them off the hook nor to make them feel better. Quite frankly, that thing you refuse to forgive, it plagues you worse than it does them. (they, more than likely, never think about it) So then, who is your unforgiveness harming? You. It keeps you trapped. God tells us to forgive repeatedly because He knows well the freedom that comes with being able to do so. God says we are to forgive as we have been forgiven. That means I am to forgive as far as the east is from the west. It does not mean that I am to say that I have forgiven someone then hold that thing in the back of my mind for future use. I am human, so it is unlikely that I will forget the offense or want that person back in my life. God is capable of forgiving and forgetting, I have yet to become quite that good at it. However, there are those people exceptionally close to me that I need to forgive and accept their faults and continue to love them. My forgiveness of someone also does not mean that I need to talk to them about the situation. Sometimes it is forgiving in silence and mending a relationship nobody else knew was broken. Father forgives you and removes the punishment of eternal hell. I do not know about you, but I sinned against our LORD in various ways and on numerous occasions. He forgave me for 25 years of being a soldier for the enemy. After that, who am I to hold a grudge? Forgive someone today. If it is hard, well, do it anyway. Choose the freedom God is offering you in this action.

Be transformed by the renewing of your mind.

Romans 12:2b

If my mind had stayed the same, I would be dead by now. There could be no real change until my mind changed first. I will forever be grateful beyond words for the altering of my mind. I did not just wake up one morning to a complete mind change. For me, it was much more dramatic. Jesus met me in my bathroom, amidst my darkness and misery. He gave me a choice between life and hell. I had already been in hell for so long in the physical I knew I did not want that misery for eternity. In the twinkling of an eye my entire life changed because Jesus became real to me. When He sat with me as I read the Word, His voice rang through the pages. As I dug deeper, I noticed changes about myself that were major. My habits were changing, my words were changing, even my clothes were changing. If on the outside I was not the same person, inside was a complete reconstruction. An author compared it with the reconstruction of a cathedral. The walls and structure remain the same, but the center, where I worship and venerate what I hold most dear was changing. The things I used to worship, the idols in my life, drugs, alcohol, men, Facebook, were being replaced with Living Water. I was filled with Holy Spirit. All of that transforming because I chose to change and renew my mind when Jesus offered me the chance. Today I know the transformation does not stop if I am invested in the Word and my relationship with the One who renews. How is your mind today? Is your life being transformed by its renewing? Or are you confirming to the world by not changing it?

He went on: "What comes out of a person is what defiles them. For it is from within, out of a person's heart, that evil thoughts come"

Mark 7:20-21a

This verse confused me for a while. I thought it was what I was putting in my body that defiled me. I loaded my body with poison of all kinds. I thought, if I could get rid of the poison I was putting in, surely I would be okay. What I know now is that what was going in was only a byproduct of the poison that was coming out. It takes an action to put something in. However, it takes a thought to create that action. My thoughts were the cause of my defilement. And they were coming from a heart that was black and stone. Nothing good could be humanly put into action because nothing good was being produced into thought. And no matter how hard I tried; I could not stop putting the poison in because I could not stop the evil that was coming out. But God! In scripture we are promised, not one but four times, that He will take a heart of stone and make it into a heart of flesh. When that happens, He does not leave the newness and go away. Jesus stays with the new heart of flesh. Suddenly, the production of evil thought is replaced by good. Good thought is then produced into better actions. And because of that, I am able to stop filling my body with poison. My actions change because my thoughts change, and my thoughts change because Jesus changed my heart. What do your actions show your thoughts are producing today? Is your heart producing good thoughts? Or are they sometimes evil, producing thoughts that cause actions you are not always proud of? Do you allow Jesus all your heart, or are there pieces you keep to yourself?

.....Jesus.....saith unto him, Follow me.

John 1:43

Following in Jesus's physical day meant, literally, "leave everything and come travel with me as I teach you the way and the truth". The disciples left their homes, their families, and jobs. When they continued to follow Jesus after His death and resurrection, they left their lives. They were persecuted, beaten, stoned, poisoned, shipwrecked, exiled, and ultimately killed. They followed. Jesus stepped into their lives and changed them as He dwelt among them physically. Jesus moved into their hearts and altered the entire world through them spiritually. Because they followed. I want to follow like that. I do not want to simply be a bench warmer, sitting in the pews like a good girl on Sunday and Wednesday with no change, mistaking admiration for who Jesus is with love. I want Jesus to be with me physically in His Word and change me and my world spiritually with His presence. I want to follow and that means putting down everything I once knew, stepping out in faith, and traveling through life with Jesus. He says, Follow me. Will you follow Him today?

For sin shall not have dominion over you; for you are not under the law, but under grace.

Romans 6:14

Doesn't that sound wonderful? Before I experienced the merciful grace of God, I was enveloped in sin. Even when I tried to be good I was still dominated by the sinful nature. I was trapped under a blanket of disobedience that I was powerless to release myself from. There was no choice. Until God gave me a choice, Him and freedom or sin and bondage. Through His grace I am no longer trapped by sin. I can be good because He dominates my choices now. This verse does not mean we are free to sin with no consequences nor does it mean we will never sin again. Through the grace of God, we are free to make choices that are based on His will. Sin no longer dominates our choices, so it no longer dominates us. We face temptations, but through grace we are given the choice to resist. I did nothing deserve the life I love today. Had I received what I deserved; I would be in hell. Through God's amazing and merciful grace, instead I received forgiveness and am a pencil, used by Holy Spirit. Take time today to ponder God's grace. Praise Him for relieving you from the dominating bondage of sin. Praise Him for allowing you the choice to resist that temptation. Then, choose Him.

The fear of the LORD is the beginning of knowledge; fools despise wisdom and instruction.

Proverbs 1:7

I like knowledge. I always have. I had always found it in places other than God though. When I thought I was losing my mind, the knowledge I had was fading. I despised the wisdom and the instruction, therefore the knowledge meant little. It could not save me. I was so sure I was right. Until that day Jesus walked into my life. That day knowledge turned to wisdom because I began to respect the instruction of the LORD. He gave me a choice, turn to Him, and allow Him to grow the knowledge into understanding and the understanding into wisdom or stay away from His discipline, instruction, and guidance and ultimately die. Today I fear my God. I value His instruction and discipline. I choose to not be a fool today. Because of that choice, my mind is restored and even growing stronger. I am living and not dying. Fear of the LORD is the beginning. It is also a choice. Which path will you choose today?

May no one ever eat fruit from you again.

Mark 11:14b

But the fruit of the Spirit is love, joy, peace, forbearance, kindness, goodness, faithfulness, gentleness and self-control.

Galatians 5:22-23a

Jesus was talking to a tree. He saw it in the distance, filled with green leaves. It appeared as though the tree should be bearing fruit. Yet when Jesus got closer, there was none. He kept walking and made this statement in hearing of the disciples. I cannot imagine they gave the statement a second thought till the next day when they walked past a dead tree. It was not just that the leaves had fallen. The tree was dead from the root, never to produce fruit again. I have had times in my walk when I resemble this tree. From far off I look like I should be producing fruit. However, had you gotten close you would have seen irritation, anger, disappointment, fear, impatience, cruelty, and loss of control. I knew that is what people would see if I let them get too close so I would keep them at arm's length. Thankfully, when I finally turned to Jesus because I could no longer stand myself, He did not curse me from the root. Quite the opposite happened. When I got totally honest with the Lord, He cultivated the soil around me. He pruned away what was toxic and with what was left, He breathed into. I began to pray with Him and for Him, not simply to Him. I again dove into the word as though it was the fountain of youth. I surrendered my will to His and I could feel the nature of the fruit in my life change. Today I am able to feed people instead of taking from them. I know that what people see from afar is different then what they see when they are close to me today. What they see is a work of God, incomplete and still growing. What they do not see is my trying to be something I am not, trying to cover up the death at the roots. What happens when people get close to you? Do they see good fruit or dead roots? In our world today, nothing is sweeter than the fruit of the Spirit. Do you bear the fruit, or only look good from afar?

If thou wilt walk in my ways …. Then I will….

1 Kings 3:14

This 'if and then' statement is found throughout scripture. It is always the same beginning, if we will walk in the ways of God, then He will…insert wonderful promise here. So, what does it mean to walk in the ways of God? We obey His Word. Not only the parts that make us smile and feel good. There are parts of the commands of God that some people believe are just for the age of which it was written. But the Word is living, breathing, never changing, always relevant. We are to be doers, not only hearers. If we do that, obey, and remain in God's will, only promises follow. That does not mean life is smooth sailing with no obstacles. That is not a promise anywhere in Scripture. But walking in His ways of goodness and love and grace and mercy and being obedient allows the Great I AM opportunity to change your life and shower blessing and promise on you. How do you walk today? Do you only hear? Or do you obey also?

I cry out to you, but you do not answer me.

Job 30:20

I just spent a season where I walked through the reality of this verse. It feels like it has been a long time of crying out to God and feeling not only as though He was not answering, He was not even listening. Some days it didn't matter, I could bypass the feelings because I know He is there. I could rest easy because I knew on those days that feelings are liars. However, as I got deeper in the season and chaos became catastrophe, I became frustrated with the silence. Calm knowing became angry irritation. I was beginning to develop a resentment towards God. That was miserable. What was a silent knowing turned into yelling at, crying to and pleading with God. At the peak of my own misery, when I had reached my end, I told the Great I AM that I needed help and I demanded God show me He was still there and listening or I was walking away. I was not as grounded in my faith as Job was. God eventually did answer Job. He heard his very faithful servant cry out to Him and, when the time was right, God answered. The same happened with me. What I know is that God always answers. While some days are easy to know He is there even in the silence, others are more difficult because He is not answering in my pain. Today I know that I am coming out of that season of torment. That does not mean that God is constantly, quickly answering me. However, it does mean that today I know He is listening and answers are on the way. Are you in a season of silence or have you been there before? I want to encourage you today that you are not alone, even when it feels like there are no answers. God hears you and answers are coming. Do not stop crying out to Him today.

And I sought for a man among them that should make up the hedge and stand in the gap before me for the land, that I should not destroy it: but I found none.

Ezekiel 22:30

We wage a spiritual war. Do you ever think of your prayers as protection? When someone you are praying for is in spiritual battle, fighting for their lives against illness or addiction or temptation that seem too big to conquer, you are praying for them to not be destroyed. We intercede for others when their defenses are weak. Warriors of old would stand on the walls already built to fight. But when the wall would crumble, they would gather there and build the defenses back up. That is what standing in the gap for our fellows under attack accomplishes. We all have people in our lives who experience times of weakness, when it feels impossible for them to hold their defenses up on their own. So, they ask for prayer. How seriously do you take that request? Do you stop what you are doing and go to battle for them? Or do you wait for later when prayer better fits into your schedule? God wants us to build hedges around and stand in the gaps of those fighting. In doing so, we are helping them to not be destroyed. We are giving them a fighting chance. I encourage you today, when you say you will pray for someone, take it seriously. If you know someone who's defenses are weak and in need of strong warriors to stand in the gaps do not shy away from that need. In reality, we can physically do very little for our fellows. Spiritually though, we can wage war. I pray for you today, as you make up the hedge and stand in the gap to stop the destruction of those that need your strength today.

Enoch walked with God, and he was not, for God took him.

Genesis 5:24

By faith, Enoch was taken up so that he should not see death, and he was not found, because God had taken him. Now before he was taken he was commended as having pleased God.

Hebrews 11:5

There is not much more about Enoch in the bible. Scripture tells us that he was a father and lived a long time. But twice it says God took him. Enoch did not die like others. I imagine, and this is purely my imaginings, that he daily walked and talked with God. That he told Father everything and that he listened to every word that God breathed into him. I imagine that God was Enoch's very dearest companion, and he showed it. Not just on those walks would it have been evident. Their relationship would have settled into every part of Enoch's life. Everyone who knew this man would have also at least known who God was. Several of them would have known Him personally because of knowing Enoch. My favorite part to think of is God taking him. He loved His friend so dearly that during one of these walks, our Lord just swept him away into His true presence. Are you a true friend of God today? Do people know who He is because they know you? I pray to be more like Enoch today.

Then Moses led Israel from the Red Sea and they went into the Desert of Shur.

Exodus 15:22a

When Moses led the Israelites from Egypt they expected the land of milk and honey immediately. They did not want to endure the wilderness. They constantly complained, they grumbled and when shown the Promised Land, they convinced themselves they could not possibly inhabit the land because they could not possibly conquer the inhabitants already there. They had allowed their physical wilderness to invade their minds and the wilderness also became an ideal. Part of why they could not leave the physical wilderness was because they had become trapped in a mental wilderness. Had the Israelites chosen to trust God and really lean on Him, their time in the wilderness could have ended. Instead, they allowed the wilderness of their minds to trap their bodies also. It is no different for us. In Psalm 23 we are told we can walk through the valley of the shadow of death because God is with us. That is possible because we are able, through Christ, to take our thoughts captive (2 Corinthians 10:5). We are able to keep from becoming physically stuck in the wilderness because God is our way to not get stuck mentally in the wilderness. By example of the Israelites, to do that is death. You have a choice today. Get stuck in your own mentality and suffer. Or, through Jesus, take your thoughts captive, know that God is with you, and walk through the wilderness with no fear of evil.

Dear friends, now we are children of God …

1 John 3:2a

How often do you hear people say, "we are all God's children"? It is a common misunderstanding. If it were true, then "all" would include those loyal to Buddha, one of Hindu's billion gods, or Allah. I venture to say that the followers of those religions do not recognize God as their Father. Yet we insist that is how it is. When John says "now we are children of God" it is because a transformation has taken place in the people who make up his audience. I think we sometimes use the thought of us all being children of God as a way to step away from the purpose we have been created to fulfill. While I absolutely do not need to do any works to gain my inheritance, there are works God created me to do with Him. For me, its spreading the Word through these writings. I see people every day walk out a lie. If, as a true child of God now, I do not walk in my purpose, if I allow myself to be satisfied by this lie, the people I come into contact with on a daily basis may never know the truth. Because I know Jesus Christ in an intimate way, and accept Him as my Savior, I repent, I turn from my old ways, and I choose to allow Holy Spirit to change my heart of stone into a heart of flesh I am a child of God. Since I am a child of God, my belief dictates that I act upon my inheritance and walk out my purpose. I have to call a lie a lie and back that up with truth. Not everyone is a child of God. Not everyone who calls on the name of God is saved. My purpose, and yours, if you are now a child of God, is to say the truth, show the truth and live the truth. In order that those who are not may become children too. Even inside of quarantine there are ways. Paul did it from prison. John did it from exile on an island. Live like you have your inheritance within your grasp now because you do. Let the world see you as child of the King. Set an example that they may follow.

Do your best to present yourself to God as one approved, a worker who has no need to be ashamed, rightly handling the Word of Truth.

2 Timothy 2:15

 Do you think of yourself as a worker for God? One given the responsibility of rightly dividing His Truth. We are privileged to have the Word of God. But we chop it up. We take little nuggets that we feel speak to us. Oftentimes we hear what others have studied out and claim it as our own truth. We hear someone else's revelation and decide that it is awesome and repeat it without ever even thinking to divide it against the Truth. Being an approved worker who rightly divides the Truth takes, well, work. I encourage you get your bible in hand and divide the truth you hear against the Word that is written. Even what you hear from your pastor, spiritual advisor, and bible study teacher. Use your concordance, several translations, a dictionary. There are study tools available to help you. I, personally, would prefer approval by God. I do not want to stand before Him ashamed because I would not take the time to rightly divide the truth. Open your Bible today.

The Lord will fight for you, and you have only to be silent.

Exodus 14:14

I am not always good at being silent. I am loud by nature. I love passionate conversation where not everyone agrees on everything. It inspires thought and reason. It allows the participants to become louder than usual as they express their side. I love that it is not always about changing someone's mind, but simply laying out why one believes the way they do. Outside these conversations it is easy to see it as fighting. God knew the issues fighting would cause. He tells us to not do that, but instead to be silent. I think its human nature to do the opposite. Especially when ideals clash. For some reason we humans think other humans should think the same and when they do not, offense occurs and fighting ensues. What would happen if someone came into your life, heard you speak of Christ and called you a hypocrite? Would you argue, or could you be capable of being silent and letting God fight the battle for you? What would that look like? Perhaps it looks like walking by faith in the sight of the doubtful fellow. Maybe it looks like giving when you have nothing left and not allowing worry to consume you. It could be that this doubter watches you deal with a very difficult situation, not allowing the fear to overtake you. It could be walking in your inheritance instead of waiting for it to come. This is how God fights. As you follow Him, grow strong in relationship with Him, in your silence God is given the chance to speak. Francis of Assisi said, "Daily I spread the Gospel. Sometimes I use words." It is a beautiful picture of being silent as God fights the battle. I am still learning which battles are best fought with my silence. I pray it is also a lesson you are learning.

For God gave us not a spirit of fear but of power and of love and of self-control.

2 Timothy 1:7

It is easy to become fearful when faced with the unknown. That inability to control the circumstances surrounding us sends us into a state of panic. We react in ways that are out of character and irrational. In a state of fear, self-control is difficult, to say the least. God tells us, several times, that we are not to be filled with fear. He wants the opposite for us. If fear leaves you weak and without control and irrational, what is the opposite of that? Power, self-control, love. Through Holy Spirit we are given power to remain calm in the face of fear. We are given love for those around us, making it easier to listen to others while making decisions. We are given self-control allowing us to retain our dignity and composure in the face of uncontrollable circumstances. Life before salvation was full of fear, why would you remain in that spirit when Holy Spirit gives you so much better? Embrace the power, love, and self-control He gives you today. As we face today, I urge you to grab hold of the power of the Kingdom in your life. Walk in love of your neighbor with kindness and self-control. Whatever is going on will not last forever, be it the good or the bad, but your reaction to it will leave a very lasting impact on those around you.

And at midnight Paul and Silas prayed and sang praises unto God: and the prisoners heard them. And suddenly there was a great earthquake, so that the foundations of the prison were shaken: and immediately all the doors were opened, and everyone's bands were loosed.

Acts 16:25-26

Paul and Silas did not beg God to release them. They were locked in a cell, probably quite deep in the prison. They were chained. It was midnight, so it had to have been a dark, and, I imagine, rodent infested place. They chose to praise and to pray. Not quietly, either. The Word says that the other prisoners heard them. They were examples of the Light we are to shine in the darkness. Their praises and prayers moved God to the point that He moved the earth and broke their chains. Perhaps He will not send you an earthquake today. However, He can shake your world. Are you in bondage? Does something have you chained down? Are you choosing to pray and praise out loud? Follow the example laid out in the Word. Pray and praise. Let everyone hear you. Trust Him to see you, even from the deepest darkness of your prison. Do you know someone in the prison? Are you standing on the outside? Free from bondage, chains already broken? Pray and praise. So that those locked up learn how. Be their light until they can shine their own. In this time of solitude, it is hard to imagine that others can hear you. Know that we are listening. God hears your prayers and praise and places you on the hearts of others and places still others on your heart. We are a connected Body, even when we feel so isolated. Sing out today. We are listening and God hears.

But I tell you that I am going to do what is best for you. That is why I am going away. The Holy Spirit cannot come to help you until I leave. But after I am gone, I will send the Spirit to you.

John 16:7 (CEV)

I read this verse in a lot of different translations. This one not only caught my eye, but my heart. A lot of translations tell us Jesus was leaving in order to do what was expedient, to our best advantage, or profitable for us. This verse makes me think of how I feel about my own kids and grandkids. I do the things I do, even when they do not understand, because I am doing what is best for them. Jesus was doing what was absolutely the best. A few days from now we celebrate the greatest three days in all of creation. As it approaches, I want to encourage you to set aside devoted time to consider what happened. As Christ died on the cross the Scripture says He gave up the Spirit. He gave Him up in order to give Him back. In giving us Holy Spirit, our hearts of stone could become hearts of flesh and we could be set free. He knew that and that is why Jesus told His disciples He was going to do what was best. The best is not always easy. Sometimes its violent and ugly. In the end though, beauty rises. Consider the coming celebration. I know this year it will be done differently, but do you not already celebrate it every day? If not, start today. Celebrate Holy Spirit inside you. Give thanks for the reason He is there. Find comfort in this time through the Comforter inside you. Remember the best Jesus had to give was given for you.

Being in anguish, He prayed more fervently, and His sweat became like drops of blood falling to the ground.

Luke 22:44

We often pray for God's will, not our own be done. I often wonder how much we mean it though. I am a member of an organization that often reminds its fellows that this prayer truly means God's will. Not God's will as it aligns with our own. Jesus understood this profoundly. It is easy to remember that Jesus showed us how-to walk-through temptation and endure weakness and bear the fruit of the Spirit. How often do you think about how Jesus showed us to humble ourselves to God's will? In the garden, moments before His arrest and hours before his death Christ demonstrated how painful and contradictory fully submitting to God's will can be. Sometimes God's will requires us to go completely against our nature. He asks us to do things that cause a tearing within ourselves, walk through fire, and tread the deepest waters. What I have found is that God knows His will is for my good. I have also found that as I war against my flesh and choose to submit to the will of God, He does not leave me to do it alone. Jesus was not alone in the garden. As Jesus agonized over what He knew was coming, God was there. God held Him and gave Him strength. God helped Jesus to follow His will. He does the same for each of us. It is my hope today that you commit to submitting to God's will in your life. Know that He will be with you to accomplish it because it will not be easy and it cannot be done without Him.

When he had received the drink, Jesus said, "It is finished." With that, he bowed his head and gave up his spirit.

John 19:30

In the last several years I have spent a lot of time wondering what it would have been like to be in Jerusalem on the Friday Jesus died. I would have been a Roman, Gentile. The events of the day would have been lost on me. There are things I could not have failed to notice though. As happened every year before, the town was overcome with Jews for Passover. They were flowing in and out of the temple, it could have seemed like the stones were breathing, giving offering and sacrifice to God. This day, I wonder if as a Gentile I would have noticed the extra commotion. Would I have paid attention to the Jew being beaten far beyond recognition? Perhaps I would have stood on the side of the road, repulsed by the sight of His blood. Maybe I would have been irritated that I could not get where I was going because of the strangely large crowd that had come to watch this Teacher suffer. Eventually they would disperse, and I could get home in time to start supper. For hours, my house would be covered in an odd darkness that I would also resent and not understand. Then the earthquake would come. Finally, there would be silence. All the strange events of the day would end, and I could get on with my Gentile life, allowing this day to fade just like all the others had. Praise God I was not a Gentile in Jerusalem on that day. I am alive now to understand the power in the words spoken by Christ from the cross. It is finished. The Passover Sacrifice had shed His blood. Every sin, not only for the past year, but for all of time had been, not atoned for, but completely covered, able to be forgiven and forgotten. I am so in awe that as a Gentile I get to experience the power of what happened that day in full awareness of what each lashing, drop of blood and ragged breath meant and caused. When Jesus declared it finished from the cross, He spoke those words into eternity. That moment kisses each moment that passes. I pray you allow it to kiss each moment of your day and all of those to come.

This is the day that the Lord has made; let us rejoice and be glad in it.

Psalm 118:24

This is the day. Right now, you are promised this right here. Yesterday is faded into history. Today you have new chances and new opportunity. What are you going to do with it? The bible tells you what you ought to do. Look around you and see who is following the Word. We are told to rejoice and be glad in this day. Seems as though I am given a choice inside of that suggestion. I do not feel like rejoicing every day. Just a few days ago I sat in a dark and quiet house alone and cried all day. I was not thinking about rejoicing and being glad. I was thinking about everything that has been making me sad, frustrating, and irritating me and I swam in the muck of that filth and chose to be miserable the whole day. Yesterday, it was completely opposite. Why were two days, back to back, so very different? I chose to rejoice and be glad yesterday. I hear people complain all the time that they just are not happy. I have to often try very hard to bite my tongue when I hear that. Generally, it means they are choosing to not be glad and rejoice inside of a situation they ultimately caused with the choices they made that led up to that point. The bible does not say rejoice only of you are pleased with your situation or to be glad only if you enjoy your companions. The Word says on this day, today, that the Lord has made, we should rejoice asks be glad. We are not promised tomorrow. If it happens that today is the last day, wouldn't you prefer to spend it rejoicing in gladness instead of wallowing in irritation?

For to set the mind on the flesh is death, but to set the mind on the Spirit is life and peace.

Romans 8:6

When life is chaotic it can be difficult to focus on the Spirit. When things do not feel good and change is of the kind you do not like, it is easier to focus on the flesh and attempt to insert your will into the situation instead of God's. I have lived in that manner more than I like to admit. In the midst of our pandemic and having to stay at home, I experienced other things that made life less than peaceful. I went through a surgery that altered my appearance. My daughter made a huge life decision I did not readily agree with. My son's senior year got cancelled. I went through a crazy break-up. My best friend and her family moved hundreds of miles in the opposite direction because her really great job offer was rescinded in the midst of a temporary reality. Unfortunately, all of that made a very chaotic time even more so. If I were to focus on all these things, well when I focused on them, in my flesh I only want to scream. Some days I give in to the stress and sadness of the chaos in life and I focus on the flesh. That makes for a miserable day. In those days, I may cry all day, become morose or melancholy or act out in anger that is actually fear or sadness. I do not behave like that often. Instead I choose to focus on the Spirit. I worship and pray. In connecting with God in those times, I can feel the darkness lift and experience peace. I do not stay there constantly. When I experience the grief of a changed life and lost friendship and those emotions are ebbing and flowing through my day, I choose to not set my mind on the feelings. By doing that and setting my mind on the Spirit instead of flesh, I can have a bad half hour instead of a bad full day. What are you focusing on today? Are you enshrouded in the death of flesh? Or are you choosing to walk in the peace of the Spirit?

But they who wait for the Lord shall renew their strength; they shall mount up with wings like eagles.

Isaiah 40:31 a,b

Have you ever seen an eagle take flight? There is no effort in it. An eagle simply trusts the wind, opens its wings and falls knowing without a doubt that it will soar. At one time, very early in my relationship with God, that is how I behaved also. The bible says that is how I am supposed to view Holy Spirit. I am created to trust Holy Spirit, spread my wings, and fall knowing, without doubt, that I will soar. In the beginning it seemed so simple. I was propelled by childlike faith that trusted without question. I read the Word and nurtured my relationship with God and because I trusted each thing the bible said to do, I could overcome everything in my life. Through Christ I was more than a conqueror. Somewhere along the way, I let humanity get in the way of my faith. I allowed what I was seeing to violate what I knew to be true. In doing that, my faith became less childlike and I began to flap instead of soar. I started to work against the Spirit without understanding thatwas what was happening. An eagle acts on instinct in order to leap from a cliff and soar. If the bible tells me I shall mount up as an eagle then that is what I should instinctively do. However, that comes after being strengthened in the waiting on the Lord. It is not easy. But I am not promised ease anywhere in scripture. If I am obedient though, then I will have victory. If I trust Holy Spirit and fall into His arms, He will catch me every time. Today I will wait. I will grow in strength because I am choosing to wait for the Lord. Because of that, I will soar. It is my prayer today that you are waiting too, so that we can soar together.

All things are lawful for me, but not all things are helpful. All things are lawful for me, but I will not be dominated by anything.

1 Corinthians 6:12

I spent a huge portion of my life being dominated by my flesh. Twenty-five of my 36 years before Christ were spent heavily veiled in a vicious cycle of a myriad of addictions. I have been controlled by men, alcohol, drugs, food, and self. The enemy of my life was not a little red man with a pitchfork and pointy tail. My enemy was the face looking back at me from the mirror. Do not get me wrong, the process was started by the lies of satan, but I am the one who almost let the domination of flesh kill me. I do not live like that today. The person in my mirror is not the same as before. Christ in my life changed everything from the inside out. Through Him I will not be dominated by anything. In this verse, Paul says he will not be dominated by anything. Sounds to me like it is a choice. Not being dominated by things apparently does not just happen. I do not believe he was capable of making that choice before he was on the road to Damascus. He was dominated by hate, anger and (probably) fear before that day. Jesus did not leave him there though. Jesus gave Paul what we are all offered. Choice is consistent throughout the Bible. God is a gentleman; He will not force Himself upon anyone. He will open our eyes and ears long enough to hear the truth so that we can decide to walk in it. If we choose to, He presents us with more choice along the way. One of those choices is whether we will be dominated by things of the flesh or be led by the Spirit. It is a daily choice. As you start your day today, you get to choose what is guiding you. Will you be dominated, or will you be led?

Amen. Come, Lord Jesus!

Revelation 22:20b

Some translations of this verse read "Even so, come". When I got saved I thought this was the most amazing sentiment. John was saying, "even though we will need to endure all of these things you have just shown me, come anyway". I hear people say this verse often out of stress or misery. I have done it myself. Life gets hard, we experience chaos inside of chaos and we only want it to end. So, we cry out for the coming Christ. I try to not do that anymore. Not because I am not ready for the end. I would be delighted to endure the tribulation, or not (whichever way it is going to go), and be raptured tomorrow. It is so selfish for me to pray for that to happen so soon though. I may be ready; you may be too. What about the person in front of you at the store? Or that neighbor I know has serious alcohol or drug issues? How about that girl who has not met the real Lover of her soul yet and keeps letting in the false ones? Or the boy who is engulfed in anger and acts out in violence? What does it say about me, a woman who claims to be Christ-like, if I pray for my salvation and not theirs? How self-absorbed is it of me to think, "I am ready for You to come Jesus, even so"? I want as many people as possible to be ready in the brightest twinkling that has yet to come. It is my purpose to show people how to be ready. Just as it is yours. Do you cry out, "Even so, come"? Or are you using your given time to show people how to be ready when Jesus does come?

You are the light of the world. A city set on a hill cannot be hidden.

Matthew 5:14

I was driving on Hwy 277 one night, several years ago now. It was late and dark, no lights except the stars. When I came out of the hills, I could see the lights of the air base and the city. It was a beacon showing that I was almost home. I think of that every time I think of this verse. Today, for the first time since that night, I saw a different light on a hill when this verse came to my mind. Jesus, the Light of the world, set on a hill, not hidden and even in death, not dimming. His light was brighter than any modern city ever could be. Neither death nor the tomb could hide His light from the world. I am called to be like Christ. If He refused to allow even death to dim His light, how can I justify allowing things of the world to dim the light God chooses to shine through me? I allow things like anger, frustration, lack of self-control and bitterness to dim His brightness within me. The symptoms of my dim light are seen in less writing, less worshipping, less praying, and less talking about God's glory. When there is less of God in my life, there is less brightness. I am supposed to be a light, a beacon, on a hill for those who are looking for home. If I have become dim, how then do I become bright again to fulfill my purpose in showing others the way to God? I open my bible and allow God's Word to breathe into my life. I begin to worship in my kitchen when nobody is looking and in my yard when the neighbors might hear. I tell others about the glory of God, fulfilled promises and those yet to be seen. I walk in faith and I pray in a raw fervency. And, for me, I write. I do find that I am not a good judge of my own brightness. I only see from the inside and that makes it difficult to see the light that is truly shining out. I have to trust those I walk with to help me see when I have become a bit dim, so I surround myself with people who care about and help to adjust the light within. How bright is your light today? Ask someone who will be honest with you. Are you a bright beacon? Or have you allowed the things of the world to cause you to go dim?

Listen to what the Lord has to say.

Micah 6:1a

God saw everything. As the foundation of creation developed in the heart of I AM, He not only knew, but He saw all things. God felt the first taste of breath and knows the last crumble of the end. He experienced every sin from the cross through Jesus. From the Alpha to the Omega, God already knew, saw, and felt it. Yet still, His grace abounds in the fullness of His love. I have had a very difficult time walking through some things. I realized that is because I have not truly been listening to the Lord. I can hear Him, like the music playing in the background. I have not been listening to the song of His voice though. If I had, I would have heard forgiveness and mercy and grace. I also would have understood the discipline coming through in the notes of His love. I could have felt God's desire to help me stop wrestling with self and the inability to do everything on my own. I was not listening to what the Lord had to say though. I was allowing the enemy to come in loud and clear. I have been believing the lies and the perversion of the enemy because somehow I find those things more believable than the Truth of God's promises whispered in my ear. I was dying by what I was hearing from my enemy because I was not listening to the truth of the Lord. I have been on the brink of complete disaster because of what I was choosing to hear. Listening to the lies always produces a form of death. Today I have decided to kick the lies to the curb. They will not do damage here today because instead of hearing them I will choose to listen to what the Lord has to say. What are you allowing to flow into you today? Is it what you hear? Or are you truly listening?

You shall have no other gods before me.

Exodus 20:3

Choose this day whom you will serve.

Joshua 24:15b

The Israelites were told over and over to have no idols before God. It is not in just one or two places in scripture. I find it hard to read through any book of the bible and not find some reference, no matter how vague, to the subject of idol worship. In the Old we read about physical idols, things carved of wood or metals or stone. Sightless man-made creations who could not hear a sound. In the New, the idols begin to change. They look like money, religious pride, lusts, and self. Today we have more idols than ever before. God knew this would be a human problem until the end of time. I imagine that is why we are reminded over and again to stop putting things before Him. I want God to be first in my life. However, wanting Him in His proper place and keeping Him there are two very different things. There are days when I put humanity first. I choose to serve my anger. I choose to serve my fears and depressions. I choose to serve my desire to sleep and isolate. Some days, I choose to serve my work. Other days, it can even be my children. Absolutely anything in my life, I put before or in place of God becomes an idol. If I am choosing to put that in place of Him, that is the thing I am choosing to serve that day. Each day, this day, this moment, I get to choose whom I will serve. Will it be some form of self-created into an idol? Or will I choose to give God His proper place in my day and choose to serve Him? As for me and my house, this day, I choose God. I pray today you choose the same.

He is not here, He has risen!

Luke 24:6a

When I experienced the cross it was the most profound and life altering day of my life. I was wrecked. It was an opportunity for truth, tears, discipline, and repentance. At the cross I made the decision to repent, to turn and go in the opposite direction. I chose to accept that the sacrifice of Christ paid my debt and I also chose to allow His sacrifice to change everything. It would have been so simple to get stuck at the cross. However, if I were supposed to stay always at the foot of the cross, Jesus would still be there. He is not though. There came a moment that His time on the cross was finished, He came down and was buried. One of my favorite parts about my cross experience was the death. For me it was spectacular. I saw my corpse and I died in my bathroom. When I left that bathroom that day, what emerged was a brand-new creation. It did not take much study for me to understand how to live from resurrection. In that victory is how we are created to live. I do not do it today like I did then. I did not change on purpose. Life happens. I went backwards, not all the way, praise God. I did go back far enough that I stopped living in the victory of resurrection and got stuck in the moments of the cross. Living outside of victory is not the reason the tomb is empty. Jesus rose so that I could walk through life in the victory of what He overcame. Today I am going to remember the tomb is empty. I am going to walk in the same victory Jesus walked out of the tomb with. Today, because He rose, I am going to live.

"Let me inherit a double portion of your spirit," Elisha replied.

2 Kings 2:9b

Elisha's stories are covered in faith. He had a spectacular teacher and a double portion of that teacher's spirit. Since I know every lesson in scripture points directly to my relationship to God through Christ, I know that the lesson here is profound. Elisha could have asked his teacher for anything. He asked for a double portion of his spirit. My Teacher also asks of me what Elijah asked of Elisha. "What can I do for you?" As much as I love having Holy Spirit, in my humanity I think of all the things of Christ. I could use a little more peace. Some joy would be great. A dash of Your strength. Today, I wonder what would happen, if when Jesus asks what He could do for me, I ask for a double portion of Holy Spirit. Isn't that how brave and bold I am supposed to be? I am supposed to run to the throne of the Great I AM and ask for more of Him. I wonder what that would look like. A double portion of faith and love and hope and joy. A double portion of miracle and humbleness and power. A double portion of struggles and pain and persecution. A double portion of the strength to overcome. How amazing would that life be? If that is the lesson here, why do I allow my human fear to override the spiritual desire to walk in a double portion of the Spirit of God? Close your eyes. Hear Jesus whisper in your ear, asking what He can do for you today. I encourage you to boldly ask for a double portion of Holy Spirit in your life. I pray that you bravely walk in the truth of receiving Him.

And after you have suffered a little while, the God of all grace, who has called you to his eternal glory in Christ, will himself restore, confirm, strengthen, and establish you.

1 Peter 5:10

We will suffer. The prophets of Old suffered. The Apostles suffered. God's chosen people have suffered more than any other nation of people. More than any of those, Christ suffered. Yet, we live in a world where people believe we should not. Perhaps excessive comfort has become detrimental to our spiritual character. Comfort and entitlement have clouded thought patterns to where people think they should have exactly what they want five minutes before they decide that is what they want. That is not what the bible tells us to expect in life. I have searched scripture and not one time am I promised comfort and ease. I am told to glory in tribulation. I learned that it rains on the just and the unjust. I read stories in which great men of God are thrown into wells, beaten, shipwrecked, exiled, and persecuted. I recently heard a preacher who had spoken with a leader of one of China's underground churches. This church has a great following of extremely devout people who could lose their lives at any moment. When asked what pillars that body stood on, what beliefs makes it strong, the answer was astounding. There was prayer, miracles, caring for widows and orphans, declaring the Gospel and they cherish the suffering they encounter. Can you imagine? They know they will suffer, and they do not shy away from it. They embrace the suffering. What? Why? Because in the suffering God Himself restores, confirms, strengthens, and establishes them. Do you know that? Is it a belief you walk in? In whatever situation you are suffering in today, do you know God is using it to grow Himself in your life? Are you allowing what you know about suffering to dictate what you see, or are you allowing the suffering you see to violate the grace that you know?

And after the earthquake a fire, but the Lord was not in the fire; and after the fire a still small voice.

1 Kings 19:12

It seems Elijah would know where the voice of God was. Just the chapter before we read about Elijah calling God's fire down and consuming not only the sacrifice but the water around it and the rocks it sat on. In the chapter before and in this passage, scripture specifically says God spoke to Elijah. The prophet knew God's voice. So why would he flee all the way to Horeb? Fear. If you look at scripture, almost everyone, at some point, was overcome by fear. It caused them to make huge mistakes. God always met them in the midst of it though. Over the sound of human chaos, each of them came to a place of hearing God and being restored by His voice in their lives. The story of Elijah and his cave speaks so loudly to me. There was a time when I heard God's voice as though He were sitting next to me all the time. I did everything by faith and fear did not live here. Things happened though and fear crept into my life. It looked like lack of finances, being alone, not being good enough, and a thousand other forms. It has become like a constant ringing in my ears muffling God's voice. I have fled to a cave in fear and God wants to know why. A pastor once asked, "How does the Lord speak to you?". Right now, He is speaking to me in the stillness. There is no earthquake or fire like there was in the beginning. I hear His gentleness calling out to me to be restored. He is beckoning me to be consumed and refined in His fires. His sweet voice is calling me to drink from His well until I am overflowing. God is urging me to the hem of His garment to become whole again. Through the people He has put in my life God shows me the way out of this cave of fear and guides me into the freedom of walking again in raw faith. Today I would encourage you to answer the same question, how is the Lord speaking to you?

"Your servant has nothing there at all," she said, "except a little oil."

2 Kings 4:2b

This woman needed Elisha's help in figuring out how to pay a debt. If she could not pay it her sons would be taken and she would be left alone. I am sure Elisha knew she did not have much. However, he did not ask her how much she had. He asked what she had. She knew she only had a little. He knew that did not matter. He guided her and she followed, and the result was an overflow. She poured out her oil until there was nowhere else for it to go. I generally have the same answer if I am asked what I have. My first answer is usually nothing. But I tend to remember that I do have a little. When Jesus came into my life, He was not concerned with how much I had. For me, that was a blessing because what I had was only a little, barely the size of mustard seed. What He did though was multiply that little bit. In the last five years, my faith has grown. Though there are still days when it is about the size of a mustard seed. What I know today is that what I have and how much I have does not matter. Jesus can make that little bit of mustard size faith overflow onto everything it touches. What size is your faith today? Who does God need the overflow to touch? Are you willing to let Him cause the overflow in your life, or are you content with the little you have?

Love never ends.

1 Corinthians 13:8a

When I think of the supernatural things of faith, I think of miracles, signs, and wonders. This verse causes love to appear very supernatural though. Paul very plainly says love never ends. He could not have been talking about natural human love. I have seen that end quite a lot. Human love has a way of hurting and stopping. This verse is also not quantified with a "but" or an "unless". Natural love has boundaries and standards. However, here, Paul simply makes a three-word statement, no humanity is wrapped up in it. Love never ends. In the verses preceding this declaration, we are told the characteristics of unending love. It is patient, kind, humble, giving, calm, understanding, and values truth. It stands up against hard times. It believes the unbelievable, and it takes the hard hits. That sounds supernatural to me. It is the love Jesus showed and it is the kind of love we are supposed to strive for. I used to skip over this whole chapter. I thought it was a part of the bible that could not possibly be true. Nobody can love like this. But God. The first time I encountered this unending love was the day Jesus saved my life. Looking back to that point, I see how love has evolved in the last five years. I do not love as pure and as raw as Christ loved, but it is defined by more of His characteristics today. I also notice, when I am immersed in the Word and in relationship with Jesus, love is amplified. Today, I will not skip over this chapter, instead, I will immerse myself in it so that I can see it. How do you see love today? Do you see the natural human love that can stop? Or do you see the unending love of God working in your life?

See, I am setting before you today a blessing and a curse.

Deuteronomy 11:26

So little has really changed since the time the Israelites were in the desert. We are given the same choices. Each day we wake up to the same presentation and God is as much a gentleman now as He was then. There is no imposition of His Kingdom in our lives. Just as the Israelites were able to wake up and choose whom to serve and the commands they would obey, we are given the same choice. As I open my eyes I get to choose if I put myself or God first. When I talk to other people, I choose if I speak with kindness or malice. If I choose to go into a public place, do I go with respect or selfishness? Do I love God with all my heart, mind, and strength, or do I have an idol? I choose to love my neighbor as myself or love no one at all. Each of these choices, and so many more, signify whether I am choosing the blessing or the curse. Some days I choose the curse, I am not even going to lie about it. There are days when I am in a bad mood and it leaks into every decision I make. I could choose to acknowledge the irritation, give it to God, put on some worship music and get over it. That would be choosing blessing. Or I could decide to marinate in the aggravation of life. I can choose to stomp my feet and just be angry. That is choosing the curse. The options come in all forms. Am I walking in the fruit or crawling in the muck? Today I am choosing blessing. Not only that, I am asking for blessing in my life and in the lives of the people I love. You have the same choices the Israelites had as they stood in the wilderness with God. Set before you today is a blessing and a curse. Which one will you choose?

There are different kinds of gifts, but the same Spirit distributes them.

1 Corinthians 12:4

Every one of us has gifts. They are given by Holy Spirit in order to edify the Body. They are given without discrimination. We do not all get the same gift; however, one is no better than the next. It is easy to get into the mindset that if we admit to our gifts it is boastful or somehow not humble. I recently took a gifts test and told my mom I was surprised by the results. She was not surprised at all. Except in the fact that I was not comfortable in admitting that these were the gifts given to me by God. It is kind of comical that as humans we do that. If my mom and dad give me a great and wonderful gift, I generally do not keep it from people. As a matter of fact, I show it off. It is an attitude of pleasure and satisfaction that they thought of me so much that they gave me the gift. I do not operate in false humility when my earthly parents give me gifts. Why would I do that with the gifts that come directly from God in order to edify His Kingdom? Can you imagine what would happen to the world if everyone operated in their gifts, leaving aside the false humility, and embracing the ability to edify the Body in the way that we were individually created to do? We could fully unify as a Body and reach the ends of the earth for the Lord. We could unashamedly walk through life offering the blessing of God on everyone we meet. If I were to fully embrace my gifts, I would need to be closer to God in order to purposefully walk in those gifts. That closeness would produce fruit and that production would allow others to see God and give Him glory. Do you know the gifts given to you by Holy Spirit? Do you claim them and fully walk in them to edify the Body? Or do you keep them wrapped up inside of a sense of false humility unwilling to share them with others?

If you love me, you will obey what I command.

John 14:15

The majority of John 14 is red letters. These words came from the mouth of Jesus. He knew the men He was speaking to loved Him more than they had loved anything else. He knew what they were about to see and endure as Jesus went to the cross. Jesus knew that His time was almost complete. One of the things He said that last night was this very simple sentence. IF you love me, you will obey. God is a consistent gentleman. Even up until the end of His fleshly life, He offers choice. The disciples were not forced, coerced, or brain washed. They were given the same choice as the Israelites and the same choice as you and me. We get to choose to love Jesus and obey the commands He gives. There are two greatest commands. Love the Father and love your neighbor. He knows the power of the action of love. God knows that if we choose to love fully, we cannot help but to obey. The disciples loved Jesus and obeyed so completely that they changed the world. Peter and John's first encounter was one of giving. They did not have silver, but what they had was of much more value. It is the same thing that you have. In love we spread the Good News of the Gospel of Jesus. If you love Him, you love others and you give His love to them. It does not matter if it is the beggar, the crippled, the healthy, the wealthy or the wise. You have a choose to love Jesus, you choose to obey His command. Take time to listen to Him today. What is His command for you to do?

Then Eli said, "He is the Lord; let Him do what is good in his eyes."

1 Samuel 3:18b

Samuel had just spoken with God and Eli wanted to know what the Lord had said. Samuel really did not want to tell him. Eli pushed and Samuel told Eli that the Lord was going to judge Eli's family. The Lord intended fully to cause the shame on Eli's family to last forever and He was going to carry out His judgment. Eli accepted that. He accepted the Lord is the Lord and He will and should do what is good in His eyes. I think that is amazing. I do not always want to be so accepting of the way God is doing things in my life. I should be though. The faith of Eli in this passage is staggering to me. He knew the end of his family was coming. He knew his acceptance of and inability to stop the things that were happening was a direct cause of the end of his family. Instead of begging God and making empty promises, He believed that God would do what He said he was going to do. I so very often want to stomp my feet and throw a fit when hard to handle things happen, Eli did not do that. Often I think of faith in a way that causes me to believe in the possibility of something that is the opposite of what God has indicated would happen. In these cases, what I should do is have faith that God will give me the strength to get through what is coming. Sometimes, I need the hope that the end will come on the other side of the fire. If I am having faith contrary to the flames, I am sure that I will end up getting burned. Today I am walking into whatever it is that God has planned for me and I am striving to be ok with what being ok with what the Lord is doing, whether it is good in my eyes or not. Today I hope that you can accept that what is happening could be the thing that is good in the eyes of the Lord, even if you don't see it as good today. I pray you have faith for His strength to get through it.

Let the wise listen and add to their learning.

Proverbs 1:5a

I often think that I know the meaning of words. I can look them up and understand them. However, I heard yesterday that Rabbis say every word of scripture has 70 meanings and 600 shades. My mother asked me if I knew what wisdom means. She is also a word person and she goes all the way into studying them. She said that one of the definitions of the word wisdom is the application of knowledge. I was stopped in my tracks. If we think of that in human terms it makes complete sense. If we have knowledge that the house is on fire, we are wise in leaving the house. Do we always apply that same wisdom on the things of God? I know that I must stay sober in order to be vigilant. I act on that knowledge and remain sober. I know that I should pray in order that I have communion with God. I act on that knowledge and stay in conscious contact with Him. I know that if I remain in the Word, I will hear direction in the voice of God. I act on that knowledge and I can hear Him speak. Those are the easy things. I do not just have knowledge of the easy things of God though. I know that I am to remain kind and peaceful. I know that I am supposed to have patience and self-control. I also know that I do not always walk in wisdom of the knowledge that I have. Today, I am asking God to show me the knowledge He would have me be wise in. I pray for the strength to put my feet in the knowledge He has given me. What knowledge is God giving you today? Do you have the wisdom to walk in that?

He will die for his lack of discipline, led astray by his own great folly.

Proverbs 5:23a

I lived this verse. I had only folly in my life. If I advised you to turn left at a stop sign, that was a sure sign that you should go right. I had no discipline in my life. It was not because my parents did not try. I did not have the capability of being disciplined by anyone. Even on probation I could not be disciplined long enough to stay out of trouble. Eventually I was put on house arrest, but even then I found ways to work the system. The lack of discipline allowed scripture to be alive in my life without me even knowing it. I was living out this verse by being led astray by my folly and into death. But God. While I could hear the discipline of no human, inside of my darkest moment, breaths away from death, I could hear God. His discipline was sweet. It smelled like love and tasted like freedom. The discipline of God changed my life. He did not shame me or allow me to stay in my guilt. God's discipline freed me from those things. He took my broken pieces and created something new. In the chiseling of discipline, I could breathe and rest. For the majority of my life I looked at discipline as a grounding that meant I was in trouble. With God, discipline allowed me to fly. Are you being led astray by your own folly? Is God whispering to you to embrace the freedom His discipline can produce? Are you willing to live in His chiseling, or would you prefer to die in your lack of discipline?

Therefore, I tell you, do not worry about your life.

Matthew 6:25a

I heard a speaker once say the most amazing thing. "If I have fully turned my life over to the will of God, my life is no longer my business." When I first heard it, I was newly sober and newly saved. Everything was still a big tangled mess. For me it was easy to give it to God. I could not even begin to unravel things, so I left it to God. It was not my business anymore. As things started to unwind I began to see specific parts that I wanted to pick up and retake control over. The biggest thing I took back were the finances. When I decided to try to retake those, worry began to set back in. I know that when I have a tight month, I instantly begin to worry about food. I have to pay the bills and the creditors do not care if I have mouths to feed is always my first thought. Even though, very consistently, at the end of the month, I always find that we have not yet starved. No matter that I know better, I always worry over finances. It is almost comical, in that dark and dry humor kind of way. God says do not worry about your life because He knew I would. He, very specifically, says to me that He will provide my needs, yet I still try to take control. I am very good at letting people take care of their own kids. I do not interfere and tell them how to do it better. Except with God. Like I know better than Him how He should take care of His child. Regardless of the fact that child is me, His care taking is none of my business. Lately I am working on really turning my full life over to the care of God and letting it be none of my business. If I can do that, I can wisely walk in the knowledge of these words and not worry. It is a definite work in progress though. Do you worry about your life today? Is there an area you try to control because you place most of your worry there? Or do you understand your life is really none of your business if you are in the care of God?

But now, up on your feet—I have a job for you. I have handpicked you to be a servant and witness to what's happened today, and to what I am going to show you.

Acts 26:16 (MSG)

I love Saul's conversion. Here was a man, intelligent in the ways of his people. He knew scripture, he lived in tradition, and he was willing to kill for the belief of his culture. He knew all the signs of the coming Messiah. Yet, until the Light of Truth blinded him, Saul could not see. He persecuted and chased and killed, in the name of God, those who believed God. Such a contradiction of life. Then we see him emerge from blindness, a changed man. Paul, courageous Apostle, writer of two-thirds of the New Testament, witness to the Gentiles. It is easy to think I could never have the impact Paul had. My devious heart tells me I do not have a testimony worth telling, or that others have already heard the story. While Jesus was speaking to Paul in this verse, it is in a place I can read it because He was also speaking to me. Jesus chose me to tell the story of what happened to me the day He walked into my life. I get to share the Truth of the death, burial, and resurrection of Jesus and how those moments centuries ago touch my life today. That is what we are all called to do. What happened to me that day and what God has shown me since touches more people than I realize; so, I tell my story. When was the last time you told someone what happened to you that day? Who knows the things God revealed to you since then? Do you say more than, "yes, I am a Christian"? Are you a witness to the miracle of your salvation? What happened to you the day Christ walked into your life could change someone else's life. Just like Paul, we are called to tell. I encourage you, as a servant, to also be a witness.

You have let go of the commands of God and are holding on to the traditions of men.

Mark 7:8

This verse makes me think of that old saying, "the road to hell is paved with good intention". The Pharisees were overcome by their tradition to the brink of hypocrisy. They had stopped looking further than their own noses. Their tradition had them backed into a corner of selfishness that restricted them from seeing the Messiah that stood before them. They could no longer truly love because they were following man and not God. When the oral law began to be passed those leaders were not thinking that they were taking their people further from scripture. It is the same thing today. Some churches dictate women's clothing. Others teach people the 'correct' way to pray. There are places that have made tradition out of the gifts of the Spirit. Then there are some who teach the correct recipe for baptism. These are all traditions of men. We hold on to these things because we are taught that these are the things that please God. They are outward coverings though, disciplines that we use to sometimes hide the truth of what is inside. I could wear a dress to my ankles and speak in tongues 20 hours a day. However, if my spirit is out of whack, nothing on the outside could compensate for that. Whether I am or 0am not following the commands of God, there is no covering for that. Not only can God see it, but the fellows on my path can also see it. If I am rightly following the commands of God, it does not matter if I am standing by the traditions of man. If my spirit is led by the commands of God and not the traditions of men, my life looks like Jesus. What is leading you today? Do you put more stock in looking like the traditions of men, or do you strive to look like Jesus?

Therefore, keep watch, because you do not know on what day your Lord will come.

Matthew 24:42

In the twinkling of an eye the rapture of the church will take place. What if it is tomorrow? Scripture says that two will be together and one will disappear. Can you imagine being in the grocery store or the park and half of the people simply disappearing? What if it is a Sunday morning and worship service is in its second song? Imagine half of the worship team being gone. Suddenly, half of the congregation just is not there. Are you sure you are going to be on the leaving side? Scripture tells us to keep watch. How do we watch for something we could miss if we blink? I think this verse, at least partly, means to keep watch of what is flowing in and out of you. I am not properly keeping watch if I am binging Netflix or scrolling Facebook or Instagram for hours on end. I am not keeping watch if I am not testifying of the goodness of God in my life. I am not keeping watch if I am not talking to God in prayer or being led by Holy Spirit. So often it is easier to get stuck in the trap of just saying, I am a Christian so I will be fine. But what if my life does not reflect that. Am I really what I say I am? Am I truly keeping watch if I am not living the life God designed me to live? I do not want to watch the person beside me disappear unless I am fading into rapture with them. I do want to keep watch until that time comes. If that means I devote my life to the things of God, I am ridiculed because I live by the morals and values God shows me in His Word, and that people see Christ when they look at me, I welcome that. Are you really keeping watch? Are there things in your life that are taking the place of God today? Get rid of them. You do not know what day your Lord will come. If it is today, will you go, or will you be one who has to stay?

Today, if you hear His voice, do not harden your hearts as you did in the rebellion.

Hebrews 3:15

I heard the calling of God when I was a kid. I went to summer camp, I sang in the choir, I did bible drill, and I was baptized. Then the rebellion came, and it would be another 25 years before I heard, not just the calling, but the desire God had for me. In the time of rebellion, my heart hardened slowly. In the end though I was so very angry with God. I know today that was such a blessing. The anger meant that I still had feeling which meant that my heart was not completely hard. The opposite of love is not hate; it is indifference. Had I been in a place of indifference, that would have meant that the rebellion had fully done its job and that there was no longer any feeling at all towards God. I would have been hard beyond repair. This verse reminds me not to go back there. I tell people in recovery that I have another relapse in me. What I do not have is another chance to come back from that. They say that when you go back, you do not start over, you pick up from where you left off. Since I know that is true in recovery, I believe that is true in most every facet of life. If I go back to the rebellion and the hardened heart of that time, I cannot ensure that I will make it back. I do know where that life leads, and I will die on the bathroom floor and go to hell. I am not willing to do that today. Today, I hear the voice of God. I ask for and receive the direction of Holy Spirit. I had a heart of stone, but God has replaced it with a heart of flesh. I am no longer angry with God; I am in love with the Lover of my soul. I actively stay out of the rebellion today by prayer and through the Word and walking with the fellowship of the Body. How is your heart today? Are you hard and in the rebellion, or do you hear His voice and remain attuned to the things of God?

Be imitators of God, therefore, dearly loved children, and live a life of love.

Ephesians 5:1-2a

There are some commands in scripture that seen almost impossible. Imitate God. Live in love. Jesus did just that. He came to show us that it is possible to live in imitation of God. He also promised when He left that He would send us a helper to live in such a way. It is easy to get caught up in how difficult it is to imitate God. Sounds hard, but with God all things are possible. When Jesus walked in flesh, He lived a life of love. He healed. He spoke only the truth. Jesus did not ridicule people. He encouraged and served and gave of himself completely. He resisted temptation through words of Love. Jesus lived a life of love as a testimony that we could live ours the same way. Each time you walk out of your house someone sees your testimony. Do they see you imitating God as much on Friday as on Sunday? Are they witnessing you living the same way you are talking? Does the stranger in the store see you living from love or from self? When you leave your house today, will the world see the testimony of someone imitating God? I encourage you to live a life of love today.

Go now and leave your life of sin.

John 8:11c

There are several different translations to this verse. However, they all mean the same. Leave your life of sin because you have been healed. Can you imagine the magnitude of that healing? This woman was embroiled in sin. Her lifestyle hinted at what happened inside of her house. There was no way, I imagine, for her to escape it. Then one day, as she was right in the middle of the act of her sin, the authorities barged in and took her out of her house in broad daylight, without her clothes and threw her on the ground. They were using her as bait for the Teacher. He would not bite though. Jesus was ever compassionate. He knew that this was a moment that could alter this woman's life forever. Instead of addressing her, He addressed the crowd. Once He had made His point, He then got down on her level and addressed this her. He did not berate her or condemn her for her actions. He lovingly told her to go and not to live in a life of sin anymore. Scripture is written as an example of how we are supposed to live. When Jesus comes and takes us by the hand and heals us from our life choices, we are then supposed to go and leave the life of sin. How many truly do that though? When Jesus came and told you to go and sin no more, did you decide that since you were now under grace you could behave like a flawed human, continuing in sin because it was covered? Or did you take Him at His command and go from that point and change your life. Often the things that we are commanded to do seem so hard. However, Jesus would not tell us to do this if there was not a way. With God all things are possible. When you walk out of your door today, will you go with God and choose to live a life free from known sin, or will you continue on as you always have with a false sense of grace and freedom that will inevitably trap you inside of sin?

In your anger do not sin. Do not let the sun go down while you are still angry.

Ephesians 4:26

There are times when I find it difficult to not let the sun go down on my anger. I have been in situations that just seem to pile one on top of the other with no break in between and it results in a time of emotion that I am not comfortable with so I often portray that I am angry because anger is the easiest emotion for me to feel. I would be lying if I said that I have not allowed the sun to go down on the overwhelming emotions of the day. What happens when I allow that to happen is that I become situated inside of those emotions instead of being situated at the foot of the Throne. The truth is that emotion is a fleeting thing. The thing I am angry about today, could simply be something better felt in sadness and then walked past. Sometimes the problem with that is that it seems as though there is a new thing every time I turn around. Historically, when I get stuck inside of emotion it is as though I cannot turn around without something else slamming me in the face. So, how do I not let the sun go down on that when I am powerless to stop the barrage and take a breath? Perhaps this verse signals a time to take a break from the pile of emotion from several days also. I may not be able to stop the barrage, but I am able to rest in the break of the reload. In the break of the evening, am I dedicating that down time to soaking in the strength of God to get me through this season? Am I using the down time to center myself in forgiveness for everything that is going on? Am I praying for whatever the pressing issues are? Am I taking whatever season I am in to the foot of the cross? If I am not doing these things, I am allowing the sun to go down on the negativity and I am holding on to it. This is where the devil gets a foothold. It is a lot easier for me to believe his lies if I am situated inside the emotion rather than at the foot of the Throne. Amidst the pain and the anger, I have to choose to not allow the sun to go down on those things. I choose to take them to God and rest in the break of the barrage. I pray you are able to do the same with the negativity in your life today.

Let this be written for a future generation, that a people not yet created may praise the Lord.

Psalm 102:18

Prophecy always fascinates me. Can you imagine being given information that is intended for a future generation? Not only that, but about a future people. Not a person, a whole body of people. It amazes me when people say wise things about the present. This verse is on a different level than that. He was prophesying about a people that would praise the Lord. I love that so many centuries ago, he was talking about us. I do not mean the generic American "Christian". Us, those who encountered the Messiah and because of that moment our lives changed course and we began to follow Him. This verse talks about a people created to live lives that are seen as testimonies to the Great I AM. We are that people. We, the people who sacrificed ourselves at the cross and died in the arms of Jesus. The author, without knowing it, referenced a people who would rise from the darkness of death to praise God in spirit and in truth far past the end of time. We are that people. We are a people, now created because the Spirit of God wraps into every fold and corner of our lives. We were created out of the pure unselfish love of God. We are a people who can use more people. When was the last time you shared the love of God? Have you ever stood by and witnessed to someone who saw God because you see God? Are you telling people your testimony? Are you part of a people created to praise the Lord? Are you doing that?

But as for me, I trust in You.

Psalm 55:23c

Scripture promises that we will have knowledge, wisdom, and understanding. If I fully understood what is going to happen next, why would I need to trust in God? For that matter, if I understood now, why would I need to trust in God? One meaning of understanding in scripture is in connection to the character of God. If I do not understand His character, how could I trust Him? That makes me consider this, why exactly do I trust in God. If it were because I was told to, I definitely would rebel against that. I did rebel against that for a very long time. I know His character. I know that He does not lie. God loves completely and wholly. I know that He only has my good in His plan. I know that He is strong and constant. God has never let me down. As a matter of fact, when I was at my absolute lowest, God reached down and picked me up. God's character is filled with amazing grace and mercy and forgiveness. Since I have known Him there has not been a day go by that I spent questioning my ability to trust God. I do not always understand why things are happening. I do sometimes question God's methods. I even get angry with Him occasionally. When I do I know that He is strong enough to take it. I know that when I go to Him, no matter when that time is, He is right there to cradle me in His arms, and He allows me to leave the baggage I came with. God takes what is broken in my life and improves it in the fixing. His character renews my mind and transforms my life. This scripture sings to my spirit today. As for me, my trust is in God. Do you trust in God? Have you taken the time lately to remember why your trust is in Him? I encourage you to do that today.

But it is the spirit in a man, the breath of the Almighty, that gives him understanding.

Job 32:8

Job lost everything in a day. We have all experienced loss. But there are not a ton of people who have experienced it to the level of Job. He did not have time to take a breath between losing all his children and his property. His legacies were gone. Everything he had worked a lifetime for was gone. His God remained though. I love Job's story. I too have lost everything. It was a slow and drawn-out loss though. However, in the end, it was all gone. The difference is that I did not have a God to trust until I had also lost myself, in the process I was losing my mind. I could not understand anything at all. I could barely form a cohesive sentence. I could not sleep, and I only wanted to die. When God came into my life, He changed that. He first healed my spirit. Where there was nothing He planted the Spirit of Himself. Even what was then a small seed, a process started that healed my mind. I used to say, "of all the things I lost, I miss my mind the most". God is a God of His word and His word says that you will be transformed by the renewing of your mind (Romans 12:2a). He did not give me the understanding of the things I had before I started losing myself. He gave me understanding of Him. That understanding caused amazing things to happen. At less than a year of salvation, God allowed me to understand things in a way I never had before. It was because I was understanding through Holy Spirit. Isn't it amazing that in this verse, centuries before Holy Spirit was released on the earth, Job knew Him and understood that through Holy Spirit is where true understanding comes from!

Three times a day he got down on his knees and prayed, giving thanks to his God, just as he had done before.

Daniel 6:10c

We all know the story of Daniel in the lion's den. How he defied the king and was thrown into the den to endure the lions for a full night. As a kid that is pretty much what we are taught so when I was saved as an adult, that is all that I knew. I did not realize the decree that he was defying. He was told that he could not pray. Can you imagine? There are people in the world today who understand the pressure of that decree. They live in countries where they are not allowed to pray even inside of their own homes. In my mind, Daniel must be such an inspiration for them. They go and meet and pray in spite of their government and decrees that tell them they cannot. What I find interesting about Daniel is that he did not go underground to continue to pray. His faith was huge. He went to the exact place he had gone every day before and he did exactly what he did before. He opened his windows and he prayed to God. Daniel was not ignorant to what he was doing or the trouble he would see. The decree specifically stated that he would be thrown into the lion's den! Daniel's story shows us how to be bold in the face of persecution. God knew that somewhere along the way we would need to know the importance of having built up a storehouse of prayer that would help us walk through very dark and dangerous times. I doubt that any of us will be thrown to the lions any time soon. There is adversity out there that will attack you though. When that happens, are you prepared to go boldly in prayer, no matter who is watching? Are you ready to stand up to those who challenge your faith and devotion? Are you willing to go to any length in order to worship God? Are you a Daniel?

Not by might, not by power, but by My Spirit, says the Lord Almighty.

Zechariah 4:6

The Spirit of God will fulfill the plan of God. The power and might of man mean very little to the plan of God. He does not intend to tell someone what He wants done and then step back while the power of humanity fulfills His purpose. That would make the need for the Spirit of God void. If we, as humanity, could fulfill even one bit of the plan of God, He would not have needed to create the plan at all. That is not the way of it. God wants mountains moved and valleys level and healings to happen and He wants a people who believe in Him. In order to ensure that His plan is fulfilled God works through Holy Spirit that lives inside of us. The mountains to be moved are supposed to be moved because of Holy Spirit. I cannot do it by myself. The valley that is supposed to be levelled should be done by Holy Spirit using your hands. You cannot haul enough material to fill it up. The healing of the person who crosses your path, that is to be the miracle of Holy Spirit working through you. The Apostles did not set out to change the world for eternity out of their own strength. They were filled with Holy Spirit and that was a feat accomplished by the Spirit of God. Your salvation was not a thing you did on your own. That was the by the Spirit of God. I am not living a life completely altered from the way it was by my own power. The miracle of me being a new creation was only by the Spirit of God. Jesus, as a man, did not walk out of the tomb on the Third Day out of His own humanity and will. He did not do any of the things that he did as a product of fleshly power. Every miracle, each supernatural moment in time has nothing to do with man. While man is the vessel that God chooses to work through, He is just as likely to use a donkey or a bush. All the things that are being fulfilled in God's plan are done not by my might or your power but by the Spirit of God. How does Holy Spirit work through you to move the mountains of the world? Are you a willing vessel for Him to work through?

It is not only the old who are wise, not only the aged who understand what is right.

Job 32:9

The speaker of this verse was the youngest of the group speaking to Job. He meant aged in the flesh. I have learned in my walk with God that this verse applies to those young in the Spirit too. Just a few years ago I was walking through the camp of the enemy. I was a liar and a cheat and a thief. Every one of my intentions were malicious because I was enshrouded in the darkness of sin. Today I do not live in that camp. What happened in my life never ceases to amaze me. God took the creature I had become and in making me a new creation, he renewed my mind. In that renewal, He gave me the gifts of knowledge and wisdom. The scripture comes alive as it is planted inside of my spirit and Holy Spirit grows it into understanding of what is right. Holy Spirit guides me to know and understand things that I could not comprehend before. I never knew how to walk in faith, today I understand how to do that. I did not know that grace is not a pass to continue sinning simply because I am human, but it is the vessel that allows me to go and sin no more. I could not fathom forgiveness, but today I know Jesus taught me how to forgive as He was dying. Before I met Jesus I only thought I knew what love was. Nothing compares to understanding how the love of God tastes, sounds, and smells though. Today I am able to understand the character of God and in that understanding I am able, through Holy Spirit, to be young in spirit, but wise in understanding. How is your understanding today? Whether old or young, are you walking with Holy Spirit in understanding, or are you sitting watching others grow before you?

Not one word of all the good promises that the Lord had made to the house of Israel had failed; all came to pass.

Joshua 21:45

All the promises of the Lord came to pass. Miriam-Webster defines "all" as the whole, entire, total amount, and every member of. God's promises did not start with Joshua. They did not even start with Moses. They started all the way back in Genesis with Abraham. There were hundreds of years in the between for God to build on His promises before Joshua was led to conquer the Promised Land. By that time God had promised the house of Israel so many things. All, the entirety of every promise God made for hundreds of years came to pass. He did not stop there. God has been making promises since before the foundation of time. Each and every one either has or will come to pass. That includes the personal promises He makes to each one of us. Often, God's promises do not come to pass how or when we expect. For me, God promised first that I would be a new creation. The entire creature that I had been would die and from that, He would create a completely new woman. That promise came to pass. There are promises God has made in the last 5 years that have been fulfilled. There are promises I am still waiting on. However, I know, beyond doubt that they will pass because God said that they would. God cannot lie. It is not that He does not lie. He cannot. That means that all, the entirety of, His promises for my life will come to pass just as those for the house of Israel did. The same is true for you. If you are a child of God, there have been promises you have seen answered in ways you could never imagine. There are also promises you still pray over. Do not give up those prayers. That thing God promised you will come to pass. I encourage you to keep faith and know that all things are working for your good if you love God (Romans 8:28). Remember not one of the promises had failed.

Have I not commanded you? Be strong and courageous. Do not be frightened, and do not be dismayed, for the Lord your God is with you wherever you go.

Joshua 1:9

God was speaking to Joshua. Why would He need to tell one of the greatest warriors and territorial pioneers to be strong, courageous, not frightened and not dismayed? He knew that Joshua was a human and as such contained the tendency to allow his human anxieties to get the better of him. Nothing is in scripture by mistake. We are told over and again by God, through His Word, to not fear. He knew that we would. God knew we would lose courage. He knew that we would feel weak and be dismayed. God, the Lover of our soul, wanted to offer us comfort through His Word. He shows us warriors and powerhouses of faith who, just like us, felt anxiety over the things they were facing and experiencing and being asked to do. God does not leave us alone in these times. Not only is He here in the good, He is here in the hard. I hear people all the time who say that while they were going through the hard times, they could not hear God. Every time someone inevitably tells that person that the Teacher is always silent during the test. I generally do not question that thought. It sounds logical. Except that it does not line up with scripture. God said He will never leave us or forsake us. Perhaps we have a hard time hearing God in these times because we are not listening to Him speak to us through other people. Maybe we are not fully paying attention when we are reading the Word. It could be that when we pray in the hard times, we are not fully listening for the response. I am so guilty of these things. The Lord your God is with you wherever you go. In the weakness, the less courageous times, times of fear and dismay, God is there. If you are in a season of feeling alone, I encourage you to listen to every avenue God is using to speak to you. Read the Word with intention. Listen to those around you. Wait in the times of tearful prayer for the response. God has commanded you to be strong and courageous, not frightened or dismayed for He is with you.

Therefore, let it be known to you that this salvation of God has been sent to the Gentiles; they will listen.

Acts 28:28

The Jews were not listening. The chosen people of God could not hear Him. Can you imagine? The God of Abraham, Isaac and Jacob clothed Himself in flesh and came to stand before His people. They knew the words. They made the sacrifices. They prayed the prayers. Yet, the God they had been waiting so long for stood before them and they could neither see nor hear Him. Even after He was sacrificed and rose they did not believe. Following that, the Apostles went and told them, yet still, the majority of them did not listen! However, God would have a people who followed and worshipped and praised. He would have a people who would lay down their lives and follow Him. God's plan for Holy Spirit to inhabit the earth would be fulfilled. The spreading of the news of the end of the Old Covenant and the beginning of the New would be accomplished even if by the Gentiles. We listened. Through extremely adverse situations in the evolution of history, we still listened. The Gentiles listened so well that even after the Apostles, the Good News was still spread around the world. For 2021 years we have listened to the voice of God, the nudges of Holy Spirit and we have followed Christ. God's chosen people are still His chosen people. Their borders have expanded to include us, the Gentiles. We are supposed to continue in the line and send the Word of salvation to the world. We begin at home, go to our neighbors and then even to our enemies. I pray that I never cease to listen. There is so much more to know and so much left to do, and I have a hunger for all of that. Are you listening today? Do you hear the word of salvation? Have you shared it?

Share in suffering as a good soldier of Christ Jesus.

2 Timothy 2:3

I have looked through the whole Bible looking for the verses that say life gets to be easy and free flowing now that I am a follower of Christ and a child of God. However, those verses are not there. What the Scripture does say is that there will be suffering. It is not suffering like there was in my old life though. This suffering will be bearable because I am filled with Holy Spirit and, thereby, the strength of God. All of the Apostles suffered. Paul was shipwrecked and beaten and bitten. John was exiled and boiled in oil. Peter was crucified upside down. The Prophets even before Christ suffered in the name of God. What makes me think that I would be spared. I cannot even imagine life without suffering. That would mean, to me, that I am out of the race I am supposed to run faithfully until the end. In my basest of humanity, I do not want to suffer. Some days I am in a place where I just want something, anything, to give. There are times when I do not consider the suffering I am enduring as an indicator that I am being a good soldier of Christ Jesus. I get stuck in what I want instead of what God needs. That opens a time that allows me to think I am not doing enough or being good enough and therefore being punished instead of blessed. It is a lie that is hard to get out of. The truth is, if I would give the suffering to God, He would give me His strength to endure it. If I would wait in the suffering, relying on Holy Spirit, instead of trying to trudge through the mud, the storm will be stilled by Christ and I would see the harvest of the enduring. Today my goal is to suffer as a good soldier and not as a two-year-old throwing a fit. Are you suffering? Is that suffering harder because you are trying to do it alone, or are you relying on Holy Spirit and the strength of God?

Turn to me and be saved, all the ends of the earth! For I am God and there is no other.

Isaiah 45:22

There are other gods in the earth. Hindu boasts of 33 million gods. Can you imagine? There is Buddha and Allah. Then there are the gods of the Mormons and Jehovah Witnesses and Branch Davidians that are based on twisted scripture. Not to mention all of the pagan gods of the Greek and Dutch and medieval times. Also, there is a plethora of gods in the realm of those who choose Wiccan and wizardry sects. Coming up with a number to total the gods that people worship would be an unimaginable feat. None of these gods can give salvation, resurrection, and forgiveness. That is because none of those other gods are God. They are not the One Who Created but the ones that man created. I know a ton of people who believe that all of those false gods are different paths to the same end. They believe that no matter what you believe, as long as you have a higher power and you are a good person, in the end you will end up in heaven. That simply is not what scripture says. The Bible very plainly states that the only way to the Father is through the Son (John 14:6). A person cannot get to the end of life and be welcomed into heaven and the Throne Room of God if they do not believe in God. It just does not work that way. Salvation comes through the belief and the living of the Gospel. Salvation comes through following Jesus. It is shown by being filled with Holy Spirit and producing fruit of the Spirit. Salvation is being washed by the blood of Christ and being robed in the righteousness of Christ. These are things that no other God can offer. They do not offer to forgive as far as the east is from the west. They do not offer love or compassion or refuge. Nor do they offer answers to prayer. Elijah so plainly showed how the Almighty God will consume even the stones, while Baal would not so much as show up (1 Kings 18:25-39). Do you believe in the One Who Created? Or are you stuck in the faulty belief of a god created by man?

He must increase, but I must decrease.

John 3:30

John the Baptist was speaking here. He had been in service to God, living in the wilderness and proclaiming the wonders of the coming Christ. He understood that his ministry would change when Jesus appeared. John the Baptist knew that his influence would decrease, and should, because of Jesus's ministry. What this verse does not mean is that the person of John must decrease. When we are given the gift of salvation that means that God sees us through the blood of Christ, we are clean. That does not mean God wants us to be Christ. While it is true that we are to strive to be Christ-like, God does not expect us to decrease so much that we are no longer the one to inhabit our bodies. What happens in salvation is a filling with Holy Spirit. My favorite way to understand this is with play-doh. I saw a preacher put together 2 different colors of play-doh. He squeezed them together and, while you could still see each color, there would never be a way to fully pull the two colors apart. However, in the entwining, there was not a decrease or increase of either color. The result in some places was a completely new color. Had he continued to mix the color together, the whole of what was 2 different colors would have become a completely new color. That is what is supposed to happen when we are saved and filled with Holy Spirit. I do not need to decrease. I am intended to be so entwined with Holy Spirit that in the mixing I become a new creation. It is in this change that God can, through Holy Spirit, use the talents and gifts He has given me to fulfill my purpose in His plan. Jesus saving me was not so that I would decrease. It was so that Holy Spirit could entwine with me like 2 colors of play-doh in order to make a new creation to fulfill a purpose for God. Are you entwined with Holy Spirit as a new creation? Or are you still trying to decrease?

If I say, "I will not mention Him or speak anymore in His name," there is in my heart as it were a burning fire shut up in my bones, and I am weary with holding it in and I cannot.

Jeremiah 20:9

Jeremiah was a great prophet. At least that is how we look at him all of these years later. Those who were there with him locked him in the stocks, he was thrown into a cistern where there was only mud and left to sink, he was rejected, and called a liar. That does not sound very great to me. This verse came after he was put in stocks. He no longer wanted to mention the Lord or speak in His name. Just in saying those things he felt bottled up with fire in his bones and exhausted from holding it in! That is how it feels when I do not write. If I am not sharing the things of God I feel as though I am often in agony. I know that sounds extreme, but if I am not fulfilling this part of my purpose, the one that I know without doubt, I can totally relate to the feeling of my bones being on fire. I have gone months without writing. What I find is that I eventually feel as though I am going to explode. I imagine that is how Jeremiah felt. As beloved children of God, we are meant to talk about Him. How do you not talk about the greatest Love your soul has ever known? Can you imagine having your life saved and never speaking about the One who saved you? What if when you spoke of Him you were thrown into a well to sink in the mud? Would you still speak? How about spending time in the stocks? Could you still let the words flow out? If you faced death if you told people about God, the things He has said to you and done for you, perhaps you would think twice about saying anything at all. Then what would happen? Someone else would be brave and speak in your place. But my question today is, what would happen to you? If you do not speak of God, do your bones burn or do you become exhausted in the quiet? If not, why not? I encourage you today to speak the truth God has given to you. Whether it is your story, a word of encouragement for your neighbor, or an act of service or giving, mention Him and speak in His name not just today, but every day. The person standing next to you may not ever hear otherwise.

Then the veil of the temple was torn in two from top to bottom.

Mark 15:38

Nobody knows exactly how thick the veil was. Some say it was 4 inches. Others say it was so thick horses could not pull it apart. We do know that it was very large. It covered a room that was 30x30x30. That means the veil could have been 30 feet tall and close to 30 feet wide. Can you imagine the size of it? For centuries, the only people behind the veil were high priests. There are stories of them having to tie a rope to themselves so that if, in the case that God chose to smite them while in the Holy of Holies, the others could pull them out. Only the elite were allowed in and even they were cautious of going in. A Gentile would never have been allowed inside. Until the day this verse is reminding us about. As Jesus died, the moment He breathed His last breath, this gigantic obstacle to the Throne Room was torn, just like the flesh of Christ. It did not rip side to side or bottom to top. God tore the veil from the top to the bottom. God got rid of the obstacle and in doing so, invited everyone into the Holy of Holies. In the tearing of the veil He was inviting us, Jew, and Gentile alike into His Throne Room. When I was a kid I wanted to be in whatever room my parents were in. I wanted to just be able to sit with them. As a child of God, I want the same thing. I want to be in the Throne Room with my Father, sitting with Him, talking to Him, relaxing in His Presence because I know that there everything is alright. I am always amazed at this part of our heritage. God wants us to be a part of Him and He has given every indication of that and the people closest did not even see it. Here I am, born centuries later and I can close my eyes and picture the man on the cross with His skin torn. I can see the veil ripping straight down the middle in invitation for everyone around to enter a place very few ever had. Today we can walk into the Throne Room of the Great I AM, not bound to others with a rope, and rest in the Presence of God. Have you been there today? When was the last time you went beyond the regular prayer and study time and really entered into the Holy of Holies just to spend time with God? The veil is torn, the invitation is open.

And He said to them all, "If any man will come after me, let him deny himself, and take up his cross daily, and follow me.

Luke 9:23

I used to think differently about my cross. I thought it was my disease that I was to pick up daily. That it was my lot in life to carry that pain and shame every single day. When Jesus found me, though, He showed me how to put that down. Since then, He has shown me how to put down all sorts of things. So, then, those things I have been empowered through Jesus to put down must not be my cross to carry at all. I was at a loss for what I was to carry daily. Until I looked at the cross of Christ and saw the sacrifice of self He carried. How do I do that? If I am to live in the resurrection, not the death, how do I properly deny myself daily, take up my cross and follow? I do as Jesus did. Every day, I commit my day to the will of God. That does not leave me at the cross, God's will teaches me how to walk in the resurrection. People inevitably make this sound way more than what it is, however, it is so important. What it is not is a chance for me to self-sabotage or sacrifice to the point of starvation or crazy things that people do in the name of daily carrying their cross. Jesus showed us how to do everything, including this. He lived His life in the will of God. He went where God said to go, did what God said to do and said what God said to say. He denied Himself daily in order to walk out the will of God. He did not stay at the sacrifice of the cross because that was not God's will. He did not stay in the sins of humanity because that was not God's will. Today if I am to pick up my cross and follow Him, it means to walk in the will of God and in the promise of resurrection. Are you weighed down by your cross today? Are you trying to deny yourself for denial's sake, or are you doing the things that are in the will of God today?

And He said unto me, "My grace is sufficient for thee: for my strength is made perfect in weakness"....

2 Corinthians 12:9a

Paul speaks about the thorn in his side, not to other men, but directly to God. Three times he asks God to remove it. God refused him. Not because God is cruel, but because Paul was to fully rely on God for his strength. I was doing a group fast last year and one of our group told me she wanted just one bite. She said in the wanting to relieve the pain of hunger she could feel the nudge of Holy Spirit. She said it felt as though God was telling her, "You are not in pain. You are only hungry. I will feed you." How awesome, in that moment of weakness God fulfilled in her a promise made to Paul! In her weakness, His strength was made perfect! There are times when I have felt so weak. Whether it was by finances, adoption, or whatever circumstances, those things were a thorn in my side. I often cry out for relief. God is always faithful to remind me that in my weakness, He is strong and if I am relying on His strength instead of my own, it is possible to endure whatever the thorn is. Do you feel stabbed by a situation or circumstance in your life that just seems to go on forever? Are you talking to other people about it? Have you cried out, begging God to take it from you? Or do your rest in the grace He gives you, having faith that His strength is being perfected in you at this time?

Weeping, she began to wet his feet with her tears and wiped them with the hair of her head and kissed his feet and anointed them with the ointment.

Luke 7:38

The ointment was the visible and tangible liquid poured on and absorbed by humans that told of the invisible presence and action of Holy Spirit. In this reference, to see Jesus as the Anointed One, you have to see His necessary association with Holy Spirit. Jesus had a required connection for a joint purpose with Holy Spirit. The anointing spoken of in this verse was fairly close to the beginning of His ministry. It is believed that Jesus was in His first year and a half. The anointing of His feet could be preparing Him for the remainder of His ministry. That definitely required connection to Holy Spirit for a joint purpose. The next time Jesus was anointed, it was in Bethany by Mary. She anointed His head in a manner to prepare for Him for burial. Again, there was a necessary association between Jesus and Holy Spirit. If Jesus required connection with Holy Spirit in order to accomplish the greatest things in humanity, it would stand to reason that I would also need that connection in order to accomplish the things I have been purposed to do. Nobody has ever poured $50,000 worth of oil over my head or on my feet as they did for Jesus. However, what has happened is so much better than that. Holy Spirit, the Spirit of the Great I AM, came to dwell within me. That does not mean that I can do the things that I am not purposed for. I am anointed, through Holy Spirit to do the things God needs me to do. I will write, but I will never be a pastor or an evangelist or probably even a full-time-move-across-the-world missionary. I will though, do my best to fulfill the purpose God wants to achieve through me with the anointing of Holy Spirit. Do you know that you are anointed today? It may not be in the act of saving the world, but it is definitely in making it better. Walk in the required connection you have with Holy Spirit and watch God open amazing doors for you.

And make an incense blended as by the perfumer, seasoned with salt, pure and holy.

Exodus 30:35

I say all the time that nothing is in the Bible by mistake. Salt is an amazing compound. It is formed when a positive ion bonds with a negative ion. That puts in mind the bonding of the positivity of Holy Spirit with humanity. Salt is a necessity of life. Humans have to have it to live. It serves as a disinfectant, cleansing, like the blood of Jesus. Salt is a preservative. An interesting fact about that is because of its preservative qualities that make it top choice as the symbol of an enduring compact. That means it was used in the bonding of covenants. For making sacrifices, the Israelites were instructed to sprinkle them with salt first. There are significant sayings about salt in several languages. In Arabic, to signify covenants, they say "there is salt between us". The Hebrews denote eating the salt of the palace as an honor. In contrast, the Persian phrase "namak haram" accuses one of being untrue to salt, dishonorable. For the English, the phrase salt of the earth shows one to be in high esteem. We are told in the New Testament to be the salt of the earth (Matthew 5:13). From everything I have seen about salt, it means we are to be held to more than high esteem. We are urged to bind positivity into the lives of others. We are called to be a sweet-smelling incense to God. Christians, as the salt of the earth, are supposed to spread the cleansing blood of Jesus. As the salt of the earth, we carry the preservative qualities of the covenant God made at the resurrection of Jesus Christ. Are you salty today? Are you seasoned with salt, pure and holy? Or have you lost your saltiness?

Religion that is pure and undefiled before God the Father is this: to visit orphans and widows in their affliction.

James 1:27a

In my church we are in the middle of a sermon series about hearing God. This week the focus is paying attention to the doors He is opening in our lives and being bold to walk through the door. It is also about remembering what doors the keys to the Kingdom really open. Since my kids were little we have always had other kids at my house. Each kid has a different story. There has not been a ton of time when my house has been empty. As they have gotten older, the kids have changed, the problems often are much more severe. My house though continues to be the refuge. I did not realize, until it was pointed out to me today, that while God is opening unimaginable spiritual doors in my life, He is also opening one very physical door for these kids. Lately I jokingly refer to my home as the house for wayward boys. Today I was tired. I physically felt the emotional and financial weight of having a home where kids feel safe. This afternoon a very dear woman said a prayer for me in which she referred to my home as God's home, a refuge of strength and love for these kids. Tonight, one of the boys found out both of his parents are facing prison time very soon. He believes that God has a plan and that God will see him through this. He also knows that he has a place here to call home. I had a hard time with this verse before today. The word religion had come to mean something different to me. However, today, I can see that Holy Spirit has opened up my front door as a way to show these kids pure and undefiled religion. It is in the love that Holy Spirit blankets this house and their lives with when they are here. People do not understand why I so willingly let these boys in when, honestly, I can barely afford it. I was beginning to question that myself. God showed me why tonight in a broken boy, full of hope in the Lord. While I do not recommend everyone open their doors, I do encourage you today to help the needy. Whether it is in prayer, a conversation, a meal, or just a hug. Love someone outside of your comfort zone. It could be God is opening a door to the Kingdom for them through you.

Pray without ceasing.

1 Thessalonians 5:17

This verse sounds so very hard. However, since it is in the Bible, as a direction, not a suggestion, that must mean that it can be done. It is so often thought that prayer is a reverent time. While it is, it is also something else. Prayer is how we communicate with God. It is a conversation. Think about the beginning of your relationship with your spouse. Do you remember how it felt to wake up in the morning and want to talk to them? How in the middle of the morning you wanted to hear their voice, and at mid-day you wanted so much to be with that person. Do you remember how you wanted to talk to them and learn everything there was to know? Prayer is the same thing. It is the most intimate conversation with the Creator and Lover of your soul. It isn't just a time to bow your head and repeat words you heard someone else say, though that is a great place to start. Prayer is constant communication with the One who loves you the most. It is waking up and starting a conversation that does not stop until you go to bed. It is not only talking, saying the deepest, most intimate things in your being, but also listening. It is the way that we come to learn the sound of the Holy Spirit guiding us. Prayer is the way we learn to see open doors and hear direction and taste love. When we pray without ceasing we are nurturing our relationship with God. We are building bridges that connect humanity with eternity. When I think of it like that, it makes praying without ceasing seem not quite so hard. What is your prayer life like? Do you give God just a couple of minutes in the morning and a few more before you close your eyes? Or do you offer Him more of you and your day? I encourage you today to pray without ceasing.

But Peter and John answered them, "Whether it is right in the sight of God to listen to you rather than to God, you must judge, for we cannot but speak of what we have seen and heard."

Acts 4:19-20

Peter and John had been taken before the Sanhedrin because they were proclaiming the name of Jesus and resurrection in His name and they were healing in Jesus name. The Sanhedrin demanded that they not speak the name of Jesus. They could not do that. Not only did they walk with Jesus and see the miracles He performed in the three years they were together, but they saw Him in the end. They saw the resurrected Christ. He spoke with them and ate with them. Peter and John saw Jesus ascend and then went to Jerusalem where they waited with prayerful breath for the Power Jesus promised. Then they were filled to overflowing with Holy Spirit. How could they not talk about that? How could they not heal and teach when that is exactly what Jesus told them to do? I do not always say exactly what is on my heart about God. In some settings it is easier. When I am with likeminded people it is easier for me to talk about the things I know and have seen and experienced. In some areas it is more difficult. People do not always take the Truth well and because of that I find there are times when I hold back. However, what I know is that I am not supposed to behave that way. I am supposed to boldly speak of the things that I have seen. I am created to speak of the miracle that my life is because of Jesus. I like to think that if I had to go before an authority and be told to not speak of Jesus I would respond in the same way that Peter and John did. If I believe that I am brave enough to stand my ground in Truth with authority, why would I also not do that with the people who really cross my path every day? Do you speak the Truth of Jesus to the people on your daily journey? Or do you let the pretense of "to each their own" quiet what Holy Spirit is really wanting to say to them through you?

Jesus said, "If you were blind, you would not be guilty of sin; but now that you claim you can see, your guilt remains.

John 9:41

The Pharisees were offended because Jesus implied they were blind. Jesus did not say that their guilt remained because they could see, but because they claimed to be able to see. There is such a difference. The Pharisees were raised in Scripture. They memorized it and they read it and they taught it. They thought they knew it. However, it did not impact their lives in a way that altered their existence. They knew but they did not believe. They were not blind, however, in the most important of ways, they could not see. Their lack of sight did not cause their guilt. Their gift of sight also did not cause their guilt. Their pretense of sight caused their guilt to remain. Because they could not humble themselves and admit that they truly could not see the truth, their stubborn ability to "see" kept them caught in the guilt of sin. While their eyes worked fully well, their spirits were blind and proud. Though they were found by tradition, they were lost to God. They could see in the flesh but were blind in the spirit. Since they could not admit to their blindness of spirit and held to the pride of being able to see, they condemned themselves to the guilt of sin. Personally, I do not want the guilt of my sin to remain. I want to truly be able to see because I know that in the sight, there is Jesus and He is the way to the Father. Do you only claim to see today, sticking yourself in the guilt of sin? Or do you truly see and walk inside of the freedom of sight?

So, because you are lukewarm, and neither hot nor cold, I will spit you out of my mouth.

Revelation 3:16

We often think that the opposite of love is hate. However, hate is still a passionate emotion. The opposite of either one would be indifference. That is what I think of when I think of someone as being lukewarm. They come to a place of indifference. Indifference signifies a place of middle ground. They are neither passionate in positive emotion or negative emotion. There is simply no response there. I do know that I cannot tell by looking at someone if they are hot or cold because I cannot see what God sees in others. To me it may look like a lack of outward praise when truly in their heart they are on their face before the Lord. It may look like the lady who goes to the church to pray for hours a day, when internally and behind closed doors she does not give God a second thought. However, I do know two sides of this verse feels like. I know that when I am cold, I am dying. There is a pit of deep despair and so much anger towards God. When I am on fire my life is ever changing. I am growing and evolving. I do not ever want to be cold or lukewarm with God again. I pray to be hot so that God does not spit me from His mouth but welcomes me to His Throne. When was the last time you truly took your spiritual temperature? Are you in a place of indifference? Or are you on fire for the things of God?

He answered, "I tell you, if these were silent, the very stones would cry out."

Luke 19:40

Jesus was entering Jerusalem on the back of a colt. The crowd was praising God joyfully as He went. They had been travelling with Him and seen the miracles and felt the love and seen the working of faith. In response of those things and of being in the same place with the Son of Man, they were praising. Like David danced before the Lord when they brought the ark into Jerusalem so many years before (2 Samuel 6:14-15), the people of Jerusalem danced this day also before the Lord. The Pharisees did not appreciate the joy. They told Jesus to control His disciples. In David's day, it was his wife who reprimanded him. On this day, it was those who were supposed to be closest to God that was reprimanding Jesus. On both days, the Glory of God was travelling the roads into Jerusalem. Both days there were people trying to nullify the praise. The response of Jesus is profound to me though. If the people did not offer praise before the glory of God, the stones would. Can you imagine your lack of praise of God being outshined by the praise of the rocks? I am like the disciples in the crowd. I have travelled with Jesus. I have seen the miracles. I have walked in the faith. I have tasted His love. Those things give me, not only a desire, but a need to praise God. Very often my praise is loud and big. Sometimes it is me dropping to my knees, arms wide and high in the air. At other times, my praise is very private, dancing and worshiping in my house. Always it is done in joy, not influenced by those who would reprimand such a showing of affection. When was the last time you danced before the Lord? Do those around you get to witness you joyfully praising God? Or are the stones standing in your place?

And who knows whether you have not come to the kingdom for a time such as this?

Esther 4:14d

Esther is the only book in the bible where God is not directly mentioned. This fascinates me because He is written all over the book. Throughout the whole book there is love, wisdom and knowledge. God is threaded throughout in courage, strength, and victory. His will is the most evident gift in the book. Mordecai spoke of the will of God in this verse as he was encouraging Esther to go before the king. God placed Esther in this place at this time. Through her placement in the kingdom God had a vessel through which to save His people. She had come to the kingdom for such a time. Her purpose was not the saving but being the vessel so that the saving could be done. She could have said no. Esther could have told Mordecai that she would not risk her own life in order to save others. That is not what happened though. Esther decided that even if she lost her life she would go to the king. The result of her courage to be used in that time was God being able to use her to speak to the king and ultimately save His people from a wide sweeping massacre. I have asked myself the same question that Mordecai asked Esther. Have I come to the kingdom for a time such as this? The answer is that God saved my life for a time such as this. I choose to let Him use me as a vessel of His light. He does things for and through me that I could never accomplish. I will probably not be used to save an entire nation from massacre. However, if in the fulfillment of the purpose that He has for me, I want my sentiment to always be the same as Esther's, if I perish I perish. I was brought to the kingdom for a time such as this, to share the Gospel and to love as God loves. I was created in a time such as this to encourage and spread hope. The strength, courage, love, and power that is needed to fulfill the purpose I was created in this time to walk in not of me. Those things are given by God, just like He gave them to

Mordecai and Esther. Have you ever asked yourself this question? What if you came to the kingdom for a time such as this? Are you fulfilling the purpose God placed you here for?

Come, follow me, Jesus said.

Matthew 4:19a

Jesus said these words to grown men. They had been making decisions based on logic and emotion for their entire lives. However, this request made no sense in either realm of decision making. Jesus was asking men with families and responsibilities to literally stop doing the things that they were doing in order to care for those people and responsibilities and to follow Him. Nothing about doing that would qualify as logical. I mean, think about what was happening. Back then when Jesus said come, follow me, that is exactly what He meant. He wanted them to leave everything and walk all over Israel with Him and learn from Him. Walk away from your job, your wife, your life and follow. Seemingly, without thought, that is exactly what they did. The decision was not made out of logic or emotion. When Jesus came to me and told me to follow Him, I cannot even describe the decision in that moment. There was no thought process. It was like being at a stop sign and knowing this is a right turn, not left, even though I had never been at this particular stop sign before. While I did not need to leave my children, I did need to leave every other thing about my life. However, I could not get where God was taking me if I did not leave where I was. Nor could I get there without a guide. When Jesus says, "come, follow me," He does not leave us to walk the road alone. Just like He did not leave the Disciples, even when He died, He will also not leave us. Do you really follow Jesus? Did you leave your life so that He could create a new one in you? Have you changed the direction you were going so that God can show you the better way? If it was an instinctive change of direction for you in the beginning, is it still that way today? Or have you changed instinct into logic and emotion?

Refrain from anger and forsake wrath! Fret not yourself; it tends only to evil.

Psalm 37:8

How hard is it to follow this wise piece of advice? If you have ever been a mother or a wife or had any human relation, I would venture to say that it is quite difficult. Lately there is a ton of change going on. Most of which is internal, with the change of my role as Mom. I do not get to fix things or kiss away the pains or make the decisions. I do not deal well with change that I do not like is the ultimate issue. I also do not deal well with the emotional part of the change, so I allow it to all be revealed in anger. It has been quite exhausting to be totally honest. This Psalm tells me why. I am supposed to refrain from and forsake these overwhelming feelings of annoyance and displeasure. I am not created to fret. I even know that it would produce evil on some levels. It is an evil that causes me to be internally callused. I found that I had lost some drive. I had a huge case of the 'I don't want tos'. I did not want to pray. I did not want to read scripture. I did not want to praise. That kind of evil begins very soon if I am not refraining from anger and forsaking wrath. When I sit in it too long, it begins to alter my appearance. My light fades. However, I know God would not tell me to refrain from anger without also telling me how to. I turn on worship music very loud. I pray and listen to God's response. I read the Word. I seek the fellowship and I serve. The wisdom of this verse is in taking the steps God gives me to follow it. He would not tell me to refrain if it were not possible. Does not make it easy, but it is simple. Do you refrain from anger? Or have you let it produce evil in your life?

Jesus answered him, "Truly, truly, I say to you, unless one is born again he cannot see the kingdom of God."

John 3:3

The book of John is so explicit in wording. I have said before that the Rabbis say the words of the Torah have 70 different meanings each. That is no different for the New Testament. John wrote of His experience with words that are shaded and hidden. If I read with common knowledge, while I gain some understanding, I will miss the deeper hues of the truth. The word truly means that what follows is a trustworthy statement. Born again speaks of a rebirth of heart and spirit. The word see in this verse is my favorite though. For years I have read past this word, thinking it referred to sight. I thought this verse meant that if I am not born again I will never get to visually see God's Kingdom. While that is true, there is a deeper meaning. Here, the words "will not see" mean I will not know the Kingdom. Not only that, I will not behold and understand the Kingdom. If I am not born again, I cannot tell (see) the Kingdom of God. I love this verse because the opposite is also true. Truly, truly, since I am born again I will see (behold with knowing and understanding that causes me to tell) the Kingdom of God. The truth of seeing this verse in literal context allows it to live in me. That living causes understanding and the understanding causes expression. The expression is what allows others to see the Kingdom inside of me. How do you see God's Kingdom today? Do you Behold it with knowing and understanding? Do you take the time to tell it? Or is it time for you to be born again?

My command is this: Love each other as I have loved you.

John 15:12

Chapters 14 through 17 of John have very few black words. I love these chapters because they are the words of Jesus edifying and preparing and praying for His disciples. That means that there has to be things said in there that is hard to hear and harder to walk. This verse is one of those things. Jesus commands that we love each other as He loved us. I know that he was talking to a very specific group of people. However, I also know that this is not one of the things that was meant for them alone. It is a command that surpasses the day that it was spoken. It also happens to be one of those things that is considerably easier said than done. Jesus loved His disciples in ways that changed their lives. He loves me in the same way. The love of Christ has caused healing and hope. It breathes into my life and gives me the courage to live in a new way. His love smells better than the finest perfume and feels gentler than the softest breeze. How could I ever love with that degree of pureness? Could my love for others ever be that truly unconditional? One thing I do know about the commands of scripture, if they are there, they are possible. However, not of my own power. Holy Spirit is the living love of Christ dwelling inside of me. That is how we are able to love how Christ loved. With His Spirit inside He is able to manifest that love in the flesh again. The catch is that I have to allow that to happen. If there is prejudice of any kind in my heart or mind, I am blocking that love from its full expression. If I am not humble and willing, I place an obstacle. Ultimately, I am choosing to not love as Christ loved. If I am giving myself as a fully willing vessel, without prejudice and humble, that allows Holy Spirit to love others through me and I am loving as Christ loved. How do you love today? Is it as Christ loved, or are there obstacles of self in the way?

Blessed are those who have not seen and yet have believed.

John 20:29b

Jesus was talking to Thomas who refused to believe the resurrection because he had not seen Jesus with his own eyes. Thomas needed to see the Man and the scars before he would believe that Jesus lived. Jesus acknowledged that Thomas had to see to believe. However, He then went further and said that those who believe without seeing are blessed. It is not a normal thing for people to see Jesus today, yet we believe. Why? It is not because we see His human form or because we can place our fingers in his nail scarred hands. We believe because we see Him in other ways. For me, He was the Light in the darkest of dark places. I see Jesus in my own healed scars. I see Him in the Words of the Bible and in the Truth of His promises that have come alive in my life. I could not deny today that Jesus exists because I have seen Him, not in the flesh, but in my life. I often wonder how it was to be a Disciple. They walked with Jesus. He looked into their eyes; can you imagine? They ate with Him and saw Him die then resurrected. I used to envy them of those things. However, I realize today that I get to experience those exact same things with Him. Every day, I wake up and Jesus is here, walking with me in life. Every time I have a meal, I invite Him to join me. I share communion with Him in the fellowship of the Body. I feel Him look into my eyes and shine His light into my spirit. While He is gone, He is also here. Blessed are we who have not seen yet believe because in that He lives with us daily, never to leave again. Do you believe? Do you see Jesus in your life in every moment of the day? If so, you are blessed.

In fact, though by this time you ought to be teachers, you need someone to teach you the elementary truths of God's word all over again. You need milk, not solid food.

Hebrews 5:12

In the passage above this verse the author of Hebrews talked about the way Jesus prayed in reverent submission. He spoke about Jesus learning obedience through suffering. The writer discussed the eternal benefit that is the result of these things. However, in the very next passage he said these truths were too difficult for those reading to understand. These people were stuck in the beginning. They only understood foundation of repentance...and of faith in God.... instruction about baptisms, the laying on of hands, resurrection of the dead and eternal judgment. That is as far as they had gotten though. Can you imagine only knowing 6 things about God's truth? I am not saying they are not important truths. They are foundational. The truths of God are meant to live and breathe, not just on the pages, but in your life. Since that is true, what lives and breathes is also meant to grow. Like a child going from milk to solid food, or children moving from sandwiches to steaks, we are supposed to grow spiritually. The foundational truths of God are only the milk of infancy. Over time we are meant to feast on more of the Word, increased intimacy with God, deeper understanding of His knowledge. I enjoy so much sitting on a pew and listening to people talk about God. I love the Gospel. And I could live on just that fruit. For me though, there is a hunger for a feast. Are you still on milk? Or are you nurtured with meat and growing in God?

Let us therefore come boldly to the throne of grace, that we may obtain mercy and find grace to help in time of need.

Hebrews 4:16

The first phrase in this sentence contains the word 'therefore'. There is something in the verses above that is meant to build confidence in us that allows us to approach the throne of God. You could assume it is some amazing thing that is difficult to obtain. You would only be half right though. What builds our confidence is the amazing gift of Jesus. The author of Hebrews talks about how Jesus is our high priest, He can sympathize with our weakness. He was tempted in every way we are, yet without sin. He tore the veil and paved the way to the throne with His blood. Confidence means boldness and assurance. Since I am a child of God, Jesus shows me the way and gives me assurance to approach the Great I AM. This verse says when we are there because we have boldly approached, we receive mercy and grace that helps us through trouble. We are also able to go in good times. God wants to celebrate with us as much as He wants to help. I want my kids to come to me in hard times and I love it when they call me to celebrate their victories. God is not different. Jesus gives us boldness to run to the Throne in hard and easy times. We can go on any day of the week and at any time of the day. I love, more than anything, to spend time in the presence of the Almighty. Jesus gives me the confidence to do that. When was the last time you boldly approached God's Throne? Did you really go with confidence, or did you shuffle out in the foyer, worried you were not good enough to be there? Get your confidence from Jesus. Grow in boldness. Run to the Throne of God. There mercy and grace await you in the good times and the bad.

Give and it will be given to you. Good measure, pressed down, shaken together, running over, will be put into your lap. For with the measure you use it will be measured back to you.

Luke 6:38

The words pressed down in this verse have always made me smile. It is like when you are baking with brown sugar. Most recipes call for packed measurements of brown sugar. You add some to the cup and think that it is full, but when you press it down, you realize that there is room for more. Generally, I can do that a few times before the cup is really measuring full. That is how the things of God are. Not only does God press it down, He then shakes so that He can add more. So much so that the cup runs over. That is definitely a good measure of things. This is not just the truth with the good and lovely things of God. If I am judging, condemning, not forgiving, and not giving, with the measure I do those things it is also measured back to me. I do not want a pressed down, shaken together, running over cup of unforgiveness and condemnation. However, God will not force me to be kind in life. That is a choice I get to make through my own free will. Very often I hear people pray for God's will to be done in matters that He has no control over. While God is sovereign, He will not cause me to be kind, even though that is absolutely His will for my life. He gives me a choice. When I wake up, as I walk through my day, I get to choose if I am going to accept, love, give and forgive. If that is the choice that I make then my cup will overflow with peace and joy. If I choose differently, my cup will be full of chaos inside of chaos. God wants to overflow your cup with the beautiful and wonderful things of Him. He is a gentleman though and you have to choose those things. What will your good measure look like today? Will you overflow with love? Or will you be pressed down with chaos?

See, I have refined you, though not as silver; I have tested you in the furnace of affliction.

Isaiah 48:10

Lisa Bevere said, "God is more concerned with our condition than our comfort". Generally, when we are in the furnace of affliction, God is not teaching us how to grin and bear it. Those are times of growth. Growth is not comfortable. What I often fail to remember is that I get to choose how long it is going to take me in the furnace. It is so easy to get in the hardships of life and throw a fit. For me, I want to fight the situations. When they start I tend to see them as a test. I begin to want to control the circumstance or be more assertive in being the one who can fix it all. I have had two very adverse situations and two very different responses. One was during the shutdown. I wanted to bang on my highchair for a month. A ton of small things happened inside of the one big thing. It was chaos inside of chaos and I was choosing to react chaotically. Eventually, I went to God and told Him I could not handle it anymore and I needed help. That furnace lasted a while. A few days ago, a payment came out of my account and left me very broke. This time, I went to God first. I did not throw a fit, I let Him have control and I had faith that He would provide. This time in the furnace lasted only a few hours. Not shockingly, I got a call that the withdrawal was in error, that payment had already been made and they put the money back. My furnace of affliction in this season has been to refine my patience and faith. Next season it will probably be something different. I have had very little internal comfort through this time. However, my condition is becoming one of greater spiritual health and growth. I have again found the Light of my fire in the Lover of my soul. Today, I did not have to stay long in the furnace. Like the Hebrew boys, I knew my God was there with me and protecting me and that allowed the flames to not touch me, but growth to still happen. Is your comfort level greater than your spiritual condition? How do you react when you are thrown into the furnace of affliction? Do you trust that God is there with you, or do you try to control your way out of it?

You too, be patient and stand firm, because the Lord's coming is near.

James 5:8

Momma told me years ago not to pray for patience. When you are a kid, things like that do not make sense. Today I know why people tell you not to pray for patience. Some things we pray for and they are gifts, like grace and mercy. Other things we pray for come only by lessons. Patience is one of those things that is learned. In the last 5 years I have learned patience to different degrees. When I first got sober I had to learn the patience to just sit still. God taught me how to stay though. Instead of giving me what I wanted at that time, He taught me patience in sitting still. Since then I have learned patience in praying. I have learned patience in kneeling. Somewhere along the way, God taught me, through those lessons in patience, how to stand. At first it was a wobble. Once my feet got under me though, I started to learn about what to stand for. The Bible is full of instructions on how to live life. I do not always follow instructions well. Some things I forget. So, I continuously go back to the Manual. I have had the opportunity to stand for things that other people did not understand. I do not believe in picking and choosing which part of the Bible is not meant for today. I firmly believe that the things written are breathing life in every generation since the words were penned. I will not lie, I have had rebellious times and have decided to stop and sit instead of stand firm. Each time that happens, the result is another lesson in patience. God is more concerned with my condition than my comfort, so He helps me up and teaches me again how to be patient and stand firm on His Word because His coming is near. He does not want me to miss that. Since He told me to be patient and stand firm, He also teaches me how to do that. It is not always a fun lesson, but every time, it is well worth the pain. Are you patient and standing firm? Are you in the midst of a rebellion, even a small one? I encourage you today to take note of your condition. Perhaps it is time to learn the next degree of patience so that you are standing firm.

For sin shall not be your master, because you are not under the law, but under grace.

Romans 6:14

Paul was adamant when he was writing to the Romans. He says over and again that we are not under the law but under grace. Sometimes that is confusing because we are taught that we are still human and still prone to sin. However, Paul's point is that sin is no longer master. Whatever it is that we serve is what we are slaves to (Rom 6:16). If I am serving my sin, then it is my master and I am its slave. However, if I am choosing to serve God, He is my Master. That does not mean that I will not sin. If I am serving sin, there can be moments that I choose to be righteous. That does not mean that God is my master in those moments because I am still very much a slave to sin, regardless that I was able to make one better decision on one day. The same is true when we choose to fully live under grace and allow God to be Master. There will be times when we sin. It will not be a place that we want to stay. Sin will not be the thing we instinctively want to do. Grace does not give us the freedom to have life both ways. It does not give us the opportunity to continue in sin while we also have a foot in the Kingdom. The purpose of grace is to change our spirit in ways the law could not. Grace forgives us for sin, but it also causes us to desire to no longer be a slave to it. Paul asks if this means we should go on sinning, then he answers the question: absolutely not. It does not mean that we will never sin again, however, the sins done overtly, outright, and with intent are supposed to no longer happen. That is why Jesus Himself told those He healed to go and sin no more (John 5:14, 8:11). Living under grace has changed my life. I am a slave to God today. I still screw up, but the life of screwing up is no longer my master. Who is your master today? Is it really God and His grace? Or do you still live as a slave to sin, hoping that grace will cover the things you know you are not supposed to be doing?

For you did not receive a spirit that makes you a slave again to fear, but you received the spirit of sonship.

Romans 8:15

In Paul's time, sonship was a big deal. It determined inheritance and place. Back then, it was a big deal for someone outside the family to receive the status of sonship. It meant that the patriarch was bypassing his people in order to give an outsider a place at the table. Inviting an outsider in and giving him sonship did not mean that the people in the family were no longer in the family, it meant that the outsider was given the blessing also. From the time he is invited in, this person would have walked in the identity of his sonship. I think sonship is used in the stories of the Bible to show us the gravity of God's plan. God had His chosen people. He could have allowed them to understand and welcome the ministry of Jesus. However, God had greater things in store. He created things this way so that he could reach out for people He could offer sonship to. In His greatness, the Lover of our souls wanted to give us identity and inheritance and a place, not only at His table, but in His Kingdom. I never knew my identity. I knew what I was, but I never understood who I was. With Jesus that changed. I finally knew my identity. I am a graft on a massive family tree. I am a woman at a well. I am a lady, made for such a time as this. I am a girl who left everything for a God I did not understand. I am a Gentile, no longer a slave to the sin that almost killed me, but a servant to the Master. I am welcome into the throne room because it is my Father who sits on the throne. I am coheir of the Kingdom of the Almighty. I am a child of the Great I AM. I am not of His people, yet He offered me sonship and by Him I cry "Abba". Do you know who you are today? Do you know which spirit lives in you? Is it one of fear? Or do you walk in the identity of your sonship?

Love never fails.

1 Corinthians 13:8a

I used to skip over this whole chapter. I could not stand to read it. Even when I was saved and I knew this love was different, I could not wrap my head around these verses and believe that it is humanly possible for humanity to love in these ways. I came from a lifestyle that was shrouded in darkness. The people I knew did not love anything anymore. I was in a place where I considered everything of malicious intent. I did not even believe my family really loved me anymore. It was so dark there was nothing. Then Jesus came and immediately I knew His love. It was a fire that ignited every cell in my body. I instantly knew that God loved me fully and that His love would never fail. I was very skeptical about humanity though. In my mind, people only "loved" you until they got whatever it was they wanted and then they left. I was thinking wrong though. This chapter was not telling me how the world is supposed to love me. When I really sat down and read it in the light of the love of Jesus, I learned how I am supposed to love them. This chapter suddenly became a guide in the way that I love people. When that happened, I began to believe that this love is possible. I stopped waiting for the other shoe to drop in my relationships and I started to see that the love of Jesus can be felt also in the love of people. Not in the fire igniting way, however, it is a love that is pure and real. I see it in my parents, my siblings, and my kids. I experience it with the women I share my time with. Love like this is only possible with God though. I cannot wake up of my own humanity and choose to love in an unfailing way. If I could do that I would not need the presence of Holy Spirit in my life. It is only with the love of God as the fire that love never fails. How do you love today? Is it out of human will or do you love with the unfailing love of God?

If you hold to my teaching, you are really my disciples.

John 8:31b

The biggest word in the entire Bible is "if". It denotes possibility and choice. God is ever a gentleman. Sometimes I think it would have been a great thing had He rethought putting that tree in the garden. The world could have gone on being perfection and we never would have had to choose. However, when I think about relationships in my life, I want those people to choose to be with me. I do not want to marry a man because he feels as though he has to. I do not want friends who talk to me out of an obligation. I want to be chosen. The same is true with God. He could have created a world of robots. That was not His thought though. Love comes with an if. We get to choose this life. We get to wake up every day and decide whether or not we will walk with God or with the world. The choice is to be a disciple or not. Jesus did not say we are allowed to hold to the teachings that we agree with either. He gives us a choice to follow Him in everything. I want to be His disciple, so I choose to study His Word. I make a conscious decision to have a relationship with God. As I do that, He teaches me great and wonderful things. He shows me how to love and obey. He leads me in submission and grace. God shows me how to be His light in the darkness. It is through the cracks in my life that His light shines. I love the if of scripture. They are always followed by a "then". If I choose to follow, then I will be led. If I choose to learn, I will be taught. If I choose to let Him, God will change my life in ways that are far beyond my imagination. What is the if in your life today? Where are you choosing the world instead of God? Are you holding to His teaching? Are you a disciple?

My dwelling place will be with them. I will be their God and they will be my people.

Ezekiel 37:27

God was talking about a covenant He was intending to make with His people, and He was telling His plan to Ezekiel. My favorite part of this verse is God's promise to dwell with His people. Sometimes things get lost in reading. It would be simple to look at this verse and think that God meant He would go back to how it was in the wilderness and the Temple. He would reside among His people in the Holy of Holies, entrance barred to all except the one most elite man in all of Israel. However, that is not what 'to dwell with' means. This verse means that God's plan is to live with His people. When people live together, they do not just share a house. To dwell together means that you are living life together. There is communication and love. Dwelling together denotes meals shared and tears shed. There is meant to be closeness and trust. The fulfillment of this promise is so much more though. God does not just share my house. He shares my being. When He said His dwelling place would be with them, He did not just mean communally. God meant that He would make His dwelling with every individual who calls on the name of Jesus. Through Holy Spirit, He does not just do life with me; He takes every step, and He breathes every breath with me. I do not have to experience any moment of life alone anymore. God's dwelling place is quite large. It involves the dwelling with the Body of Christ. However, it also is within every cell of that Body. He is our God, and we are His people. This is the new covenant. Where does God dwell in your life? Is it just in the church where you sit on the pew. Or does God dwell with you?

Jesus said to him, "Receive your sight; your faith has healed you."

Luke 18:42

This was a blind beggar. He was sitting on the side of the road begging and when he heard that Jesus was there he did a very bold thing. He stood up and yelled over the crowd. He caused such a ruckus that the disciples were trying to quiet him. Jesus was not having that though. He called for this man to come forward. The man had not seen any of the things that Jesus had done. However, he had heard and believed. Jesus asked him the simplest of questions. "What would you have me do for you?" He just wanted to see. As natural as anything, Jesus said yes. When his eyes were opened, the first thing this man saw was Jesus. It is that way for all of us. Most of us have always had our sight, but there was a time in all of our lives that we were blind. My first request when Jesus asked me what it was that I needed was not sight. I just wanted to live in a way that allowed me to not crave death. In that though, my eyes were opened. When Jesus gave me my life, He gave me sight and the very first thing I could see clearly was Him. Jesus was in everything. He was in my mirror and in my healing. I only had faith the size of a mustard seed and I have no idea where that came from. That small amount of faith allowed healing far beyond the imagination of even the most devout people that I know. I cannot tell you the praise that God got. It has been several years now that I have been able to see and the praise for the miracle of sight in my life still goes up. Jesus still heals today. It does not always look like we imagine. Healing varies from the physical to the spiritual. Each time though, it brings the gift of sight. We are able to see love and grace and mercy and sacrifice. That sight causes change and healing. It allows faith that is small to grow into something that others can see. There are still so many areas I am blind to. I am constantly standing up and asking God to let me see. Are you blind today? Are there things that are blurry? Ask for sight. Look into the face of Jesus. Let your faith, no matter how small, heal you where God needs to heal you.

Then he said to them, "Watch out! Be on your guard against all kinds of greed; a man's life does not consist in the abundance of his possessions."

Luke 12:15

I know so many people who have to have possessions. They feel as though they have to make a certain amount of money, drive a certain vehicle, and live in a specific neighborhood. While there is nothing wrong with those desires, if someone becomes obsessed with the things and the money it is detrimental to their spirit. I have seen people who have the world and lose it all. What generally happens is that they also lose themselves in the loss of the things. They fall into depression and shame. Their worth and their treasure was in the things of the world and when those things are gone, so is the essence of the person. Do not get me wrong, I have lost everything. At one point I lost not only all of my possessions but also the people. I did not have God then, so when everything was gone, so was I. Today I have possessions. I have a spectacular job. I have a nice house with a yard. I have a car. However, these things do not provide abundance in my life. The things in my life do not cause wholeness and peace and joy. Those things, the things in life that are true abundance come only from God. I would prefer to never experience loss to the level that I have in my past. If I do though, I know today that I would not lose myself also because I find myself in God, not in my things. My life is not the abundance of my possessions. It is the abundance of God through Jesus. He breathes into my life through Holy Spirit. My relationship with God gives love and joy and peace and all of these things come in such a quantity that it is beyond my understanding and imagination. As I learn to be on guard against greed, I also learn the true abundance of God. Are you greedy? Do your possessions mean more to you than God?

Now faith is the assurance of things hoped for, the conviction of things not seen.

Hebrews 11:1

Today we hear all the time about the faith people and how they ask God for things and if they believe hard enough that they will get it, then God will give it. Their faith resides in the receiving of the things they want God to give them. I would like to have a 1969 Jaguar E-Type, storm cloud gray with white leather interior and a rag top. Where in the bible does it say that my assurance should lie in the desire of that car though? Should my faith rest in the conviction that I want that thing and I should assure myself I will have it even though I cannot see it? Knowing what I know about God providing things I need; I do not think that is what this verse is talking about. Faith is not being assured I will receive a thing. Faith is being assured that I will receive the promises of God in my life. I wish He had promised me a Jag. However, I have a Nissan. What He has promised me is so much better. If I delight myself in Him, He then places desires on my heart (Psalm 37:4). Those desires are His promises. He has promised me peace, joy, love, a Comforter in Holy Spirit, a help meet, and abundance in Him. I do not store up my treasures in the earthly things, but in the eternal. That is where my faith lies today. Not in the fading want of a Jag, but in the Creator who gave me the true and lasting desires of my heart. He is where my assurance and convictions stand. Is your faith in receiving the things God can give you? Or is your faith truly in God?

He said to him, "Love the Lord your God with all your heart, with all your soul, and with all your mind."

Matthew 22:37

This is the first and greatest commandment. It is not second or third. We are not told to love our children or spouse first. First, love God. Why are we told so descriptively how to love God though? The commandment could have simply said to love God. However, we are commanded to love with all. God wants us to love Him with our whole being. It is a love that is intellectual, emotional, and deep. This love is meant to be so complete that it touches every moment of our day and every cell of our being. God's love for us is so great that it transforms a heart of stone into one of flesh. When that happens and fully takes hold it becomes life changing. You start the day going in a direction that will only lead to hell, encounter this amazing love along the way, and you completely change direction. It is a love that changes your thought process. It creates in you a new being. God offers this love that causes the dead to live, chaos to become peace, fear to be faith, and sorrow turns to joy. What He asks in return is very simple compared to that. Love Him, first, with everything He has given you. I find, when I do that, loving everyone else, including myself, is not such a difficult thing to do. Do you love God with every part of your being? Do you keep part of it back and put something else first? Do you follow the greatest of commandments?

Do you not know that your body is a temple of the Holy Spirit.

1 Corinthians 6:19a

In times of my life when I am attempting to make serious life changes, this verse is often the first that comes to mind. I start to think about how very much I do not treat my body like a temple. While I am not nearly as neglectful of my temple as I used to be, there are still things that need to be changed. This verse makes me consider the gravity of this truth. Holy Spirit, the Spirit of the Great I AM, resides inside of me and how do I treat His house? I fill His temple with carbs and smoke. I do not exercise. I am sometimes lazy. Are those the really important things though? While they matter, a lot, those are surface things. Do I truly treat my body as the temple of God? Do I put anything before Him? Do I pray as I should? Am I truly a servant or do I prefer to be served? Usually when I am in a time of renovating my temple, I look at things like the smoking. This time, however, I am choosing to pull back the veil and allowing God to show me what He would like to change. God's changes to Holy Spirit's temple is not always comfortable. If I am truly walking in the way of Jesus though, I am willing to be uncomfortable. How is the condition of your temple today? Do you honor Holy Spirit living inside you, allowing the uncomfortable changes of God? Or do you prefer the comfort of your own design?

I tell you the truth, anyone who will not receive the kingdom of God like a little child will never enter it.

Luke 18:17

This verse used to confuse me. Paul later says that we are supposed to mature and grow in spiritual manners. So, if we are supposed to be mature in spirit, how are we still going to be like a little child? Think about when you were little. Do you remember the unwavering trust you had in your parents, or the best adult in your life? That trust gave the freedom to run into their arms. It offered the ability to charge into any room of their house. As you grew older, you did not ask before you ran every inch of their yard. You asked for the things you needed. The relationship you shared allowed you to rest knowing that all that they had belonged to you. There was no question. In my own life, there was a time that I forfeited those things. However, as I got older and I changed my life, I was again able to go to my parents like a child. When I go to their house today, I walk in without knocking. I open the refrigerator. We have coffee on the patio. I walk into the living room and kiss my dad on his head without worrying that I will be kicked out. I have faith as a child when I go there that I am home, and I am blessed to be there and so much more than welcome. Once again, because I come in a childlike manner, I am forgiven and what is theirs is also mine. That is what it means to mature and to grow, yet to still go like a little child to receive the kingdom of God. How do you approach the kingdom of God? Is it in the maturity of growth? Are you dignified, knocking on the door of the Throne Room? Or do you charge into the kingdom? Do you have the unwavering faith of a four-year-old running to his favorite person for a hug, confident that you will receive everything the kingdom has to offer?

Everything is permissible – but not everything is beneficial.

1 Corinthians 10:23a

Paul was exceedingly wise. He knew his place in the Kingdom and he did not fear that. He embraced his sonship and took ownership of the blessings that God bestowed on him. In that, he understood that he could now do everything. He could eat any meat, wear any cloth, go to God without the assistance of the high priest. He knew that people would no longer need to be circumcised in order to believe, but at the same time, it did not matter if they already were. Paul knew that every law of the Old Covenant had been fulfilled inside of three days. He knew that God now sees His children through the righteousness of Christ. Paul did not fear to live inside of that belief, and he did not hesitate to walk in the truth. He knew that he could now do anything and in that, he chose to live like Jesus. Following Jesus was the only thing that was beneficial. He could have settled down and led a quiet life. He did not have to go through the shipwrecks, the beatings, the prisons. Paul knew that would be permissible, however, living that life would not have been beneficial. As children of God, it is permissible for us to simply sit on the pew. It is allowed that we only choose to open our bible on Sunday if we remember to bring it to church. We are even able to never mention the name of God to those outside our own house. While those things are permissible, they are not beneficial. A life that is beneficial is one that follows Christ. Speak the name of God to the world. Sing His praises and live a life of worship. It is better to be a servant rather than to be served. Open your bible and build a strong and solid relationship with God. These are the things that are truly beneficial. How do you live your life? Do you follow self, knowing that all things are permissible? Or do you follow Jesus, knowing He is the only way that is beneficial?

Submit to one another out of reverence for Christ.

Ephesians 5:21

I know a ton of people who have a problem with any verse that talks about submission. They see it as their free will and choice being taken from them. They see is as loss of self and independence. That, however, is not what submission really is. When we submit to the people in our lives it is a humble gesture of respect and trust. Submission is admitting that we do not have all the answers and may need help. It is lowering our guard and taking suggestions that are meant for our good. Real submission is releasing control and allowing people to speak into our lives and our process of living. It is knowing that we cannot do life by ourselves. I am a strong, independent woman, self-supporting, very few outside contributions. However, one of the things I am working on within myself is submission. I pray to be able to do this better. I want relationships that cause me to want to submit to those wiser, more knowledgeable, those with more understanding. I want to be able to listen to others with an open mind and be willing to take suggestions and apply them to my life. I cannot do that if I am unwilling to submit to others. I do not have a problem submitting to God. He is my Master, my Teacher, my everything. As such, He places people in my life I am meant to submit myself to in order that He can work through them. So why would I not submit myself to those guiding lights? How does submission work in your life today? Are you fully submitted to God without allowing anyone else to speak into your life? Or are you fully submitted to others out of reverence to Christ?

In the morning, as they went along, they saw the fig tree withered from the roots.

Mark 11:20

I love this story. The day before, Jesus and His disciples were walking, and Jesus saw the tree from far off. When they got closer He saw that there were no figs and Jesus said to the tree, "may no one ever eat fruit from you again." The disciples heard it and when they saw the tree the next day, the tree was not merely dead, but withered. The roots had died. That part makes me smile. Jesus does the same thing to the sin in our lives. When we encounter Jesus in our flesh, He does a very important work in our spirit. As He walks into our lives He speaks to the sinful nature of our spirit. Jesus tells the sin in our lives that He has overcome it. Jesus removes the sin that has occurred and covers those to come. The hold of sin in our lives withers at the root. Then we have a choice. Jesus kills the hold of sin; however, He does not remove us from the temptation to sin after that. We are given the choice going forward. We are no longer bound to the slavery of sin. That truth alone does not make the choice for us. So many times, I see people who are saved remain in sin. They either have a false idea of faith or they do not believe that they are strong enough to overcome the temptation in their lives. It is as though they did not hear Jesus banish sin and so they do not believe that it has happened. I also know those who fully believe the truth of the withering of the root of sin. These people grow strong in faith and hope. They think on things that are true, honorable, just, pure, lovely, and commendable (Philippians 4:8). They are full of joy and suffer trials with God's strength in their weakness. These people spread love and forgiveness because they fully embrace the love and forgiveness they have been shown. Which side of the withered root are you on? Do you embrace the death of the root of sin in your life and live according to that gift? Or do you forget that the sin is withered and choose to remain in the life you were meant to leave?

But grow in the grace and knowledge of our Lord and Savior Jesus Christ.

2 Peter 3:18a

In the passage above, Peter was giving his readers a warning about being led astray by those who are ignorant, unstable and those who distort the scriptures. We are told by Peter to be on guard so that we are not carried away by such people. I have learned to test everything by the word. If it is not there, it is not true. False teachers very rarely step outside of scripture though. They take the words written by the breath of God and they twist them. The words of the bible can have 70 different meanings, so how are we to know which teachers are false and which are not? We spend time growing in the grace and knowledge of Jesus Christ. The bible never tells us to do something without also telling us how to do that thing. The disciples walked with Christ. They knew Him in ways we cannot because we were not there. However, Jesus said that He was leaving so that He could send the Comforter. The very Spirit of Jesus lives inside of us to guide us in growth and knowledge. When we seek to understand the Word, we are not left to do that alone. We are offered guidance and knowledge with revelation through Holy Spirit. God did not leave us to our own imagination when it comes to the deeper things of Him. Paul taught us many things that are hard to understand of our own accord. Peter even pointed this out. That is why Peter said to grow in grace and knowledge, not to turn from what we were first taught, but to build on that foundation with Jesus, not necessarily with man. Do you study the Word? Or do you trust the man behind the pulpit to consistently speak only the truth? Do you know that man is fallible? The knowledge of Jesus Christ is not. How is your relationship with God? Have you grown in His grace and knowledge? Or is God more of a distant acquaintance in your life than someone you know? Do you grow in the grace and knowledge of Jesus Christ as you were meant to? Or do you leave that for other men?

They triumphed over him by the blood of the Lamb and by the word of their testimony.

Revelation 12:11a

I have a story. It is the story I know best because it is my life. I can smell the scents. I can taste the flavors. I know the faces. I experience the emotion. When I tell my story, I can say it in such a way that the people listening can understand it in their senses. That story caused my enemy to believe that I would forever be on his side. It is just a story though. The story is not my testimony. The word of my testimony is that Jesus Christ held me as my heart of stone completely destroyed me. He then breathed into me a heart of flesh and in that I became a new creation. When I walked away from that encounter, I did not walk away from Christ. He never leaves me. Holy Spirit lives inside of me. He breaks the bondage of sin and allows me to walk in freedom. My testimony is that I was blind, and Jesus made me to see. I was a drug addict, and an alcoholic and Jesus caused me to be recovered. What happened before that is just the unexciting part of my story. It is only different than others' stories in the details. When you talk about the word of your testimony, do you tell about the falling down? Or do you put most of the focus on what happened when Jesus altered your life? Do you only tell the unexciting part of your story? Or do you shout your real testimony?

And so through Him the "Amen" is spoken by us to the glory of God.

2 Corinthians 1:20b

We use the word "amen" in a variety of ways. It is how we end our dinner blessing. We say it out loud in service to show we agree with what is being said by the preacher. It is a word that has become common and misused. It is only used 73 times in the Bible. Every time it is used its meaning is powerful though. "Amen" means faithfully, trustworthy, surely, and verily. At the beginning of this verse Paul says that no matter how many promises God has made, they are "Yes" in Christ. Our response to God's "yes" is "amen". The word is so powerful because it is how we agree with God's yes. When we say "amen" we are declaring that we believe God's word of promise is trustworthy in our life. We are taking a stand in that declaration that we surely believe the truth of God will come to pass. When God promised my mother that "yes", He would restore what the locusts had eaten (Joel 2:25a), she declared with her "amen" that she believed His promise would come to pass. God told her she would see the Lord in the land of the living (Psalm 27:13). Her "amen" of faith and hope is evident in the rebirth of her family. God does not need us to respond with an "amen" to His "yes". What He says will pass either way. However, when we have faith to stand on the truth of God's word, we are able to see miracles happen and truths unfold. What does your "amen" sound like? Do you use it until it has no meaning at all? Or do you say amen in a declaration of faith that God's promised word is trustworthy in your life?

For my thoughts are not your thoughts, neither are your ways my ways, declares the Lord.

Isaiah 55:8

I like to think I know what is best. Lately though, I am being shown that is not the case. The lesson is not coming in an easy-to-swallow-take-it-one-time pill. God is asking me to step out in faith and trust that His is the best way. He wants me to believe that since He can see the beginning from the end, and all possible outcomes of all different scenarios, this is right. In most situations, I do not have a problem understanding that. I accept it in my singleness. I welcome it in my friendships. I acknowledge it in my career. When it comes to my children, sometimes getting on my knees and submitting to His will is the hardest thing to do. I am not a fan of our current circumstance. However, God whispers reminders to me through my people. Throughout this time, my people have reminded me that if things were supposed to be going differently, they would be. They tell me that if I have given my kids' life to God's will, what He does with it is none of my business. Last night I was reminded that God sees the beginning from the end. Since I do not understand or agree with what is happening, this is the time for me to step out in faith, trust God and know that His ways are higher, and I do not have to understand to trust. Are their situations in your life that are stretching your understanding? Do you confine yourself to your finite ways, wanting to be able to make the decisions even though they are already outside of your control? Walk in faith, trust God's ways in all things, especially the hard ones.

And also, some women who had been healed of evil spirits and infirmities: Mary, called Magdalene, from whom seven demons had gone out.

Luke 8:2

When Jesus crossed Mary's path she was tormented. Her body, mind, and spirit were ravaged by demons. She was left with only one way to feed herself and pay her debtors. Yet Jesus loved her anyway. He could see who she was created to be, not what she had become. He knew her name and her pure identity. His voice breathed life into her ravaged body. His touch healed the wounds of her spirit. His gaze allowed her to see. The love of Jesus changed her life. How long do you think Jesus pursued Mary? Maybe it was from when He saw her possessed by demons. Perhaps it was from her first breath. I imagine He pursued her from the foundation of creation. When did Jesus's pursuit of you begin? Remember the first time you breathed His breath, saw His eyes and felt the power of the love of Jesus in your life. Know that Jesus knows your name and gives you your identity. How do you honor the pursuit of Jesus in your life today? Do you pursue Him as He did you? Do you really know His name?

When the righteous cry for help, the Lord hears and delivers them out of all their troubles.

Psalm 34:17

I have a very full life. I have grown children trying to make their own path in the world. I have beautiful grandchildren. I am blessed with friends from all walks of life. I belong to wonderful organizations. I have a spectacular career and a boss who is nothing short of an answered prayer. Yet there are still troubles. I am in the middle of quitting smoking - again. The medication makes it difficult to rest and I often have terrible headaches. I suddenly have a very empty, very quiet house. My very best friend and guardian of my oldest granddaughter is moving all the way across the country. I feel very alone despite the fullness. My mind tends to dwell very heavy on the difficulties. It is easy for me to surround myself with people all day and cry myself to sleep every night. Lately the sadness is overcoming the fullness. I just knew I was becoming depressed. When I was in church Sunday though, I had a realization. I have a spiritual malady. While I am trying to cover the emptiness of my life with an overwhelming amount of busy fullness, I am forgetting to treat my malady with the only solution that works. I pray, but in these times, not as deeply. I sing, but I fail to praise. I bow but forget to worship. I weep, yet do not cry out. When I go to God recently, I am not leaving anything with Him. I talk to but have not rested in Him. Therefore, my troubles remain. Today, I want to start changing that. I am going to cry out to God for help. I will boldly go to the Throne Room and lay my burden at the feet of God, prayerfully leaving more than I take back. Is your life full and troubled? Perhaps it is simply filled with troubles in this season. When was the last time you cried out to God? How long has it been since you rested in Him and allowed Him to fill you with peace? Cry out for His help and let Him deliver you from trouble.

I believe that I shall look upon the goodness of the Lord in the land of the living! Wait for the Lord; be strong and let your heart take courage; wait for the Lord!

Psalm 27:13-14

Waiting could possibly be the hardest thing to do. We wait on all different things. Some wait on COVID. Others wait for addictions and abuses to be recovered from. There are those waiting for the radiation to end. There is even a community of people simply waiting for the end of the final breath. Scripture tells us to be strong and take courage in our hearts during these times. From experience, God would not tell us to do those things without reason. God knew it would be hard to wait. He knew we would have to wait on big things and some of those things would take a long time to come. So, God gave us a promise to hold on to through the waiting. I was going to say that the promise follows the waiting. I do not know if that is a completely true statement though. I am in a season of waiting. I have no control on almost all of the changes and am waiting for this season to end. I am often sad and there is underlying anger. I am like a child who has been held too long in the waiting room, almost ready to explode. However, if I stop and take a breath and really look at what is going on around me, in the midst of human chaos, I see God. He is orchestrating this beautiful masterpiece that looks like chaos to me because of my finite view. When I look closer though, I see Him in the life around me. He is mending shattered lives. God is smiling at me through my best friend's tears. He is healing me inside of intimate conversations. God is in the encouragement of my sister and the wisdom of my mother. He is constant in my father and so very passionate in my brother. Every day I can see the Lord in the land of the living. I only have to be strong and courageous enough to stop in the middle of the chaos to see Him. Stop today and look at the chaos of life, see the Lord in the living.

Peace I leave with you; my peace I give you. Not as the world gives do I give to you. Let not your hearts be troubled, neither let them be afraid.

John 14:27

One of my favorite things is to watch verses come to life in the lives of others. I love watching it in everyone, but it affects me when I get to watch it in the life of someone I care about. I have a friend who embraces the peace of God. He has been going through some stuff and, while he is not getting upsetting answers, he has yet to get any answers at all. Sometimes the not knowing is the scariest part. If it were me, I would sit around thinking of the worst possible answers and driving myself nuts. I do not know if that is really what my friend is doing in his downtime or not, I only know what I see. I do not see a man who is driving himself crazy with thought of what ifs and maybes. I do not see a man with a troubled heart or fear. When I look at him, I see peace in the face of the unknown. He shows that God is in control, and he is alright, whatever the outcome is. This guy knows that Jesus left him peace and he draws on it constantly. He does not walk through this alone, however, there are less than a handful of people who know there is even anything on the horizon. Can you imagine going through months and months of testing and not really talking about it? He says since there are no answers, there is nothing really to say anyway. I have seen people handle some really tough stuff in my short time on earth. I do not believe that I have ever seen it done in the true peace of Christ. I pray for him constantly because that is all that he needs me to do for now. Do you know the peace of Christ today? No matter what test or answer or tribulation you face, do you draw from the peace that Christ has given you? Or is your heart troubled and in fear?

Whatever you do, work heartily, as for the Lord and not for men, knowing that from the Lord you will receive the inheritance as your reward. You are serving the Lord Christ.

Colossians 3:23-24

Oddly enough, this is not one of my favorite verses. It is the first three words that get me. Paul says, "whatever you do". That means any activity I am part of from the time I wake up until I lay down, I am meant to do it as though I am doing it for the Lord. Monday through Friday I am generally pretty alright with that. I do my job, which I do not mind giving God complete praise and a full day's work because I know that without Him, I would not have this job. Generally, in the evening I am doing something with Alcoholics Anonymous or I am at church. Those things are simpler to do unto the Lord. My problem comes in when I have a ton of free time, or I am doing something that I really do not want to do. It is very hard to remember that when I am hanging up laundry I am supposed to be working as unto the Lord. I do not find it easy to have a lazy day on my couch as unto the Lord. When the verse says to work as unto the Lord and not unto man, I qualify as man in the context. That does not mean that I am not supposed to enjoy life and do things that I want to do. What it does mean is that I am supposed to keep my priorities in order, first serve the Lord, then serve myself. That goes against the selfishness of human nature. If it were easy though, it would not really be worth it. I am going to be conscious going forward about devoting everything I am doing to the Lord. I wonder, if in the process, how many things I will quit doing. How do you work and play today? Is it unto the Lord, or unto self?

Be angry and do not sin.

Ephesians 4:26a

It is very taboo for a believer to say out loud that they have been angry with God. He is, by definition, love and grace and mercy. How could someone be mad at that? The anger comes from not being able to understand His timing and His "no". I have been angry because God promised something and as of yet I have not seen the fruits of that promise. Does that mean that I will never see it? Of course not. God promised and God cannot lie. However, I am not God. I am a human with human perception and a human frame of time. While to God the promise was made only minutes or seconds ago, for me it has been years. Lately I am angry that I do not have the results in my hands. I have thought about sinning in my anger. I have considered multiple ways that I could express my discontentment. I have not done those things though. What I have done is gone to God. I have taken my anger to His Throne. When I do that, He is fully accepting of me. God does not turn me away because I have this high-strung fearful anger lately that is directed at Him. He wraps me in His arms and lets me cry it out. God has put women in my life who have directed me to scripture in this time, He has comforted me through them and given them His words to speak over me. God cares that I am angry with Him. However, my human emotion does not surprise Him. He is okay with me being angry with Him. God is not allowing me to sit in the anger though. He convicts me to move forward and find peace in Him and not in the fruition of the promise. God is allowing my anger to pinpoint where my faith lies. For so long I relied on the fact that what God says comes to pass quickly and without fail. However, in this I am learning to trust God because He said and not because He produced. Have you been angry? Did you sin in that anger, or did you allow God to walk you through it?

So also, faith by itself, if it does not have works, is dead.

James 2:17

I am saved by grace. Salvation is a free and clear gift of the loving God. There is no work that I can do for salvation. This verse is not about salvation though. This verse is so very often wrapped up in salvation and the reality of humanity is disregarded. I am absolutely saved. That being said, I have the option of sitting around and resting on my own strength. I can be untrusting of God's plans and focus on my own. I do not have to read the bible or walk by faith in anything except the fact that I am saved. That is how a lot of Christians live their lives. They do not put work into their faith. I know if I want to have a pleasant earthly life there is an element of work that I need to put in. I get up every day and go to work and socialize and make an effort for the things that bring my happiness. If I want heaven to invade earth, isn't the concept of putting action behind that logical? I want a life full of joy, peace, blessing, promise and hope. If I do not actively pursue those things and produce those things, I am not going to obtain those things. I enjoy living a life defined by walking in faith, however, if I am not going after the Word of God and seeking Him, how will I know what true faith is? If I do not care for the widows, the children, and the poor, who will do that for me? These are not things that will get me into heaven. However, they are works that will allow heaven to invade earth allowing others to see the beauty of glory. If I am not showing my faith in God through the works of Christ, how will unbelievers know He is real? Faith should be visible, and it is only visible if there are works to show it in. I pray today that you do not think that there is anything you can do to receive salvation or to lose it. I also pray that your faith is out loud and working to allow heaven to invade earth in the ways that God intended for it to be.

Therefore, if anyone is in Christ, he is a new creation. The old has passed away; behold, the new has come.

2 Corinthians 5:17

There was a very long time that my mother thought I would never darken the door of a church again. She was not totally wrong. The person I was never did darken the door of the church. Prior to salvation, I had grown into a raging, angry agnostic who refused to be in the same room as believers. I spent my entire life trying to get away from the church and all of her judgmental trappings. If that was the way Jesus people behaved, I did not want to be part of it. Every person I knew was a sinner. I hung out with drug addicts and drunks and whores. I spent time with the dredges of humanity because that is what I was. Then Jesus came and met me at the bottom of the pit. He pulled me out of the muck and mire and when He set my feet on solid ground, I was a completely new creation. I was no longer defined as drug addict, alcoholic or whore. I received a new definition of identity. I became a beloved daughter of the Most High and co-heir of the Kingdom. I am grace saved and blood bought. I am the dwelling place of Holy Spirit. Today, I am associated with a variety of people. I get to mingle with believers because I am one. I also get to walk with the sinners because I am one. The only difference now is that I am not there to actively partake in that sin but to help them to see the way out of addiction and alcoholism. Today I am both sides of the same coin. That is what Christ showed us how to be. Jesus walked through humanity with both sinner and saint. He came to show us how to be loving to all and faithful to Him. Because of Jesus I am a new creation. How is the new creation of your life being evidenced? When people look at you, do they see the old or the new?

I can do all things through him who gives me strength.

Philippians 4:13

I had a week full of emotion. It was the type of draining that leaves you completely exhausted. I felt as though every time I turned around there was a new rejection, or the same rejection stated a different way. I have been extremely sensitive to external stimulation of my emotion. Inside of that I have felt like I am not enough and obviously there is something wrong with me. I have not been content in my circumstances, internal or external. I have noticed something though. I am in a state of unforgiveness. It is raw and invasive. It is the type of unforgiveness that keeps me up at night and makes me sick. It is not about anything outside of me. I am not having a problem forgiving the rejection of other people. I am fully accepting of the outside things. I can forgive other people because I know they are not responsible for my reaction. Essentially, in this equation, the people or circumstance perpetuating the rejection do not matter, they are only a symptom of the cause. My issue is with myself. This verse says I need Christ to do all things. Since this is a scriptural truth I will only be able to achieve forgiveness of self with Christ. Since I am a beloved child of God I am able to go to the Throne Room and lay all of my internal chaos at the foot of God and He will take it. He will forgive me which will in turn allow me to forgive myself. Life is not always positive. However, through Christ, I am given a way through the negative. What is the thing you need Christ to help you do today? Do you need to get through a season or over an issue? Through Christ you can do that thing.

Until then, there are three things that remain: faith, hope, and love—yet love surpasses them all.

1 Corinthians 13:13

I really used to skip right past this chapter and verse. I just did not understand that we were created to love without getting anything in return. In the world I lived in, you could not get something for nothing. That simply was not how things went. Everything had a price and the price for love was very high. There was no such thing as unconditional love in that world. You could not even buy that, and you could buy everything. Every concept in this chapter was foreign to me. But God. When it was time for me to feel the full force of His love, there was nothing to compare it to, nothing to stop it and the only thing I could do was share it. In humanity we tend to think that we love in order for it to be reciprocated. If that is true, the love is not pure. It is not real. I know that this is truth, but recently it is a lesson that I am learning firsthand. It is a difficult lesson, but it lets me think of the love of Christ. He did not need me to love Him back in order for Him to love me. That does not mean He is stuck in a weird unreciprocated muck. He simply loves, unconditionally, and moves forward. When I did not return that love He did not sit around and wait for that to happen. God went on about His business. He loved others and never stopped loving me too. That kind of love is beautiful. I did nothing to deserve Him loving me like that. I did not encourage it or feed it. It is love that just is. Then it changed my life. God created me to love others like that. I am not always good at it. However, today, I know that I am capable of loving just to love, nothing to gain, nothing to chase. I am alright with that. How do you love today? Is it like Christ loves? Or do you love in order to be loved and to get something out of it? Do you stop and throw a fit if someone does not love you back, or are you ok giving and not receiving?

For He has said, "I will never leave you nor forsake you."

Hebrews 13:5b

I love how God sprinkles promises throughout scripture. This is one of my favorites. God, Himself, promised to never leave me. I have heard my whole life that I could lose God's love. If I step out of line, if I go backwards, if I do not follow the rules, I have disappointed God. I lived most of my life in total bondage to addiction. God did not matter to me there. When I came to know who the Lover of my soul truly is, that changed. For a while I knew absolute freedom. Then the legalities came back. If I could not keep the whole law, I needed to attempt to at least keep the ten commandments. On top of that, I needed to keep the rules that were cherry picked out of the old covenant. If I could not do that, I was going to be in trouble. Except that is not what God said. Nothing that I do is a shock to God. When I screw up, He does not turn to an angel in confusion wondering what just happened. The Great I AM told me He will NEVER leave me or forsake me. Last time I checked, God cannot lie. If I take it as truth that God cannot lie, then I also take this verse as truth. Since I do, I get to relax in the grace of God. I do not have to work to attempt to meet a ton of rules and regulations. I get to freely walk in relationship with God. Through the relaxing in the grace of God, I get to rest in the promise of Him not leaving. Do you know that God does not lie to you? Do you know that He will never leave you?

A thorn was given me in the flesh.

2 Corinthians 12:7b

I am a suck it up buttercup kind of a lady. However, I do believe that there are actions one needs to take in order to be able to walk forward from pain. I have been in one of those spots myself recently. For as much as I have tried to suck it up buttercup, that method did not work well this time. Instead of sitting and hoping that it fixes itself, I have taken the action needed in order to be able to walk forward. First of all, I go to God. He never ceases to amaze me. Sometimes His answer in my life is a beautiful life altering miracle. Other times, Holy Spirit has breathed into my life through the Word. There have been times when God heals through the people He puts in my life. This time, God's solution and His strength are taking the form of people. Through my sponsor He led me to science in the form of therapist. Through a wonderful lady in my life group through the church He has led me to His strength through His word and the more intricate parts of warfare. I am being reminded about things I already knew. God created everything for a purpose. He created science so that we could have doctors. He created people so that we will not have to trudge alone. He created the men who went before us so that we could understand our humanity. People go through hard times. It does not mean that person has done anything wrong. We are meant to struggle. The bible says that we will. It is how we deal with the struggle that matters. Today I have a struggle, it is fear, and it has a solution. The solution is in God. I am willing to be open to the many different ways God presents His strength and solution in my life today. Are you struggling with a thorn in your side? Go to God, let Him give you His strength, but be open to various ways His strength may come.

He said, "It is finished!" And bowing His head, He gave up His spirit.

John 19:30b

What was finished? It was not the pain Jesus was enduring. It was not the taunting. It was not even anything anyone could see. Life as humanity had known it from the beginning of time was finished. The law was finished. The time of Gentiles being on the outside was finished. Unforgiveness and wrath were finished. And then Jesus gave up His Spirit. In the breath that released His Spirit, the veil ripped from top to bottom. In the death of the ultimate sacrifice, God opened the pathway, allowing us full access to His throne. Wrath was replaced with mercy. Unforgiveness was removed and we were given grace. Law was covered by faith. As a Gentile, I am so grateful for the finishing. I was never invited to know God through the law. That was not for me. Through Jesus though, I get to be a child of the living God. Because Jesus came and declared it finished the veil is torn and I am able to boldly approach the Throne of God any time I want to. The sacrifice has been made and there is a covering of my sins, not only an atonement. When Jesus declared "it is finished" and breathed His last, creation changed. Are you living in a time that has been finished? Do you drag the law into the present? Have you recreated the veil? Or do you walk by faith in the mercy and grace of the finished works of Christ?

But be transformed by the renewing of your mind.

Romans 12:2b

I have always heard that insane people do not know they are insane. In my own experience, there is a place where the mind can hover between sanity and insanity. When Jesus stepped into my life and pulled me back into sanity He helped me renew my mind. Not only that, but He also anointed my mind and thought process and gifted me with the talent of words. He took a part of me that was shattered and recreated His purpose within it. In 2020 I started to feel as though there was something wrong though. I thought it was stress and change causing me to be manic. I assumed readjusting to not being on some medication was causing me to not be able to sleep. The anxiety increased at an alarming rate. There were symptoms that indicated a struggle. I discussed the issue with a woman from the church. She encouraged me to consider the struggle as spiritual warfare. The enemy cannot entice me chemically or physically, so he is attacking what I hold dear, my mind. Seemed quite logical to me. However, I am very aware that by not seeking medical help I would be putting myself in danger. God created therapists just like He created neurologists. God still heals today in amazing ways. Sometimes it is miraculous, often it is through the hands of the medical field. It is hard to write this because mental illness is often disregarded. We are told to suck it up or pray harder. I have tried those things. I will continue to pray and seek God's guidance through this. I cannot suck it up anymore though. For me, God is leading me to healing with a therapist, His Word, and the support of His people. Do you know someone who is suffering with a mental illness? I encourage you to help them renew their mind with prayer and the Word and support them in finding someone qualified to talk to. If you are struggling, seek help. You are not alone.

We are being transfigured into his very image as we move from one brighter level of glory to another.

2 Corinthians 3:18c

My favorite part of humanity is growing and learning. I constantly want to be better tomorrow than I am today. Lately I have not been able to figure out how to do that. I hear sermons and bible studies and even general advice about loving others, taking courage, or resting in identity. I am not hearing how to do those things though. It may very well be that the answers are being given and I am not in a mindset where I can hear them. Recently I am in a season of being stuck between things happening in my life. I described it recently like being stuck in a whirlpool, steadily treading water, not being able to move forward. I cannot figure out how to regain momentum. I am, it appears, in a season of laying fallow. I am still being transformed in this time. Resting and not moving definitively forward is not my comfort zone. God wants to teach me how to do that though. He worked for 6 days and rested on the seventh. Since I am reborn in His image, learning to rest is a thing God wants me to do. I find that resting is like patience. It is a lesson, not a blessing. Also, it is something that I do not seem to be good at. The goal for me right now is to let God move me from moment to moment, not thing to thing. It does not seem in the moment as though I am moving from brighter levels of glory. I am sure, when I look back, I will be able to see how God lit up each moment as if it is a new level of glory. God knows how to help me propel. He is teaching me to move forward, I can hear Him tell me how. What season are you in? Are you moving from moment to moment or thing to thing? Either way, you are transforming from glory to glory and God is causing you to shine brighter along the way.

You did not choose me, but I chose you…

John 15:16a

I will never understand why God chose me. Had you known me before, you would not recognize me now. I was a soldier for the enemy. I broke almost every law and committed almost every sin. I was so angry with God. I was enveloped in chaos and darkness and hate and lust. Still, He chose me. When He told me, I was so near death and so consumed by my own destruction I would not have heard Him if anyone else had been there. He patiently waited until I was so shattered and so alone that He knew I would be able to not only hear His love but be healed by it. God chose me long before He created me. He knew the decisions I would make and the damage I would cause. He knew it would be 36 years before I could hear His still small voice. But He also knew how loud it would be in my life. I know today that God did not choose me so I could just sit on a pew. He chose me for His purpose, to plant seeds, produce His fruit and tend His harvest. He chose me knowing I am strong willed and hard headed. He chose me fully aware that I am a rebel greatly in need of a cause. I did not choose Him. I ran from Him. But in His choosing me and knowing exactly the moment to present Himself to me, now I run desperately towards and with Him. He chose you too. If you are feeling unworthy, not enough, or lacking, know that God Himself, before the foundation of creation, chose you. He put on flesh and died because He chose you. He walked into hell and out of the tomb because He chose you. You have a purpose in Him. Be brave and bold and courageous today. Walk with confidence because you are chosen.

You are the light of the world. A city set on a hill cannot be hidden.

Matthew 5:14

I do not feel bright lately. In the spirit of transparency, I feel as though I have dimmed to the point of only a smoldering ember. I seek after God and I pray and do all of the things I am supposed to. I am just tired in my spirit. It is hard to be a light to others when I feel so dull. Oddly enough, other people do not see those things. A few weeks ago a lady gave me a very encouraging compliment. She said joy exudes from me and infects everyone in my vicinity. I could not believe it. There are a thousand cracks in my life right now. I am discouraged. I am disappointed. I am tired. I feel so very empty. I, me, mine. Often I forget, it is not about me. I am the light of the world. Only because Jesus shines His light through my cracks. Jesus does not ask me to be on top of my game at all times. He does not expect me to feel like a bonfire constantly. God knew I would hit a point of emptiness. He knows in these times I lean into Him. Jesus opened the way to the Throne Room so on my weak days I can crawl in for His strength. He is why I am full of light, even when I do not feel bright. The raw truth is, I am not the only light on the hill who feels dim. We have all been empty and weak. My hope today is that you encourage someone. It does not matter if you know their story. Stoke the fire within them. If you know someone is having a rough time, reach out. Let them see your light, they may not can sense their own.

A woman from Samaria came to draw water.

John 4:7

I have been reminded lately that God is not surprised by anything. He shows up in the places of our lives where we least expect Him. For me, He shows up in different ways. Lately I have been in a funk. I have been disappointed, somewhat heartbroken and walking through a shadow in life. It has not kept me from going on with my daily activities. I have a pretty set routine. Though I find it amusing that in this season God isn't coming to wait for me in places in my routine. He is showing up in places I do not expect Him, but He fully expects me. Jesus knew the Samaritan would be at the well. He was aware of the exact moment He would hear her footsteps on the path. She had no expectation of Him. Yet, there He was, ready with conversation of truth and love and redemption. Jesus can hear the sound of my footsteps before I even get out of bed in the morning. He knows the course I will take. Jesus sees the exact places I need Him much more than I know. He is positioned in the exact right spot. It is not always about Him being in a place. I do not always feel His presence when I walk in a certain room. His scent does not consistently linger on a specific outfit. His voice breathes to me through Holy Spirit in moments. I see His face in people I have never seen before and will never see again. For the Samaritan, it was a place she was not necessarily fond of going, but life demanded she be there. For me recently, it is finding Him waiting for me in the remote places of my life that catch my attention. In these sweet encounters Jesus speaks to me in love, about truth and redemption. Where is the place you find Jesus? Is He in the thing you dread most to do? Perhaps Jesus is waiting for you in the randomness of your chaos. Maybe He is listening for your footsteps in your everyday routine. Take time to stop and talk with Him. He is only there to change your life.

My sheep hear my voice, and I know them, and they follow me.

John 10:27

I know that I have heard the voice of God. He has spoken to me in very profound ways. Once a lady asked me why, in my opinion, does God not speak to everyone in the way He spoke to me on the first day of the rest of my life. I do not have an answer for that. I do know that God speaks to each individual person in the exact way that they will hear Him. For me, I needed to see and hear Him in order to believe that the greatest treasure in the world is something I cannot touch. My situation was not out of the ordinary, everyone is at the point of death spiritually when they truly meet Christ the first time. I love the thought that there are people who can hear the voice of God on the wind. Or the stories about people who feel the tug of Holy Spirit deep in their soul. Those are people who believe without seeing. They hear the Shepherd's voice, and they follow. When I was young I heard His voice and instead of following, I went my own way. I committed overt and out loud sin until my life was so enveloped with darkness that the only way for me to feel God calling me was for Him to stand in front of me and give me the choice of Him or hell. There is such raw beauty in those who did not doubt the truth of Jesus. We all hear Him in the precise way that is necessary for us in the first day of the rest of our lives. It is easy to hear the testimony of someone and disregard our own as not dramatic enough or possibly too over the top. I encourage you to be grateful today for the experience that was created exactly for you. Be amazed that you heard His voice and that you are His sheep. Listen for His holy sound again today and follow where it is He is leading you.

Wait on the Lord.

Psalm 27:14a

I have been in a prolonged season of waiting, When it started it was considerably easier to wait than it is now. Then I could still hear the sound of Holy Spirit whispering the promises into my spirit. Now waiting is not so exciting. The further I get from when the promise was made the more I wonder if I really heard right. God very often seems to be very slow. Funny how the slowest result can very often be exactly on time. I have recently been reminded that waiting on the Lord applies to everything. There is a conversation that I want to have with someone. It is a conversation that would change everything inside of that relationship. I was told last night that person had postponed having a conversation with me because it was not yet time to be that raw. The thought of it not being time to be that raw stuck with me. I began to think of waiting on the Lord in terms of conversation with people that you love. It is very easy to think that because you love someone, and you are a very active part of their life that everything you think needs to be said. Conversations get rushed into and the end result can very often be disastrous. Last night I was reminded that it is not always the appropriate time or circumstance to be that raw. In my situation I have decided to stop pushing into what I want out of this conversation. I am waiting on the Lord to show me when or even if the discussion needs to take place. When was the last time you went to the Lord before you went to the person? Do you ask God before the hard conversations then wait on His answer? Or do you rush into the rawness of intimacy and risk causing more harm than good?

Not that I am speaking of being in need, for I have learned in whatever situation I am to be content.

Philippians 4:11

Sometimes it is very difficult to be content in the situation I am in. I am ready to be through this part. I know that the next part with have its own set of issues, but this section of life I am experiencing right now has been going on for a very long time. Like Paul, I am not in need of anything. Sometimes it is the circumstances that wear on me. I am waiting on God to fulfill promises and in the waiting I am becoming discouraged. Jennifer Rothschild said sometimes the waiting feels like a drip, drip, drip. Its slow and difficult. It isn't that the end result will not be worth the wait. I know that when fulfillment of the promise and change of situation comes, it will be more wonderful than I could ever dream or imagine. I am finding it ever more difficult to be content though. I become discouraged when I see others so easily get the thing I'm waiting on. It tough to see them wait 6 months when I have waited 6 years almost. I am not jealous. I am genuinely happy for them. I celebrate with them. I am left with a longing for change that feels like it's not coming. I have become discontent. I have started to look for the promise and not the Promise Keeper. God means for me to be content, even in the waiting because Holy Spirit is here with me. I let fear of being stuck here drown out the love of Him being here. So today I am not doing that. I'm going to praise God for the present and choose to be content. I am going to rest in the comfort of Holy Spirit, and I am going to look to the Promise Keeper. Are you content in your situation today? If not, I encourage you to get out of the fear that has discouraged you and praise God for this moment.

And He said to her, "Daughter, your faith has made you whole."

Mark 5:34a

I love this verse. When I got sober I really lived off this verse. I had touched the hem of the garment of God and I was healed. There was all this other stuff though. I had totally trashed every relationship in my life that meant anything at all. I had never really worked, I could not take care of myself financially. My emotions were shot. Mentally, I thought for a little while that a commitment to the State Hospital was surely on my list of things to do. I could barely form a sentence that was cohesive. Then I started to read the Bible. Story after story of healing in the New Testament spoke about complete and whole healing. It was not just physical healing that Jesus accomplished when He touched or spoke to these people. He was making them whole. The more I read the Word, the more I wanted to read the Word. I fed on it like it was my daily nourishment. There was nothing as healing in my life. As I read, things began to change. I was being transformed from the inside out. Nothing on the outside was changing, my financial and living situation was the same, but my abundance and peace was from the Lord. My lost relationships were beginning to change and mend. When I began to grasp my identity in Christ my emotional instability began to heal. I could be confident in my position in life as a child of God. I walked in faith and I was able to take responsibility for myself. The greatest change, for me, was in my mind. Scripture said I would be transformed by the renewing of my mind (Romans 12:2). The touch of Jesus had healed my body. The Word of God had and continues to heal my life. I believe every word of the Bible. I know that this verse is a part of my own story. I am made whole today through the faith I learned through the touch of Jesus and the Word of God. Do you need wholeness in your life? Open the Word, let God pour His truth into you, it is through Him that we are whole.

O Lord my God, I cried to you for help, and you have healed me.

Psalm 30:2

Before salvation, my life was dirty. My preferred method of drug use makes most normal people cringe and my drug of choice instantly labeled me as trash. My heart was stone, and my spirit was diseased. For all intent and purposes I should have been filled with sickness in my blood, in my organs and my muscles. The only time I ever cried out to God was when I was begging Him to make it stop. Not only the pain, but the breaths. I just wanted to die. So, that is what He allowed me to do. In order to rise into salvation, something had to die. In my life, it was complete death of the thing I had become. When that happened, Christ raised me as a new creation. I was completely different, completely changed, completely healed. I read over and again in the bible that when Jesus touches you, He produces healing and wholeness. I believe with every fiber of my being that is what happened to me. The proof was in the beginning stages of a new cleanliness of lifestyle. Obviously, I stopped doing drugs, I had a heart of flesh and a healthy spirit. God healed me. I always thought that meant His touch healed everything, including the blood, organs, and muscles. My blood flows completely clean. Most of my organs are healthy enough for donation. I should have had residual health effects for the rest of my life. Instead, I am healed. Healing is different for everyone. Sometimes it is physical, sometimes spiritual. Always, if you cry out to God, He will heal you.

But in your hearts honor Christ the Lord as holy, always being prepared to make a defense to anyone who asks you for a reason for the hope that is in you.

1 Peter 3:15

When I was a kid it was assumed that everyone was Christian because they were American. When people asked why I was a Baptist the answer was because my mom was. When my addiction took hold I became indifferent. I knew there was a devil. I lived inside of his hell. For me, knowing there was one meant I knew there was an opposite. At that time though, God meant nothing to me. I was not good enough for Him. I am exceedingly grateful today that everything has changed. Today I am very aware that I absolutely was not good enough and I know I deserved hell. However, I also know God's grace, mercy, and love. I am no longer a Christian because I am American or Baptist because my mom is. I know today that Satan is not the opposite of God. The reason I have hope today is the love of God. He clothed Himself in flesh, walked as one of us and taught us how to live. He endured more pain than imaginable and died an agonizing death on the cross, where He also took every sin for the entirety of creation. He walked through hell, conquered death, and rose, then released Holy Spirit to dwell in me. I did not have to be good enough. Regardless that I deserved hell, God not leave me in hell, and I also never have to go back. I have hope because I know I am a child of God. I spend time reading His love letter. I feel Holy Spirit breathing into my life. I see Christ in the lives of the people I do life with. I felt the arms of Jesus as I died to my old self and rose, a new creation in Him. I am not a Christian in word but in action and life. I have experienced Christ in life changing moments, and I will forever worship the Alpha and Omega. If someone asked why you have hope today, what will your answer be?

Love the Lord your God with all your heart and with all your soul and with all your mind.

Matthew 22:37

The things I love get priority. I know that if I am doing things on a daily basis to nurture what I love, then those things will grow in my life. The things in my life I do not give priority to usually seem to wilt and wither away. What I know is that when I am putting God first and above every other thing, there is very little in my life that is wilting. In AA they say either God is, or He is not. In my life, either He is everything or He is nothing. There have been times when God has come in second or third in my priorities. I have taken care of self before taking care of the things of God in my life. When I do that, everything seems to unravel. I have to work harder at keeping it together. I have no peace and there is no joy. I like to have God at the top. As I take care of Him in my life first and foremost, the other things fall into place. I do not lose peace and joy because the provider of those things is the priority in my life. After a while, there are benefits of putting God first that begin to shine through. He starts placing people in my life who have the same priorities. They do not think my convictions are out of place and they support and encourage me to walk in the purpose God has given me. In turn, I am able to pray for them, encourage them and shine God's light into their lives. Putting God first allows me to walk in the gifts that He has given me. I get to be bold in my writing and brave in the ways I choose to live my life. There are a ton of things in life that are very important. I have children and grandchildren, am a homeowner, have an amazing job, and I am an active part of the Christian and the recovery communities where I live. If I am not prioritizing God above all of those things, I am proficient at none of them. Where does God come in your life? Do you love Him with everything first, or does He get the leftovers?

Weeping may tarry for the night, but joy comes with the morning.

Psalm 30:5b

When I heard this verse the first time I was very excited. I thought it would be awesome if I only needed to cry over anything for a night and the next morning feel joy. Now I know that sometimes the night is very long. There are seasons in human life just like in nature. Sometimes in nature the night falls and morning does not dawn for months. God was not surprised humanity would encounter similar seasons of darkness. The dark times I experience now are nothing like the darkness before Christ. Before salvation, the night was an impenetrable darkness that lasted for decades. With Jesus the darkness has never been quite as deep. God provides starlight throughout the hard times. He provides full moons through my night seasons that allow His light to continue to illuminate my path, even when I feel as though I am enshrouded by the night. These times in life are difficult. However, they are also strengthening, and if walked through by God's grace, are times of learning and building hope that produces faith. It is not an easy season to walk through. However, the sun must rise. When it does, I know that there will be joy because in the night, God has reminded me of my identity through His presence. Joy will come with the dawn because on the horizon, I can see the beautiful purple of the King. For me, dawn is coming. Are you in a season of night? Look for the light of God's presence. Do you know someone in this season? Be a beacon for them.

Paul, an apostle of Christ Jesus by the will of God, To the saints who are in Ephesus, and are faithful in Christ Jesus.

Ephesians 1:1

Today when we think of saints, it brings to mind the Catholic church. The saints of Catholicism have a very distinct difference than the original saints. The holy people Paul wrote to were alive. To be considered a saint today you have to be dead first. You also have to meet several qualifications. The original saints were simply believers. They were called saints because they heard the good news and they believed. They did not do anything perfectly in order to be called a saint. They were because that is their identity in Christ. I have had a difficult time with my identity lately. I had allowed the rejection, lies and overwhelming feeling of not being good enough to take over and begin to create in my mind a new identity. That is what happens when I allow life to get in the way. I create a place in my mind where I no longer remember that I am a saint, just like the Ephesians. It is like I have created a prison cell in my mind and trapped myself in it. I know that Holy Spirit dwells in me. Since that is the truth, the only way that the negative thought processes can cause damage is if I trap myself with them and stop allowing Holy Spirit to free me from myself. That is the box I had brushed myself into the last few months. Understanding that has sent me on a quest to relearn my true identity. Part of it is in this verse. Like the Ephesians, I am a saint, a holy person. I have every spiritual blessing lavished on me in love. I am one with Christ and ordained through Him. I am an adopted child of the Great I AM. I wear His armor and bear His name. That is the identity that I walk in today, throwing off the chains of self and walking in the freedom of Jesus. Do you know who you are today? If you do, celebrate that truth today. If you are struggling, go to the Word and let God Himself remind you of who you He recreated you to be.

For I know the plans I have for you, declares the Lord, plans for welfare and not for evil, to give you a future and a hope.

Jeremiah 29:11

Some days it is difficult to look at my life with finite eyes and see the truth of this verse. There are also days when it is completely obvious that this verse holds nothing but the truth. Today, though, I do not believe this verse has anything at all to do with what I can see right now. This verse was penned by Jeremiah, several thousand years before I was created. God breathed these words into his prophet for a people who were lost and bound and could only see desolation of their people around them. That had nothing to do with me. This verse feels good so it's put on coffee cups and t-shirts and wall hangings so that comfort comes from thinking that so very long ago God had a plan for my welfare, my future and my hope and that those things did not include evil. That is a very different picture from what the Israelites were seeing and even what I see today. By making this verse a slogan of good feels for the moment, the amazing truth slips through. The promise God makes in this verse, in my opinion, is deeper than what is seen and stronger than anything in that time or this. God does have plans for welfare, not for evil, for a hope and a future in the infinite being of eternity. While amazingly good things happen right now that are hopeful for my future, nothing compares with the plan of eternal being with the Great I AM. I do believe this verse is for the now. God has also planned a good life for me. He saved me in this life, that is for my welfare, so that I will have a future and a hope with Him for all of time. Some days, I am sure, I will still look at this verse with finite eyes and see the plan God has for me here. I pray that most days, I will look beyond the finite and see with hope for my future the true plans for good God has given to us all. I pray when you read this verse again, you will remember the hope there as well.

This is the day that the Lord has made; let us rejoice and be glad in it.

Psalm 118:24

On December 9, 2014, my life was forever and irrevocably altered. I walked into my bathroom one way and walked out a new creation. I would like to say on that day everything stopped. It did not. Five days later I did my last shot of dope. Twelve days later, I mark my last drink. The next day is my sobriety birthday. All of those are great days and they make for an emotional month. December 9 is an altogether different milestone though. This was the day God marked out before the foundation of my life was set. He knew the exact moment I would look into the mirror and see His face. He knew I would be so close to death the only thing I would be able to hear would be His voice. All these years later and I can still feel His breath fill my lungs. I believe we all get a day like that. Each one is uniquely designed for fulfillment of God's purpose. The only thing not set is the response. I could have told God no. He gave me an option and I could have picked the other one. If I had, I would not be writing this. I would not be alive right now. I would have gone on to the bitter end and gotten the hell I deserved. That is not my story though. This is the day the Lord made for me. I will rejoice that I walk in the grace and mercy of a living God. I will spend my day immersed in gratitude that God did not give me what I deserved, instead He gave me hope and a future. I will be glad because God gave me a choice. Rejoice that God gave you this day. Be glad He also did not give you what you deserved.

Be still and know that I am God.....

Psalm 46:10a

Lately I have been laying at the feet of God crying. It has not been pretty crying, it has been ugly and raw and broken. I couldn't think of anything to say at first. Then I remembered a verse where God told Isaiah to put Him in remembrance of His promises (Isaiah 43:26). I reminded God that He promised to be my Provider, the Lover of my soul, and my Comforter. I reminded Him that He promised to be strong in my weakness and not leave me. I also pointed out that I was very weak and I felt so alone. God reminded me to be still. I didn't need to do anything else. God has shown me loud and clear that He hears me and I absolutely am not alone. In my stillness He provides, He comforts, and He shows me that He is truly the Lover of my soul. Today I feel His strength. Being still can sometimes be exhausting. When a crisis strikes and all you want is some semblance of control, being still and knowing He is God can be difficult. Knowing that God is good and God is good at being God is tough when all you can see is that the situation in front of you went from a molehill to a mountain. But, if you are still and you know that you know He is God, you can see Him move that mountain. Find stillness in your situation today. Know that He is God, He is good, and He is good at being God.

For in one Spirit we were all baptized into one body—Jews or Greeks, slaves or free—and all were made to drink of one Spirit.

1 Corinthians 12:13

I have heard a ton of talk recently about the unity of the body of Christ. I have been part of two denominations that have changed my life and they could not be more different. They are on completely different spectrums altogether. Does that mean that one group has the whole truth and the other only part? I do not believe so. What I believe is that, for the body, one is the right hand and one is the left. For me what is most significant is where they are alike. Both sides believe you cannot come to the Father but through the Son. They agree that Jesus was God, clothed in flesh. Each section believes that Jesus lived as a man, died as a sacrifice, and rose as Savior. What makes one different than the other is semantics. This man translates the Word differently than that man. Does that mean that one is more right or that one side is condemned? Of course not. What it does is allow for the greater works (John 14:12) of Christ to be done. If one is the left hand of the body and the other the right, it allows for each to reach different things for the purpose of God. In the end we will all be united under the rule and reign of the King of Kings. When that time comes, we will all bend our knee at the same time. If we are operating in the Holy Spirit and fulfilling our purpose in our given part of the body, we will hear, "Well done my good and faithful servant." I have spent quite a while thinking I need to pick one side. My purpose, though, is the unified middle, knowing both sides drink from the same Spirit. Do you know where you fit in the body? Are you willing to walk in unity with all other parts, knowing we all drink from the same Spirit?

And John bore witness: "I saw the Spirit descend from heaven like a dove, and it remained on him.

John 1:32

How often do we hear people say they want more of God? In recent times it is a phrase that crosses denominations and factions. I have heard people assume that this phrase means there is more Holy Spirit to be had. They make it sound as though we are not all filled with the exact right amount of Holy Spirit and are therefore lacking and that is causing a desire to want more of God. What happens when Jesus comes and saves our lives is a simple process. He comes and opens our eyes and our ears. When we choose to believe in Him and repent, which means we change our ways, not say we are sorry, then what happens is that Holy Spirit comes to dwell within us. At some point, if possible, baptism needs to occur. In my personal walk, the process was not precise and not in the same order as most. That did not matter, the result was the same. When I was saved, I was filled with Holy Spirit. When I was filled I was filled completely and fully, anything less would have been God not finishing the job and that simply does not happen. After that though, I wanted and craved to know more about God. I wanted to understand His word and I needed to talk to him. I craved the things of the Lord. The only thing capable of satisfying that craving was more time, more knowledge, more revelation, and closer relationship. When people say they want more of God, this is what they mean. It is not about having more of Holy Spirit fill you because we are given the perfect measure of Holy Spirit from the beginning. That being said, every day of my life I want more of God. It is like the couple who has been together for 75 years. When they die, they will have had more of each other on the last day than they did on the first. It is about maturing and growing and learning. That is how we get more of God. Do you want more today? Or are you simply satisfied with what you had yesterday?

Shepherd the flock of God that is among you, exercising oversight, not under compulsion, but willingly, as God would have you.

1 Peter 5:2

Peter is teaching the elders in this verse. I have to wonder who the elders were. What makes an elder an elder? Sometimes I can sit in church and believe that I visibly see someone who would fit in this category. They are white headed, stooped from their former height, and seem to be wise. There have been many times I go to speak with them, and they astonish me when they say they have only been in the church a short time. Occasionally, I see a boy who is barely old enough to grow a beard, I would, at first glance, not consider him an elder. However, he chooses to live a life devoted not only to the Word of, but to the things of God. I have also known people who have been in the church their whole lives and they neither know the words God has written nor walk in the footsteps of Christ. Seems as though age means very little. I think that the elders are the ones, no matter the age, who have chosen to fully live the life of Christ. They are the ones who step out in faith, especially in the private times when there is nobody watching. They are the ones who admit that this life is not easy. When they lose courage and endurance, they seek the counsel of those who can offer encouragement. An elder is one of those people you look at and see Christ long before you see them. They do not necessarily teach a bible study, but if you watch, they tend to live one. Where are you in your walk? Are you an elder? Do you shepherd the flock around you by the way you live your life? If not, I encourage you to mature in your walk, so that one day, you will be the elder who shepherds the young.

Therefore, if anyone is in Christ, he is a new creation. The old has passed away; behold, the new has come.

2 Corinthians 5:17

I was not supposed to stay the same way. The day Jesus found me, I walked into the bathroom one way and walked out different. For me, I had an experience that changed my heart of stone into flesh. Jesus breathed Holy Spirit into my being and everything changed. In my bathroom that day, I died to everything I had become. Now that those great big changes have taken place, I get to choose if I am going to allow God to finish the work He started in me. I have all of these small issues I either choose to keep or let God continue making new. If I choose to hold on to them, I am choosing to remain the same. There is no growth in that and even though the really big issues in my life have changed, if I insist on holding on to the rest, I am only part of a new creation. I get to choose to hang on to the anger, the control, the selfishness, the whatever it is, I am choosing to stop changing into God's full version of myself. These things are hard to let go of. After all, its only my family I want to control and make decisions for; I have a right to be angry; the things I am selfish about are already my things. God wants to refine me to be the person He created me to be. He does not want me to stay the person I had created. What I know is if I ask God where he wants me to change, He is going to point those places out to me. The changing is hard. When God chisels at the parts of your character that are engrained, it can even be painful. That is how the newness in life comes though. What parts of self are you holding on to? Are there things in your character you know need to change but are so engrained you are having a hard time letting God chisel them away? It is my prayer today that you continue in letting the little things in your life become new. It is time for the old to fully pass.

Have faith in God.

Mark 11:22

I like things that are straightforward and uncomplicated. This verse is both of those things. Have faith in God. Seems that, since it is so straightforward and uncomplicated, it would be an easy thing to accomplish. In the beginning it was. I did not work, and I spent hours and hours praying and reading and just being with God. I had stopped watching tv mindlessly and I was devoted to knowing how God could change every facet of my life. When I am immersed in God that much, with that kind of intentionality, having faith seems so simple. As time went on though, things began to change. I had to work, but Holy Spirit was still the air I breathed. Then I had to change jobs and then that company closed, so a different job. Then I got a house and changed jobs again and started school and worked 3 jobs, then back to one job but that job was like having 2 but being paid for 1 plus full-time school. Then another job and still school. I was struggling every day to make ends meet and breathe and I was sleeping 4 hours a night so I could do everything. Life was demanding that I take from my faith in God and put it in my schedule, myself and whatever was left over He could have. I stopped breathing Holy Spirit and started holding my breath. I had stopped following this straightforward, uncomplicated command. Now, just a few years later, I am still trying to recenter. I still struggle with taking faith out of the schedule and the job and the life and am placing it back in God. I know that when my faith is in God and I am walking in the God kind of faith, no matter what is going on, I will be where I am supposed to be. While I cannot spend hours in the Word today, I can spend my entire day in the presence of God. I had forgotten that. Where is your faith today? Is it in the 'to do' list? Maybe your alarm clock that starts your schedule. Where have you taken faith from God and given it to life? I encourage you today, no matter what is going on, have faith in God.

Go therefore and make disciples of all nations.

Matthew 28:19a

Making disciples does not sound like an easy command. It has to be time consuming and aggravating. On top of the fact that I am not qualified to teach other people things. After all, I have only been doing this life for a few years. I mess up all of the time. And Jesus wants me to go and make disciples. Not only that, he wants me to go to more than the people I know and am comfortable with! It is easy to think that this is one of those verses that was not written with me in mind. Except for the fact that it was. I am created to go out and make disciples. So what does that mean? Am I supposed to leave a long day's work and go teach a class or spend hours away from my family every week so that I can fulfill this command? I do not think so. I think, as humans, we like to overcomplicate things and use the overcomplication to convince us the command is too hard to follow. When the Apostles went to make disciples, they simply spoke the truth. They told people about Jesus and from that they built communities. Within those communities they broke bread together, they supported each other. They not only spoke of Christ, they lived like Him. It was not a command that took away from their lives, but one that enriched it abundantly. It is not about teaching people the rules and traditions and shaming them into changing their lives. It also is not about only being inside of the community that you have built and feel comfortable in. It is talking to the new people in church. Inviting someone you have just met to coffee. Keeping the kids of the young parents who would otherwise not have time to pursue the things of God. Making disciples is giving to others what has so freely been given to you. It is showing love and compassion to everyone, not just a few. Do you live the life of a disciple maker? Do you follow this command? Or do you overcomplicate it, convincing it was not commanded for you?

I not commanded you? Be strong and courageous. Do not be frightened, and do not be dismayed, for the Lord your God is with you wherever you go."

Joshua 1:9

I have, in the last month, been experiencing anxiety for the first time in a very long time. There is a level of chaos in my life that comes with the presence of a person. I knew when the anxiety started what the cause was. Instead of walking in the strength of the Lord and removing the cause immediately, I have allowed this person to remain. Each day the anxiety has gotten worse. I have an attack at least once a day. Over the weekend it was so bad I was physically ill. What I know about anxiety is that it is a byproduct of fear. It is generally future based, caused by what ifs and thoughts that could be. For me recently, it is a process that is happening at the same time life is happening. I can be perfectly happy and content, yet still have an ever present sense of anxiety over this person and what might happen. Knowing the problem does not make it easy to solve it. However, I have been trying to do this myself. My thought was, "I got myself in to this, I have to get myself out". That isn't how God works though. All I needed to do was go to Him. When I finally did that yesterday I found that He is right here with me. In that knowing I found courage and strength to be very vocal in telling this person to stop contacting me. In the last few weeks I have been dismayed and that has grown in to fear and then into a physical reaction. God knew this would be a reaction to fear. That is why He tells us over and again that we do not need to fear, He is here. It does not matter if we cause our own fear or if it is external, God wants to give His strength and courage for us to walk away from the fear. That is what I am choosing to do today. Do you have great in your life? Do you know the Lord is here with you? Take His strength, be courageous and through Him, do not fear.

Now may the Lord of peace himself give you peace at all times in every way. The Lord be with you.

2 Thessalonians 3:16

I am constantly amazed by God. Last year we had a very small incident at my house. Though it was small, it was a situation that could have been tragic. In the end we lost very little and the injuries were considerably less than what could have happened. After everything had calmed down, I felt an amazing peace for the next few days. I was overcome with gratitude the whole time. Days later I got a message from a lady I used to go to church with. She told me that days before the Lord had laid me on her heart and she prayed for me and since that time the Lord had been nudging her to check on me. Through the course of our conversation she told me that she prayed for me only hours before the thing at our house happened. The amazing part is that I have not spoken to this woman in a year or more. We were friendly when we went to the same church, but we are not a part of each other's lives. We are connected by the Blood though. Not only did God use this woman to pray over my family, He also used her to remind me that He is with me. Usually in situations like the one we had I would have freaked out. There was no anger. There was not could of and what if scenarios. What I experienced even moments after the adrenaline stopped, everything was full of peace and gratitude. If the Lord had not been with me, that would not have been the outcome. And days later, He did not want me to forget that He is still here and reminded me through an obedient sister. Do you know that the Lord is with you today? Do you feel His peace? I encourage you today, if someone is on your heart, reach out so that through you, they may feel the peace of God today too.

Those who make them become like them; so do all who trust in them.

Psalm 115:8

The Psalmist was talking about how idols are not able to use their eyes, mouths, ears, hands, or feet. He was showing how the gods made by the hand of man were good for nothing except sitting on a shelf as a trinket or standing as a statue. We all know that those gods are good for nothing. When was the last time you considered the person who made that god though? They were men, they had families and friends. They had eyes but could not really see. What they could hear would have been only muffled and the sound that came from their mouths untrue. The things that they touched would have felt numb in comparison to the real things we feel, and their feet led them nowhere. Those who worshipped those gods were no different. They loved with a shadow of the true meaning of the word. Teaching and knowledge was only a partiality of what could have been known. The beauty of creation was lost on them. The only difference in the old gods and those of today are how they are created. Today they look like Facebook, Netflix, YouTube, and a variety of other websites. They look similar when they manifest as selfishness, anger, lust and a thousand other overpowering emotions. The things in our lives that we choose to put before the one true God are the things that cloud our vision, muffle our hearing, and silence our voices. They make life numb to the touch and led us in circles, constantly going nowhere. However, when we put the Great I AM first in our lives, everything becomes open, beautiful, and pure. We are able to live life in the fullness of sight, sound, touch, and motion because the One who created those things is the One who is guiding us. What is first in your life today? Do you have a god that is clouding your senses and walking you in circles? Or is the Almighty purifying your senses and leading you to eternity?

If anyone gives an answer before he hears, it is his folly and shame.

Proverbs 18:13

I am a listener by nature. People will meet me and tell me things that they would not generally tell people they know, much less a total stranger. It does not happen with everyone, but people feel comfortable telling me their stuff. Usually they don't need or want a response or a fix. Sometimes people simply need someone to stop and take the time to hear them. Some of my best friends have come to me in this way. We start just casually talking, and then the things that they are saying are no longer casual. Since I do not mind listening, people do not mind sharing. When that happens with people I am around frequently, a bond cannot help but form. Where I am not so great at this is with some of the people I am closest to. I often pray for the calmness to hear my children before I respond by rushing in to fix their problems. I am especially bad about it in the midst of arguing when I have a significant other in my life. I allow my emotions to get out of whack and my ability to listen and really hear is clouded by my need to also be heard. Scripture does not tell us to choose which situation we want to be a good listener in though. Scripture teaches us to listen with the purpose of hearing, not with the reason of response. If we are truly hearing what the person in front of us is saying, we may realize that a response is not needed, only love and support. How do you listen? Do you hear those closest to you better than the stranger on the street? Are you choosing how to respond before they have even finished their first sentence? I encourage you to slow down in conversation today. Listen to hear what the person in front of you is trying to say.

Iron sharpens iron, so one person sharpens another.

Proverbs 27:17

I like to be challenged. Because of that I tend to surround myself with people who enjoy learning and questioning. Every person in my circle sharpens my outlook on life. You know that this has been a tough time for me lately. In this time my circle has evolved. I realized that I was focusing only on certain parts of my mind to be sharpened and doing that had dulled out other areas I only recently realized are important. I don't think God intended for me to only sharpen my intelligence or simply focus on my spirit. I also do not think He intended me to only have one group of people to sharpen me. I am in recovery and have a group of women I hang out with who sharpen that aspect of my life. I also love knowledge and I have a group of people who sharpen my intellect. For my spiritual sharpening I have a vast network of people I can question, and who question me. God did not mean for us to sharpen ourselves. He created us to help grow each other. This scripture makes it very clear that we are not to walk through life dull. We should be sharpened by the people we choose to keep in our lives. Are you choosing people in your life who give you a more defined edge? Or do your people assist in keeping you dull?

But when he saw the wind, he was afraid, and beginning to sink he cried out, "Lord, save me."

Matthew 14:30

It was the middle of the night and the wind was blowing so fiercely it was buffeting the boat. Regardless of the wind he could feel in the boat, Peter still stepped out onto the water because he knew Jesus was there. When he was out in the middle of it though and could see the wind, he doubted and began to sink. I imagine it happened quickly. One minute, Peter was full of faith because he heard the voice of Jesus, the next he allowed circumstance to overpower him. I do the same thing. Stepping out in faith is exactly like Peter stepping out onto the water. As soon as doubt creeps in I start to sink. Unlike Peter, I do not always immediately cry out for Jesus to help me. I thrash around in the sinking, honestly thinking, if I put in just a bit more effort, I can keep my head above water. I also do not always doubt. There are times I step out in faith and take hold of the hand of Jesus and I follow Him onto waters so deep I cannot see the shore or the boat. In those times, I feel exactly placed by God. Its Him and me in a vastness with no fear and no uncertainty and no doubt. God does not want us to step out in faith only to be consumed by fear. He knows that will happen though and He ensures that He is there, waiting to catch us. I think, though, the moments of sinking doubts are meant to be the lesson that He is always there. In learning the lesson, we are able to step farther out every time He calls us. Where in your life are you being called to step out in faith, onto the waters, trusting in Jesus' presence? Have you tried and allowed the doubt the crept in to now keep you anchored? I encourage you today, step out onto the water. Hear Jesus calling you. Walk with Him into the vastness of a life of faith. That is where God wants you to be.

Grace and peace to you from God our Father and from the Lord Jesus Christ.

Romans 1:7b

The introductory blessings of Paul's letters are easy to bypass. Sometimes I read the bible so often that I pass through them like I do the dinner blessing or those that follow a sneeze. Rarely do I stop to consider the magnitude of what the blessing means. Paul is blessing his readers with the grace and peace of God. I was astounded when I looked up the definitions for grace and peace. I mean, they are words I thought I knew. However, Strong's defines grace as the merciful kindness by which God, exerting his holy influence upon souls, turns them to Christ, keeps, strengthens, increases them in Christian faith, knowledge, affection, and kindles them to the exercise of the Christian virtues. When I looked up peace, the meaning is just as powerful. The peace of God is the tranquil state of a soul assured of its salvation through Christ, and so fearing nothing from God and content with its earthly lot, of whatsoever sort that is. To think, this is a verse simply skimmed over! I love that Paul took time in writing to bless his readers. Also that he took the time to use two words his readers would have understood the deeper meaning of. Today, I want to leave you with this blessing and its very deep meaning. It is my prayer that you bless someone in your life with these words. When you do, I encourage you to prayerfully speak the depth of these words into that person's life. Grace and peace to you from God our Father and our Lord Jesus Christ.

He makes me lie down in green pastures, He leads me beside still waters.

Psalm 23:2

This verse always makes me think of our family tank. It is really a hole dug out on the edge of the property line. It is filled with fish and fresh water from an underground source. Our tank is surrounded by trees filled with birds and at night you can hear the bull frogs from the house. I recently told a friend that the tank is an oasis in the midst of chaos. While our pastures are not green, I imagine the places God takes me to restore my soul are a lot like the tank. The difference is that when I go to God and allow Him to restore my soul, it is a restoration that has a profound and lasting effect on my life. The still water God leads me to is not simply an oasis in the midst of chaos. He takes me to a place in Him. There not only are the pastures green and the waters calm, but there is restoration of sanity and peace. He fills me with His joy and strength. This is not a one-and-done kind of treatment. He wants me to go there, not only as often as needed, but as often as possible. I want to be there every day. It is the place in the universe He has made the most comforting, the most calming and the most restorative. It is His presence. When was the last time you were restored in the green pastures and still waters in the presence of God? Do you only seek that place when something is wrong, or do you strive to be in God's presence every day?

Not only that, but we rejoice in our sufferings, knowing that suffering produces endurance, and endurance produces character.

Romans 5:3-4a

This verse always gets me. I have been through a lot of suffering. The majority of it was from my own really bad decisions. Self-inflicted or not, suffering is never fun. The definition of suffering is the state of undergoing pain, distress, or hardship. I have a friend who is suffering right now. Not that anyone would know it. This person wakes and goes to God. He prays for others and is of service throughout his day. He cares deeply for the people in his life, and he is stronger than anyone knows because very few, if really any, know that he is in the midst of what can only be described as an undergoing of pain, distress, and hardship. He rejoices in this time. It is not simply a rejoicing in a time set aside at church to praise. He lives a life of worship inside his suffering. I have been able to see his endurance. He runs this race in private, but not alone. I am watching his character grow. He shows love, patience, and care of others instead of drawing attention to, what could only be, the present thorn in his side. This passage in the bible goes on to talk about how these things produce hope. I get to watch the growing of that hope through being able to watch my friend rejoice as he suffers. Suffering is never fun. However, when it is done with God and in this manner, it can be a beautiful thing to witness and is a spectacular testimony for the people who need to hear it. How do you suffer today? Do you rejoice in your hardship, holding the hand of Jesus and standing in the Throne Room of God? Or do you let it get the better of you?

Bear with each other and forgive one another if any of you has a grievance against someone. Forgive as the Lord forgave you.

Colossians 3:13

I generally think I am a pretty forgiving person. I do not hold grudges because my mind is not equipped to remember that stuff for very long. There has been a situation in my life lately though where I haven't been willing to extend forgiveness. My heart was hurt. I was sad, and for me, that comes out in anger. I said a ton of things I did not mean. I let it fester and I nurtured that anger until it became like a stone in my shoe. Every time I took a step I felt unforgiving anger. I thought I was keeping it to myself. Apparently it was seeping into other parts of my life. It tainted my words, my writing, my interaction with my kids, all of it. Today, I stepped into forgiveness. I had a conversation with the person who hurt my heart. The anger reverted back to sadness and I cried instead of yelled. I asked God to forgive me for my unforgiveness and in turn I offered the forgiveness that was so very freely given to me. I do not feel great right now. My heart is feeling the pain I had been studying for months. However, I am better than I was because I can take a step without feeling the searing pain of anger. Jesus, from the cross, forgave all. Who am I to keep my forgiveness from one? Is there someone in your life you need to forgive today? Call them, give them what God through Jesus has so freely given you.

Set your minds on things above, not on earthly things.

Colossians 3:2

I find it so easy to get stuck on earthly things. It is life. A part of humanity is concerned about finances. There are questions as to whether or not I am on the right path. I get lost in being thin enough and pretty enough. There are a constant barrage of questions about reputation and other people's perception. It has not always been like this since my salvation. In the beginning, my mind, my eyes, everything were set on things above. I stopped caring about the things of the world. My finances did not matter because I knew my Provider. The path I was on was right because every step was prayed over. It did not matter what I looked like because I knew I was created in God's image. I ceased wondering what others thought of me because I knew what God thinks of me. Somewhere along the line, I shifted my focus. I was told I was too heavenly minded to be earthly useful. Today, in this moment, I plainly see the untruth of that statement. When Jesus walked the earth, He spent every moment being heavenly minded. His earthly good was astounding. It is not supposed to be different for us. Jesus taught us how to walk this world with, not only our eyes, but our minds set on things above. That is where my mind will be fixed today. Where is your mind? Are you fixed on things of the earth? Or is your mind fixed on things above?

Let what you say be simply 'Yes' or 'No'; anything more than this comes from evil.

Matthew 5:37

This passage centers on making oaths. When the bible was penned the word oath meant solemn promise. It was a thing made in reverence and seriousness. The bible said, and it was believed, that it was better to not make an oath than to make one then break it. We still have wedding vows, vows when we enter some offices, and things like that, but we do not make oaths like they did in the old days. We do, however, make promises we do not hold near as seriously. We make and break plans all of the time. We are inconsistent with our children and the people in our circle. We even make promises to God we then fail to keep. We say things, that, while we mean them in the moment, we do not hold ourselves to the standard of keeping our word. The bible still means the same thing today it did when it was penned. Just because society has changed does not mean what was meant in the bible has. Today it is still better to say nothing than to break your word. If I tell my children something, I am meant to follow through with it. If I say I'm going to be somewhere, I am meant to be there. If I tell God I will follow Him, that means in all areas, not just the ones I agree with. How do you treat the words you say? Does your yes actually mean yes? If you say no, is that what you stick to? Or are you inconsistent, making it difficult for people to believe what you say?

Do not be unequally yoked with unbelievers.

2 Corinthians 6:14a

I was discussing this verse recently with someone. When I mentioned it, I was referring to the context of friendships. He said that he had never heard it in reference to friends, usually only to husbands and wives. He then asked me what my biblical basis was to pull this verse away from the marriage and apply it to other areas of my life. So I had to go back and look. Nowhere in this passage is the marital relationship mentioned. In fact, no specific relationship at all is discussed. Paul is referring to believers and their relationships with unbelievers. My friend then pointed out that Jesus did not act like that, after all, He ate with sinners and came for the sick. What then is the point of this verse being in the Bible. Apparently we are supposed to dine with the sinners and the sick, but we are supposed to live our lives with other believers. There is a difference. The people I want to surround myself with, those who are my support group, my confidants, the ones who surround me in crisis, I want those people to be believers. Not simply people who believe that there is a god. I need the ones closest to me to believe in the one true God. I need them to know that the only way to the Father is through the Son. I want my closest circle to follow the one who I follow. Does that mean that I do not have other people in my life? Of course not. It simply means that if I attempt to walk toward my goal with people who are not like minded, I will not get very far. Who are the people in your closest circle? Are you dining with sinners while living with believers? Or are you dining with believers and living with sinners? Who are you choosing to be yoked with?

Thus says the Lord God to these bones; Behold, I will cause breath to enter you, and you shall live.

Ezekiel 37:5

Every time I read this verse I close my eyes and take a deep breath. When I first was saved God breathed breath into my body that brought me to life in the same way He brought the bones in this passage back. I was dead in every way except physical, but I was not far from dying a complete death. That day though, God's breath filled my lungs. It was like I had never taken a full breath before. Every inhale before that moment had been shallow and unfulfilling and weak. In the moment that God wrapped His arms around me and breathed life into me, every fiber of my being took that breath. All of me was completely full for the first time in my life. It took only a second, but it is one second out of my life that is etched so completely in my mind I will never forget it. I even remember the exhale. I blew that breath out very slowly. Looking back, I can see that in that experience, I breathed in new life and I breathed out the old. I generally take breathing for granted. It is just something that I do. On that day though, the breath not only changed, but saved my life. In the valley, Ezekiel was able to see what happens when God breathes life into the dead. When it happened to me, there were witnesses also. When was the last time you saw dry bones come to life? Have you ever told someone about Jesus and were able to watch them come to life before your eyes? That is what is supposed to happen. We are supposed to tell people about the life, death, burial, and resurrection of Jesus. We are supposed to speak about the glory of God. When was the last time you spoke into someone else's life? When did you last see God breathe life into someone?

But He would withdraw to desolate places and pray.

Luke 5:16

I have been in, it seems, several seasons of chaos. When I think about the chaos of life, I often wonder how Jesus would have handled it. As I look and read back over His life though, it was definitely chaotic. He had 12 guys He was always talking to. People were constantly crowded around Him, listening to every word He said and wanting Him to do miraculous feats. There were people trying to silence Him and those who wanted Him gone. He was even raising people from the dead!! It is strange to think about the life Jesus lived as being anything but peaceful because He is the Prince of Peace, however, there was chaos. He would not have experienced something on earth and portrayed it in the Bible if there were not a lesson in the situation. Often Jesus would withdraw from the chaos, go somewhere by Himself, and pray. He would take time to intentionally be with the Father and, in human terms, reset and rejuvenate. He came here to show us how to live here. When was the last time any of us did as we were shown to do amongst the chaos? I cannot remember the last time I took some real time, turned off everything electronic and was completely intentional about giving hours, or days, instead of just an hour or only a few spare moments to God. No wonder I get lost in the chaos with little notice of peace. It is easy to think there is no time for these things. Is that true though? What can you cut out of your life today that will allow you more time with God? If you can take a few days for vacation, can you not take a few days instead to retreat to a quiet place to reset and rejuvenate with the Father? I encourage you today, to withdraw as Jesus did and take the time to pray, to listen, and to grow in God.

And such were some of you. But you were washed, you were sanctified, you were justified in the name of the Lord Jesus Christ and by the Spirit of our God.

1 Corinthians 6:11

The two verses before this are a list of the things that we were. In a nutshell, we were wicked. Even worse than that though, we would not inherit the kingdom of God. I qualified for 8 out of 10 on the list of wickedness. When I first read this I had a hard time making it to the next sentence. The lies of my mind would not let me go any further than to read all of the bad about me. When I finally continued, the third word of the first sentence of verse 11 gave me hope. It says "were". That very small word means past. What I know about God is that if something is in my past and I have repented of that thing, I have been forgiven of it. Not only that, God has forgotten it. So not only was I, but it is so much in the past that I am no longer that thing. In this case, I am no longer wicked. Now I can inherit the kingdom of God. By the blood of Jesus Christ I am made clean. By Holy Spirit I am made new. It no longer matters what I was. Today, what matters is Whose I am. Today I am a blessed child of God. I am co-heir with Jesus Christ. I am forgiven and loved. Because of Whose I am, I am sanctified and justified. When you read this verse today, I encourage you to thank God for the gift offered here. Praise Him that it no longer matters what you were. Today it matters Whose you are.

One night the Lord spoke to Paul in a vision: "Do not be afraid; keep on speaking and do not be silent."

Acts 18:9

I am amazed that Paul felt fear of speaking. When I think of Paul, I think of boldness and courage in the face of persecutors. If our Lord appeared to him in a vision and told him to speak and not fear, that could only mean that in the deepest recesses of Paul's spirit there was fear. God knows even what others would never imagine was there. Speaking out in the name of God is hard. Saying the Gospel is sometimes scary. I could walk into a room of like minded people and say whatever I want about the Father, Son and Holy Spirit. That is only supposed to be practice though. I am called to open my mouth and tell people about the love of Jesus. I am supposed to declare the death, burial, and resurrection of our Savior to people who have never heard the Truth. I probably will not go to a synagogue or a mosque and preach the Word. That is exactly what Paul was doing though. He was teaching us that though it is hard, this is what we are called to do. I am not always the best at walking into a room and declaring the Truth of Jesus. However, I am good at putting words on paper. I often pray that believers are not the only ones who will read these words. This is how God has chosen to bless me with the ability to reach people who may not otherwise hear Him. He has done the same thing for you. It may not be with words on a page or standing in a mosque. He has given you a voice to speak with. It could be with prayer, service, encouragement, or kindness. The gifts God has given you are the way He has chosen for you to speak. Do you remain silent? I encourage you today to not be afraid. Speak God's glory into the lives of those around you.

"My brothers, I have fulfilled my duty to God in all good conscience to this day."

Acts 23:1b

Ananias slapped Paul in the face when he made this statement. These were not just Paul's own people. They were his peers. These men studied together. They celebrated the same festivals. They sacrificed together. They obeyed the same laws. They did life together in ways we could not understand today. Each of these men believed in the Messiah. These men knew the prophecies and understood them better than any of us ever could. However, when Jesus walked among them, they were too blinded by their tradition and their interpretation to see Him. Even Paul. Saul had gone to the Sanhedrin and requested permission to persecute people who believed in the finished works of Jesus. He hunted down believers and killed them. He was Pharisee among Pharisees. Until he was not. When Saul met Jesus, his life changed. He became Paul, he spent three years in Arabia learning of Jesus, by Jesus, through Holy Spirit. Then he went back. The Pharisees must have been as shocked as the Apostles initially were. Paul was a completely different man on a much greater mission. When he sat in front of the Sanhedrin on this day, he was not ashamed or guilty. He said with boldness that he had fulfilled his duty to God. While people change their lives in drastic measures today, I very rarely hear them boast that they have fulfilled their duty to God. I often hear people who say they could never measure up, or that they have so much left to do. I never hear them boldly proclaim, "whether you kill me or not, to this day I have fulfilled my duty to God". What would happen if this were the way people really acted? What if we were all bold instead of shy about the work of God in our lives? Can you look anyone in the eye and say, without doubt, that you have fulfilled your duty to God to this day?

He is like a tree planted by water, that sends out its roots by the stream, and does not fear when heat comes, for its leaves remain green, and is not anxious in the year of drought, for it does not cease to bear fruit.

Jeremiah 17:8

Some verses sound strange when you first read them. How can a man be like a tree? A tree never worries and does not feel fear. A tree does not consider tomorrow and fails to remember yesterday. A tree lives in determined cycles and simply grows and produces fruit. I have a friend who, for all outward appearances, resembles this verse. He is like a tree. I have seen him wilted, though only ever slightly. What is amazing to me is that his down times never seem to last as long as other people's. I do not know what is going on with him internally, however, what I see is someone whose roots shoot into the water that gives him life. His arms reach to the Son who gives him endurance. His voice speaks the truth of scripture in whatever situation that is attempting to consume him. It is a beautiful thing that even in his darkest of days, what I see is the light of Christ shining from the cracks in his life. He stands how this verse says a man should stand. This man does not cease to bear fruit even in the moments when he does not seem to feel fruitful. This is what Jesus must have been like as He walked the earth. Though there were moments He felt weak, He found His strength in the truth of God. When things looked like they could fall apart, He persevered, and the ending became the beginning. When the heat came, the storms blew or darkness tried to prevail, in faith He called for peace. In all things, He bore fruit. That is the example my friend follows. Do you have people in your life like this? Do they set their eyes on Christ and dig their roots deep? Do they seem to rarely have an off day, and when they do, it seems gone as quickly as it came? Do you see Jesus in them? Tell them that today.

Wait for the Lord; be strong and let your heart take courage; wait for the Lord.

Psalm 27:14

I recently heard someone say that they do not think that God meant for them to be still while they wait. Of course, God does not want us to sit still. If, when I began my walk with God, I had literally waited for the things He promised me, I would still be sitting on my couch. Some things have come to pass. They did not get here by me sitting around and waiting though. I prayed for things then waited on the answer. Sometimes the answer was yes, right now. God was going to open doors for me if I got up and did the foot work behind the promise. When I thought about school, I prayed about it, I waited, quickly God said yes, and I applied. Some things do not go so fast and so smoothly. There are promises that God has made to me that I have been waiting on the fruition of for a couple of years. In the waiting, I am growing strong in the Lord. I would not be able to wait in my own strength, so I lean into Him and His strength allows me to wait. I find courage in Him also. Some of the waiting gets scary. There are days when I let the lies take over and start to think that the promises will never come to pass. However, God does not lie, and He has promised me this. In Him and His Word I find the courage to not rush ahead and attempt to fulfill the promise of my own volition. In all situations, I continue to move forward in my walk with God. I know that if I am delighting myself in Him, He will give me the desires of my heart. As I wait in His courage and strength, my relationship with God grows deeper. Are you waiting for something of God in your life today? Have you prayed over it? Do you continue to pray, reminding God of the things He has promised in your life? Are you sitting still, or are you moving forward? God does for us what we cannot do for ourselves. He will fulfill the promise, but He will not move your feet to get you there.

This is my command: Love each other.

John 15:17

This should not be such a hard command to follow. The people I see in my day, I am supposed to love them. It's funny, but sometimes I have an easier time showing love to the stranger than the people who are active in my life. I can see the actions of the people in my life. I hear their words that betray them. I know the color of the wool they think they are pulling over my eyes. It is easier to show love to people whose flaws are not known to me. In this verse Jesus was telling the disciples to love each other. These men knew each other. They knew Peter was stubborn and that Thomas would doubt. They knew John thought Jesus loved him most. It is no secret how they felt when Paul joined their ranks. These men knew each other intimately. They knew each other's flaws and annoyances. Jesus was telling them to look past those things and love each other. I do find that this is an easier command to follow when I'm living in gratitude. I am then able to bypass the flaws of the people in my life and am able to see what God sees. I can love them as I am supposed to because I am looking with the eyes of Holy Spirit instead of my own. It is not always hard to love my people. However, in the times when it is, I remind myself of the way Jesus loves me. Do you have a difficult person in your life right now? Try to see them as Jesus sees them. Love them as He loves you.

So I went down to the potter's house, and there he was working at his wheel. And the vessel he was making of clay was spoiled in the potter's hand, and he reworked it into another vessel, as it seemed good to the potter to do.

Jeremiah 18:3-4

The vessel was spoiled in the potter's hand. Seems an odd statement. How does something that is in someone's hand spoil? Unless that thing does not realize where it is at. Obviously, the lump of clay does not know that it is being molded. Clay has no clue that when it is finished and it is put through the fire that when it comes out on the other side, it will be a beautiful new creation with purpose and reason. The clay is not human. Why would it know human things? There was a time when I did not know it either though. I started life, having been weaved together with so much love and compassion that my Potter knew how many hairs I would have on my head. I was born and went through infancy, being a toddler, and childhood. Somewhere along the way, I spoiled. It wasn't because God took His hands off of me. I started to think that I was doing the molding of my life. I wanted control and I wanted everything done my way. Inside of that, I made terrible decisions that wreaked havoc on every person I came in contact with for decades. I became sick with self and I spoiled almost to the point of decay. One day, God reminded me, in a life altering way, that He never left me. Then amazing things started to happen. When I turned back to Him, He allowed me to become an unformed lump of clay once again. He does not allow me to stay that way though. God reworks us as a potter does a lump of clay. He takes what has spoiled, and reworks it into a new creation. He puts us through the fire and on the other side we are beautiful, given purpose and reason. He even takes parts of my old life and weaves them in so that there is raw testimony and message that others can see. He leaves in imperfections so that people closest to me can also feel when He refines those places out. God has taken what I had spoiled and created a new vessel in Him. Where are you in this process? Are you spoiled? Are you back in the lump stage? Have you already been through the fire? Do you know the purpose the Potter created you for?

Remember not the former things, nor consider the things of old.

Isaiah 43:18

There are two types of people in my life, those who tell me to not spend too much time remembering the past and those who advise me to never forget where I came from. In AA we use our past. For some it is a way to relive their war stories. For others it is a stepping stone, meant only to help others to know they are not alone. For me, personally, usually, its like watching reels from a completely different life. That is how salvation is supposed to be. When I died spiritually in my bathroom and Jesus breathed life into me, I walked out of there a new creation with a new life. I was given complete grace and forgiven as far as the east is from the west. In the beginning I knew what it was to not consider the past. The choices I had made before that moment held no bond over who I was now able to be. Fast forward and things have sort of changed. With all of the changes going on I often catch myself wondering if I did enough for some or said the right things for others. Most often I think about how I raised my kids. I have spent a lot of time considering the past. The truth is that I am not the same person who did the doing or the saying, or even the majority of the raising. That was the old me and she is dead. I have times when I stop looking at the past as an old movie reel and start again to dwell on it. We are told not to do that because it drives us mad. Jesus did not make me a new creation in order for me to go backwards and get stuck in what I was. His purpose for me is to move forward while constantly remaining in this moment. If I am considering the past, I cannot be with God in the present. Where are you today? Are you stuck in what ifs and could have been that can never occur? Are you dwelling on what has already gone? Or are you walking in this present moment where, as CS Lewis said, eternity is touching humanity?

There is neither Jew nor Gentile, neither slave nor free, nor is there male and female, for you are all one in Christ Jesus.

Galatians 3:28

Looks like Paul left out a few categories. I am sure he meant, also, that there is no Baptist, no Church of Christ, no Apostolic. If there was to be no difference in Jew and Gentile, how could we be so naive as to think there would be divisions inside the body? We are to be one body, with one mission. Jesus gave us a very specific assignment before He ascended. We were to go, make disciples, baptize, and teach them to obey. Leave it to humanity to mess that up. One group of people heard the words in one way and another heard them differently. If satan could not get the individual to turn back on their convictions, the least he could do was to separate the body. Now we hear sermons on unity and cannot determine why there is not a sense of togetherness. Preachers want their people to unite and regardless of the fact that they fill their buildings with people who are very much of one mind, they cannot decide why they still feel the need to give a sermon on something that appears to have been accomplished. If we are united in the walls why is there such an emphasis on the need for unity? Could it be because the issue is less unity in the church but more unity of the church. We are created to be one under Christ.

In the beginning ...

Genesis 1:1a

Generally we think of the Christmas story starting in Matthew and being retold in Luke. That is only the time that it starts for us. For God it began long before that. God is able to see the beginning from the end. He was there before the beginning. Before the foundation of creation, God knew the exact moment each thing would happen, down to how many times you blink as you read this. On the bigger scale of God's plan, He knew the moment Eve would eat the fruit. He was not surprised by the need for the flood or the plagues. He was aware that David would take Bathsheba and kill Uriah. God already saw the kings who would rather worship the idol and He knew His centuries of silence before it was felt by His people. In seeing the beginning from the end, He witnessed the birth long before it happened. God felt the calluses on His feet before he took one step. He breathed the love of His disciples and felt the wrath of their rejection before He stepped out of heaven. Before the foundation of creation God felt the flesh rip across his back and saw drops of His own blood hit the ground. The Christmas story is so much more than the birth of a baby. It is the presentation of pure love wrapped in flesh. It is love that comes in spite of the outcome it already knows will come to pass. The Christmas story as we know it did not start with a birth but with a breath. It was not the breath of flesh but the breath of time. However, this week we celebrate the beauty and merciful grace of that breath putting on flesh and stepping out of eternity into humanity so that He could fulfill His greater works of placing Himself inside of us. When was the last time you pondered the true reason of the season? Do you simply look to the birth and the death, or do you go further and stand in awe of God's plan from beginning to the end?

And she gave birth to her firstborn son and wrapped him in swaddling clothes and laid him in a manger, because there was no room for them in the inn.

Luke 2:7

There was no room. I was always intrigued by this part of the story. Mostly because it is not just a part of the story of the birth of Christ. This part of the story is exactly the same in the life of every human. I am the innkeeper. There are times in my life when I just do not have room for Jesus. While these times were prevalent before salvation, there are also times since salvation that I have not had time to include Jesus. To put it in the view of an inn, I fill all of the rooms with the things and the people that I like to have around. I compartmentalize things like AA, work, church, life group and people in my life into all of the different rooms of my mind and spirit and I fail to invite Jesus into any of the spaces. I am not made to just ask Jesus into the rooms in order to occupy the spaces I separate my life into. I am meant to first give the space to Jesus. However, sometimes I forget that. There are times when I fail to allow Christ to be master over my life. He wants room in my life and I get so full and so busy that I do not include Him. When that happens, I rob myself of the miracle of Him. Essentially, when I am too full I miss the beauty of Jesus because there is no room for Him. You are also an innkeeper. You stand watch over the rooms of your life. Do you allow them to get overly full, not leaving room for Jesus? Or do you allow Jesus to come in and take space in each part of your life, ensuring that there is always as much room in your life as He wants?

And the angel answered her, the Holy Spirit will come upon you, and the power of the Most High will overshadow you; therefore the child to be born will be called holy- the Son of God.

Luke 1:35

Christine Caine said that the thing God asked Mary to do was not just hard, but it was impossible. Can you imagine being asked to give birth to Jesus? It must have been completely overwhelming. Then Joseph was asked to do what seemed to be impossible for his walk. It was unheard of for a man to keep a woman who was impure in the eyes of society. Later Jesus asked His disciples to do the impossible for their own lives by leaving everything they knew and following Him. From the cross He asked God to do the impossible and forgive us all. God is not in the business of asking anyone to do easy things. When He came to talk to me, what He asked me to do was an impossibility in my life. People had been asking me to get sober for years. When God asked me, however, He was not simply giving me a choice between being sober and being high. He was asking me to make a decision that would decide the fate of the rest of my life. It was not just hard; for an addict like myself, it was impossible. But God. He did not ask me to do any of it alone. Holy Spirit immediately caused a reaction inside of me that created inside of me a new being. He did the same for Mary. While God asked her to do the impossible that would alter the history of creation, He gave her the exact same help that He gave to me. That is the same help He gives to you when He asks you to do the impossible in your life. Do you feel as though the things God asks you to do are so hard that there is no way you could ever achieve them? Do you know that He gives you Holy Spirit to accomplish the impossible in your life exactly as He did so Mary could accomplish the impossible in hers?

For unto you is born this day in the city of David a Savior, who is Christ the Lord.

Luke 2:11

Before God planted the tree in the Garden, He knew that Eve would succumb to the temptation of the enemy. When He breathed the first moment of time into existence God knew that we would need Jesus. However, by putting the tree in the Garden He gave us the choice of Jesus. When the angel of the Lord spoke with Mary, she had a choice. Joseph was able to make a decision about staying with Mary. When the Wise Men saw the star in the sky they had plenty of time to discuss the 500 mile trek through the desert and change their minds before making the trip. Peter, John, and Matthew all had the option of walking the other way and not following Jesus. At salvation we are given the choice of accepting our Savior, who is Christ the Lord. God left heaven and put on flesh. He slept in a feed trough. Jesus was a boy and a man, living a meek life. He was the greatest Teacher. Christ the Lord was the ultimate sacrifice. All of that He did so that I would have the choice of calling Him Savior. Jesus Christ was born so that you could choose this day to decide to allow Him to be Lord over your life. Joshua said we choose this day whom we will serve. As for me and my house we will serve the Lord. Today we celebrate the birth of a baby who was already our Savior. You are not obligated to serve Him. It is your choice because He is a gentleman. I pray this Christmas that you know our Savior who was born in the city of David. I pray you choose to allow Him to be Lord over your life.

But to the two men who had spied out the land, Joshua said, "Go into the prostitute's house and bring out from there the woman and all who belong to her, as you swore to her."

Joshua 6:22

Rahab was a whore. Every time her name is mentioned in the book of Joshua it is made clear that she was a prostitute. Here her profession is used in place of her name. In present times women who sell their bodies are treated like trash. When these words were penned a prostitute was less than trash. Regardless that her services were used, she was not thought to be much of a human. When reading her account in the Old Testament it is easy to think of her as an opportunist. She saw the spies for what they were and used that as an advantage to keep her family safe. Once the siege was over she surely could have moved her family to the other side of the Jordan, started over, and looked out for herself. It would not have been a surprising outcome, after all, whores are known for looking out for self. Scripture does not say that though. Rahab stayed with the Israelites. She heard of the wonders of the Lord and she believed in Him. When given the chance, she became one of His people and allowed Him to change her life. The change of Rahab was so spectacular that she is mentioned again in the New Testament. In Hebrews she is mentioned as a powerhouse of faith. Most astoundingly though, is in Matthew 1:5 where it says she is in the direct line of Jesus Christ. God took a prostitute and allowed her to be the great grandmother (to the 31st generation) of the Savior of the world. Imagine what He will do with you.

Consecrate yourselves, for tomorrow the Lord will do amazing things among you.

Joshua 3:5

Joshua was preparing the Israelites to cross over the Jordan so they could begin the conquest of the Promised Land. God spoke with Joshua, gave him direction, and told him how to prepare. They knew when tomorrow came something amazing was going to happen and they needed to be prepared. In my life, when something is going to happen tomorrow, God is not coming to tell me what to expect and how to prepare. Just because He is not doing that does not mean He is bypassing me and doing amazing things only through other people. I do not know anyone who hears from God in the manner that Joshua did. However, I do know people God does amazing things through. The majority of those people are doing things today to unwittingly prepare for the amazing thing tomorrow. I try to follow their example. These people have a growing and conscious relationship with God. They pray constantly. These are people in service to others. They are humble and live lives of love and compassion. They are believers who constantly share the Gospel through their actions and occasionally with words. When I think of consecrating myself today for the amazing things of tomorrow, it is striving to be a woman closer to God today than yesterday. Do you know that the Lord wants to do amazing things through you? Are you prepared for Him to work through you?

Because they exchanged the truth about God for a lie and worshiped and served the creature rather than the Creator, who is blessed forever! Amen.

Romans 1:25

In this passage Paul is talking about acts of unrighteousness. He was talking about idol making and self-serving impurities. I find that it is easy to make an idol out of anything and in the process of making that idol and then spending time with it, most actions become self-serving. I have been known to make something of an idol even out of the promises of God. I do not always realize that is what is happening. However, I receive a promise and then I start looking for the fulfillment of that promise. I will fall asleep and it is the last thing on my mind and when I wake up it is the first thing that is there. As I go through my day I am constantly wondering if today will be the day that the promise is kept. Since God makes promises without time frames, I become so frustrated when there is no fruition that I even get angry with God for not holding up His side of the deal. When in truth, there was no deal, He is simply going to bless me when He wants and how He knows is best. The waiting for the promises can cause the promise to be an idol because I serve the anticipation of the promise instead of seeking the One who made the promise. Most recently, for me I have been searching for the fruition of a promise made long ago. I see the same promise fulfilled in others and am standing in wonder of when it will be my turn, why has God forgotten me, maybe His promises are not actually real. See the spiral of disappointment and how it can take you from seeking God down to exchanging Him for a lie? Today I am going to seek the face of God. I know that when I am truly seeking Him and His glory and not His promises, I am constantly fulfilled. Are you seeking the face of God, or have you exchanged His truth for a lie and turned it into an idol in your life?

Bearing with one another and, if one has a complaint against another, forgiving each other, as the Lord has forgiven you, so you also must forgive.

Colossians 3:13

I am a firm believer that the bible is written for me. The words may have been said to or about someone else, but, with maybe the exception of genealogies, I believe that there is something I can learn or take away from every verse. There are verses that I do not particularly wish that I knew though. This is one of them. The glaring takeaway is that I should be forgiving people as God forgave me. God released me of some pretty big things. Everything from petty theft to murder is was on my rap sheet. I even had the less thought about sin of being a human without belief in Christ. God forgave me for each of those. Forgiving me for not believing the absolute truth of who He is was the biggest thing. After He forgave me of those things, He proceeded to forget. Not in the human way of forgetting. He did not just put it at the back of his mind to bring it out and remind me of it the next time I screwed up. He forgave and forgot. Thankfully, scripture does not ask me to do that. However, I am told over and again to forgive everyone, not just the ones I want to. At first forgiving is hard. Once I did it though, I realized one very amazing thing about forgiveness. It makes me feel better. Forgiving makes space in my mind and my spirit that would otherwise be occupied with resentments that cause me to be angry and grouchy and eventually send me to the drink. I do not believe that God ever tells us to do something that will not in some way benefit our spirit and mind. So, as difficult as it may seem, if you have anything against anyone, forgive them. You do not have to call and tell them. Odds are they do not even know you are mad. Forgive as God has forgiven you today.

Therefore, confess your sins to one another and pray for one another, that you may be healed.

James 5:16a

James is a very controversial book. Some people believe that it should not be included in the bible. I love it though. This verse especially. I probably appreciate it so much because I have a lot of experience in seeing it work. In Alcoholics Anonymous it is said that my secrets make me sick. What I know about secrets is that while they are hidden in the very small space that is my mind, they seem very big and powerful. However, when I speak them, and they are then out in a bigger space and not confined inside of me, they lose the power of keeping me sick because they become small. In AA we have a 4th and 5th step that are derived from this verse. Part of the program is confession. We sit with someone and tell them everything, our anger, fears, sadness and mistakes. In doing so, we take away the decaying effect that a secret can produce. There is healing in sharing. It allows others to know that they are not alone. Telling others my story has allowed this fantastic relief inside of myself. I can see where I need to take responsibility for my own part in whatever secret I am telling. I am also able to pinpoint where I need to make amends in a situation or forgive someone. It also gives me permission to forgive myself, which is often considerably more difficult than forgiving someone else. The bible is the inspired breath of God. Scripture is called living and breathing because over time it does not lose validation. A very long time ago James said we should confess to someone, pray together and that process would lead to healing. I encourage you today, if you have a secret, share it with someone you trust so that you can heal. If someone comes to you with a confession, hear them, pray with them so that they can heal. It is a simple instruction to a great miracle.

Pray for one another that you may be healed.

James 15:16b

Healing very rarely looks how I think it should. It is easy to get stuck believing that healing is going from being sick to not being sick. That puts God's miracle of healing into a very small box. The people in my life prayed for my healing for a very long time. When that healing happened none of those people were near me. There was not a laying on of hands. There was no speaking over me in tongues. I was alone and Jesus found me. However, I firmly believe those years of prayers helped usher Christ into my life. I was blind, but now I clearly see, though I still wear glasses. I could not hear, but I clearly knew Holy Spirit was whispering in my ear. I was dead, but Jesus breathed life into my lungs and changed my heart of stone into flesh. I was an alcoholic but the Living Water quenched my thirst. I was an addict, but my love of dope was replaced by the Lover of my soul. Today I have a new battle to face. Though I know that God can heal me physically, I will praise Him if He doesn't because spiritually I am healed, whole and restored already. Sometimes we pray for a physical healing and are confused when that person does not seem to get better. We only see the outside though. Healing is deeper than the physical body. Healing is meant to change the hungers of the spirit to crave the Bread of Life and the Living Water. Are you praying for someone to be healed today? I encourage you to climb out of the box. Broaden your view on what healing completely is. Know that the healed body is only a bonus to a healed heart and spirit.

For you know that the testing of your faith produces steadfastness.

James 1:3

Last night I was again challenged with conversation about God. It was really just a simple question, "Do you think God tests us?" My knee jerk reaction was yes. I mean, look at Job, the prophets, Paul had a thorn in his side. Not only that, Paul was Saul. God converted him then set Paul in front of the disciples hoping that through trusting God, they would also trust Paul. What a testing that must have been. Although, the bible does not use that word in relation to that part of the story. I think that I have had a misconstrued view of the word test as it is used in scripture. In my humanity I think of being tested as an opportunity to either pass or fail. If I pass I level up. If I fail, hell is the first thing that passes through my mind. I am a finite human and try to make things fit inside my box of understanding. What if testing means a stretching though. I have been waiting on the fulfillment of a promise for a number of years. I know that the promise is of God. I know He has put this desire in my heart. I also know that I cannot see the fruition in the near future. That makes me sad. I cry out to God. In my crying, He urges me to go deeper, to keep trusting Him, He says He sees me and He has not forgotten. He wants my faith to keep a steadfastness. God is ultimately testing my faith. Not to see if I can withstand the pressure, but so that I know since He is with me in this, I can have faith that He will be with me through the rest. He does not test me in order that I may pass or fail. He stretches me through testing me so that I will trust Him, so that my faith in Him, not in my situation or circumstance, will remain steady. Do you think God tests you? Are you in the midst of something you thought was a pass or fail moment? Maybe it is simply a time to learn to trust in the strength and presence of God.

I will make with them an everlasting covenant, that I will not turn away from doing good to them.

Jeremiah 32:40a

This promise was made regarding God's people and it was made in the Old Testament. So often when I think of God's people in the Old Days, I think strictly of the Israelites. That is not an accurate picture though. Even then, there were already Gentiles who were considered His. People have been seeing the great works of God and converting to being His people long before Paul was designated to take the Good News to the Gentiles. Since that is the case, this covenant was made for the whole of the body, not just for the Israelites. It is so easy to get lost in the legalities of the Old Testament that I forget it was written for me as much as the New was. This verse is a promise to me. When God told Jeremiah He would make an everlasting covenant, God meant everlasting in His infinite understanding. I think of everlasting and in my humanity there is a stopping point. For me, everlasting is the duration of my life. God knows further than that though. God knows not only the beginning from the end, but He sees past the end of that. Since God was before time, He will be after time. In that eternity, His covenant will remain. As believers we will be in that eternity with Him and when mortal time ends, He will still be doing good for us. God said He will, for an everlasting amount of moments, do good to His people. The Israelites were not the only people He was referring to. He sent the prophets, the disciples, and every other believer since then to gather more people so that He could be good to us all for an amount of time none of us can even begin to imagine. If you are God's person, this promise is yours. The best part is that there is still time for you to share it with others. Tell someone about the goodness of God today.

And as they were stoning Stephen, he called out, "Lord Jesus, receive my spirit." And falling to his knees he cried out with a loud voice, "Lord, do not hold this sin against them." And when he had said this, he fell asleep.

Acts 7: 59-60

Stephen's story never changed. From the moment he knew the Lord, Stephen proclaimed His goodness and mercies. Stephen was a servant who was filled with Holy Spirit and with power. He knew grace and he showed it to those around him. Stephen spoke of the goodness of God until he took his last breath. He was the example of what it looks like to never waiver and to remain steadfast. Those are hard lessons. I like to think that I remain as an oak in all situations. However, there are people in my life I become very lax around. It isn't that they do not know that I love God. Sometimes it is hard for them to tell that I walk by faith and not by flesh. My mouth often shows that I am still more human than spirit. I say that I trust God, but sometimes when things are tough, I find that I hold my breath in hope that God will come through rather than breathing in faith that He already has. In my life there are situations where I rely more on human will than God's will. That is not how I am supposed to function though. I am meant to proclaim the Truth of God even unto death. The people I encounter in my everyday life should know that I am Jesus' girl. Not always because I use words, but they should know by my actions, the words I don't say, the way I carry myself. As St. Francis of Assisi said, "Daily I share the Gospel, sometimes I use words." Being like Stephen does not mean I need to be stoned to death. It means that everyone around me knows that even until my last breath, I am a believer in the one true God. Do the strangers you encounter every day walk away from you knowing that they have encountered a child of God, or do they wonder to whom you belong?

Jesus answered, "Have faith in God."

Mark 11:22

It is easy to walk around on any given normal day and declare that I have faith in God. When life is good and going how I anticipate I do not have a problem walking in faith knowing that everything is going according to God's good and perfect plan. When something happens though, and I am not sure of the outcome, or fear hits about something inside of that situation, it is harder to walk in faith. In those times it is simple to say that I am leaving it in God's hands. Usually what happens though is that I am walking through life worrying about how it is going to turn out, what I am going to lose or how the ones I love are going to be caught in the crossfire of the result. Essentially, there are times when it is easier to say that I have faith in God than it is to walk in that faith. So what does it look like to really walk in faith in the hard situations? For me, it means I am talking to God and not to other people. It is fine for me to ask others to pray into the situation, but it is not okay for me to sit and complain about the situation or the people concerned. It means that I do not allow the circumstance to be the only thing I think about. If I am obsessing over a thing, I am worrying and not laying it at God's feet. Walking in faith means that I am doing only my part and not trying to control what the other people are doing or saying. Having faith in God means I am reacting out of love and not anger. It looks like I am having a good day even when it is bad. Are you trying to have faith in God but feeling like you are not? What are you doing that is causing you to rely more on people and self than on God? I encourage you to change those things today. When you want to complain to people, talk to God. If you find that you are only thinking about the thing, change your train of thought. If you are trying to do something other than your part, don't. Choose to have faith in God then take the action to walk in that faith.

The sun will no more be your light by day, nor will the brightness of the moon shine on you. The Lord will be your everlasting light, and your God will be your glory.

Isaiah 60:19

I know well what it is like to live in darkness. There was a time when my life was so dark I would leave every light on that I could find. I stayed in a two-bedroom apartment and every light, in the closets, the hall, the entry, in every room was constantly on. I was terrified of what was in the dark. I was not scared of anything in the apartment when it was dark, but what was in the darkness inside of myself. No matter how many lights I turned on, I could not stop the darkness within from getting deeper and more terrifying. Eventually, there was no light left at all. The lights I could turn on through other people, my family, my kids, could no longer penetrate the darkness. Everything was black. It was a terrifying time in life, not just for me, but for those who were watching and were unable to help me see the light. But God. He came to me in a light that has never left. There was no human thing that could have rid me of the darkness that had come over me. Jesus did not have any problem though. His light shined so brightly I could see everything. I saw the mess I had made in the process of becoming the monster that I was. Jesus showed me love and forgiveness. What His light did not show me was shame, regret, or guilt. The Light of Jesus helped me to understand the act of repentance, not just the words, and the difference in conviction and condemnation. There is no dark thing in Him. Then He gave me a gift of words so that every day I can proclaim His glory to anyone who will listen and sometimes even to those who do not want to. By sharing the miracles that have happened because of the Light coming into my life, I get to give God all the glory and all the honor. Just like the miracles of old, those things help to point people in the direction of the Light when they are in the darkness so deep they cannot see Him. Is He the light that shines in your life? Or do you rely on the artificial switches of humanity? Is God your glory today?

Whoever says he abides in Him ought to walk in the same way in which He walked.

1 John 2:6

I have read the Gospels. I like to think I know how Jesus walked. So when I read this verse it is easy for me to become enveloped in the thought that I could never live up to this one. I mean, Jesus was perfect. He fasted for 40 days and at the end of it was tempted and still resisted. He was mocked and kept His mouth shut. Jesus was beat and, quite literally, turned the other cheek. He is the Master and servant. Jesus is the Healer, but in His darkest moment He refused healing of His own body. In His humanity He prayed, while sweating blood, that the cup be removed from Him, but in the same prayer, He fully accepted the will of God as His own. He cared for the sick, made the blind to see and the lame to walk. He did not play the victim card. He did not set out to be worshipped. He was never selfish. He displayed every emotion yet did not sin. Every step of His humanity was walked out in love. I am supposed to walk in the way that He walked, the way that Jesus walked was in love. I am no more or less human than Jesus was, so why do I, very often, find it so difficult to walk in love? God is not asking me to take on the sins of all of creation in a death that will be discussed and mourned for centuries. He does not ask me to walk the desert healing people. He does not even ask me to fully resist all temptation every time I am tempted. God is simply asking me to walk in love. He wants me to feel compassion for the plight of my fellow man. He wants me to think of others before I think of myself. God gives me two commandments in Jesus, love the Lord with everything I have and love my neighbor as myself (Matt. 22:37-39). If I am doing those two things, I am walking as Jesus walked. How are you walking today? Is it as humanity says you should walk, or do you walk as Jesus walked?

So Jesus said to the Jews who had believed him, "If you abide in my word, you are truly my disciples.

John 8:31

Jesus said this of those who believed. I often forget that the bible is written for believers. When the Old Testament was penned it was meant for the edification and knowledge of the Jewish community. The New Testament is written to show believers, Jewish and Gentile, how to abide in Christ. I very often hear people criticize other people. They say someone is not behaving in a Christian manner or that what they are doing is not biblical. What is not considered is the other person's relationship with Christ. If they are not a Christian, why would they be held to the standard that Christians are held to? How can they behave as a Christian and in ways that are biblical if they are not that? If the bible is written for believers, how does one become a believer? Could it partially be by the testimony of their neighbor? We are called to love our neighbor as ourselves. Does that not also mean that we fight for the salvation of their spirit? If the written Word of God is instruction, then the living Word of God is direction. We abide in Christ and Christ abides in us. Instead of judging people for not acting like Christians, perhaps we should be Christians and show them the way to Christ and how to be a Christian. We live in an age of offense and judgment. While we say we don't do those things, when was the last time you went to someone and gave your testimony, discipled them, and showed them how to abide in Christ? Compare that to the last time you even thought that your neighbor should be more Christian in manner. Do you know that when people see you in public those are not the same thoughts they are having about you? In your daily walk, do you show people how to abide in Christ? Are you a disciple of Christ in action, or in word only?

At that moment the veil in the Holy of Holies was torn in two from top to bottom.

Mark 15:38

How many times have you read the story of Christ's crucifixion and, while moved by it, you did not hear all of the words or pay attention to every sentence? The veil being torn is recorded in all except John's Gospel. (Matthew went so far to include that the earth shook and the rocks were split.) It is so easy to stop retaining the words written after reading that the veil was torn in two. I mean what else do we need to know? The last four words of this verse are the sweetest. God could have shredded the veil, erased it fully from existence, torn it side to side or diagonally. He did not do those things though. God tore the veil from the top to the bottom in the moment that Jesus breathed His final breath. Can you imagine standing in the temple? It was not empty. Since it was Passover there would have been people everywhere. Peoplewho understood the process of creating and making the veil and the purpose of its existence, would have stood there, and watched it tear. In my mind, I can see God reaching down, grasping it, and simply splitting it in two. Why tear it from top to bottom though? Maybe it was because God did not want any doubt as to how the veil tore or Who was responsible for the events of the day. God did not want anyone to mistake the invitation for a coincidence. Perhaps it tore from top to bottom because our Father wanted us to know that we are able to run to the Throne Room, to sit in His Presence, and that we no longer are barred from personal relationship with Him. I think He tore it in the manner that he did out of love. Humans are often ridiculous and need to be convinced. He knew that Christ's death wouldn't be enough that day. So He caused the skies to darken as Jesus took our sins. Then He caused the earth to cry out since no one else would. Finally He tore the veil in the ultimate act of invitation as Jesus breathed His last in the ultimate expression of love. I encourage you, as you read the Word, to read every word. Even if you have read it over and again, read it fully. Hear the love God is showing you.

He said to them, "Where is your faith?"

Luke 8:25a

This verse comes at the end of Jesus calming the storm. When I read the story I wondered why Jesus would ask that. By this time in His ministry the disciples had seen amazing miracles. They just witnessed Him feeding 5,000 people. The disciples knew they could have faith in Jesus. However, they get in this boat and Jesus goes to sleep and the storm comes. They were frightened. Man, have I been right there. I have been able to see God do amazing things. He pulled me right out of hell. He provides when I am not sure how I am going to eat. In what seems like the darkest times, He reminds me that I am no longer in darkness, simply in the shadow of His wing. I have faith that God will show up and provide and be my refuge. There are times when I am like the disciples too though. Regardless that I have seen the miracles and heard His voice, when the storms come, I cry out to Him in fear. Why do I do that? I would think that I have seen enough to know that God is here and working and even though I can't see Him or hear Him, I should have faith that it is going to be okay because He is lord over my life. Jesus could ask this same question of me. Where is your faith? Does that mean my faith is gone though? Perhaps it has simply been misplaced. I recently experienced a time when this question was logical. In the moment that I was freaking out and crying out instead of resting in faith, Jesus did not even need to ask the question. I already knew the answer. I had taken my faith from God in the situation and placed it in my humanity. I thought, for a minute, that I could solve the problem. What happened is that the storm got worse. So, when I cried out and Jesus asked where my faith was, I knew my faith was, at that moment, wrapped up in my fear. So how do I move my faith back to Jesus? I have to intentionally take the thoughts causing the storm captive. I say out loud, "that thought is not of God." I then remind myself of the times God has shown up in this same situation and remember that He provides victory every single time. I have to stay in an intentional state of remembrance that God is good and He is good at being God. I know that He created the winds that cause the storms and He also calms them when they blow too hard. Sometimes it is harder to see the silver lining on the storm clouds. When I can stop and find it though, the rainbow appears. Where is your faith today? Are you trapped in thoughts of chaos? Is your faith trapped in your fear? Stop, breathe, and remember the victory of your God who calms the storm.

And the Lord gave Job twice as much as before.

Job 42:10b

I find Job a hard subject to write about. Until this moment I always thought there was nothing I had in common with him. He was so righteous. I was never that. He was faithful. I was never that either. What connection could I possibly have with Job? Well, he lost everything. I did that. While the manner to the losing was vastly different, the losing was the same. I lost my kids and my marriage and my house and finances. One day it was just all gone. The glaring difference there is that Job's loss was not his fault and mine was of my own making. What I know about God though is that fault does not matter. I was so angry with God that I refused to talk to Him until He took the time to come and stand in front of me and let me hear His love and feel His voice. I say it like that because that is the truth of how it happened. In every cell of my being, I clearly heard the voice of God when He called to me. In that moment I felt love for the first time. Do not misunderstand. My family loved me. However, I could not truly feel their love until I knew God's. God's love for me began when His love for Job began. Before the foundation of creation God knew every hair on my head, each breath I would take. He knew that I would lose everything and be so angry with Him. God knew I would be ready to die until He presented me with the option of His life or hell. Given those choices outright, how could I go on to the bitter end? I would have been content walking forward with only Him. The truth is that I would have understood if the kids and the rest of my family would have chosen to have nothing more to do with me. That is not how God works in my life though. He gave me back everything, different, but double. I got a double portion of my kids because they choose to walk through life with me. I get a double portion of my family because they chose to heal with me. I did not keep that husband, but my Maker is my husband (Isaiah 54:5) and He has promised a help meet for my life. All of the return on the choice I made in the bathroom that day is amazing. It would mean nothing if I did not first get God through Jesus though. The promises are great. The Promise Maker is exponentially better than all of the double combined. Have you lost things you held so very dear? Press into God, He will replace it all, better, but different and He will give you the best in giving you Himself.

As they passed by in the morning they saw the fig tree withered away to its roots.

Mark 11:20

I generally sidestep this verse and go straight to the verse about having faith in God. However, today I read this verse in relation to the woman with the issue of blood (Mark 5:21-34). That made me think about my own experience with Christ. I am obviously not a fig tree and my issue was not blood, however, when Christ came into my life, He fully healed me from my disease. Anyone in AA reading this will object and say that we only have a daily reprieve from our disease. Is that not what the woman with the issue of blood had? Each day she woke up she had a reprieve from her disease, meaning that she did not have to contend with the effects of that issue for that day. It is the only day given. Tomorrow is up in the air for everyone. The difference in what I believe and what most in the program believe is, for me, Jesus is enough to maintain the withering to the roots. In Him, by faith I am made whole. I use the tools of the program to be more self-aware and to be a better human to the other humans that I am walking with. I was not looking for miraculous healing when I was healed. I was looking for death. Jesus had a different plan. When He came into my life He offered me death in two forms. I could have chosen true death and gone to hell. Or I could choose to die to my old life and live forever in Him. I chose life by choosing death. Jesus, in that moment, gave me Holy Spirit so that while I live in Him, He lives in me. As I withered and died to my roots, Jesus resurrected me into a new life with Him. Today I get to boldly go to the Throne Room of God. I am able to lament to God when life is not what I imagined. Not only am I loved by God, I am in relationship with the Great I AM and He delights in me. As I delight in Him, God gives me the desires of my heart. So this verse is as true for me as it was for the tree and the woman with the issue of blood. Jesus has caused the old me to wither and die at the roots. In place of that, a new tree has grown, bearing fruit for the Kingdom of God. Can you relate to this verse today? How has Jesus come into your life and cause a withering so that something new in Him can grow? Share that gift with someone today. Help them to see how in death they too can live.

Even so, come, Lord Jesus.

Revelation 22:20b

As I reflect back on the last week, I can see very specific moments when I thought, "Come on Jesus." The unprecedented time of 2020 had several people saying the same sentiment. The record breaking winter storm of 2021 caused folks to scream it from the tops of their lungs. People just wanted God to make it stop. That did not happen though. What did happen was completely amazing. I got to go on my first mission trip during the storm and I never left my county. James (v 1:27) said religion that is pure and undefiled before God is to visit the orphans and widows. I saw the church do that and so much more this week. Our community saw faith through a great work. People without power and water opened buildings and homes, hearts, and spirits to help others with less than what they had. My pastor says that there is ONE church. The storm of 2021 proved that to be so true. Whether it was the physical church building that was open and serving those in need or a friend opening her house and rescuing another from complete solitude, Jesus walked through this storm with us through those people. When John penned this verse, he had just had the vision of Revelation. He knew what was going to happen. He did not ask Jesus to stop it, he simply asked Him to come regardless of the knowing. I wonder how many people, if they would have seen the last week coming would have asked for it to happen regardless. Would their comfort have outweighed the outpouring of love and compassion that happened and is still happening? Would you ask God to make it stop so that the hard stuff wouldn't happen? Or would you put on your boots and ensure that as many people as possible could see Christ's face as He worked through you? In saying "I have a relationship with Jesus", chances are I have more than most and enough to share with all. So tonight, as I sit in my house that is warm and with water that runs, my prayer is earnestly, "Even so, come Lord Jesus. As long as you tarry though, let the people see You through me."

But be doers of the word, and not hearers only, deceiving yourselves.

James 1:22

How in the world do I do the word? That was my question when I first read this verse. I mean, there are a lot of words. Am I supposed to be a doer of the Old or the New? Do I follow the Ten Commandments or the Sermon on the Mount? I like direction and to know when to do what and how to do things properly. So I searched the scripture. I thought that there had to be more direction. I tend to make things harder than they need to be. The answer is very simple. Jesus is quoted in Matthew 22:37-40, Mark 12:30-31 and Luke 10:27 telling me how to be a doer of the word. Love God with everything in me and love my neighbor as myself. In Matthew Jesus says that on these commandments hang the Law and the Prophets. That means that every command in the bible can be lived out through the act of love. That is easier said than done. It means that I love everyone in the same way that Jesus did. He did not let everyone inside His most intimate of circles. Some people Jesus left at a definite length away. However, He loved everyone. Some people get on my nerves. There are people I do not like as a person, their personality wears on me or they have characteristics that drive me crazy. I am supposed to love those people too. I know mask wearers, anti-vaxers, carnivores, vegetarians, Republicans and Democrats, and religious believers from every sect. I love them all, without needing to agree with them or wanting to allow our differences to interfere with that love. When I am striving to love like Jesus loved, I am being a doer of the word. I do not always do it right. Sometimes I fail miserably. There are times when I have a hard time loving you because I have a hard time loving me. There are moments when I have allowed flesh to override Spirit and I put things before God in my life. Those moments are when self-deception is at its peak in my life. However, when I am setting my eyes on things of the Spirit and am walking in His love, it overflows onto those I encounter and I am being a doer of the word. Does being a doer of the word confuse you? Are you trying to obey and do everything or are you walking in a love so pure that your steps allow you to be the doer you are longing to be?

I therefore, a prisoner for the Lord, urge you to walk in a manner worthy of the calling to which you have been called, with all humility and gentleness, with patience, bearing with one another in love, eager to maintain the unity of the Spirit in the bond of peace.

Ephesians 4:1-3

I have been stuck on these verses for the better part of a week. How cool would it be to be able to say, "I am so spiritual I walk in the manner worthy of my calling all of the time."? I cannot say that. I attempt to be all of these things but I very often fall very short. Right now the test is with my patience. My adult daughter and her daughter have just moved back home. I love having them home. However, I have essentially lived by myself for a year and absolutely lived by myself for three months. Until recently, when I came home everything was in its proper spot. There were not so many dishes, and the laundry ran less. My off time was my time, and my weekends were quiet. Now everything is different. I get to play games and paint canvases. There are sweet kisses along with the sound of the most magical laughter ever. We have hard conversations and the most comfortable silences. There is nothing quite like the relationship with your kid. I am not always patient as I try to bear with her in love and attempt to maintain unity of the Spirit. I am rarely gentle (though I am rarely gentle with anything). I am finding humility in asking for help in the things that are important. I very much wish that Paul would have declared that it is easy to walk in the manner worthy of your calling. I often find it easier to walk that way in front of you than I do my family. I leave situations where I have not walked like this feeling as though I have fallen short. I wonder if Paul portrayed this verse every moment? Since he was a human, how could he? In urging us to walk in a better manner, perhaps he was encouraging himself also. In our humanity we strive to be better, that does not mean that we are at our best in every moment. I have taken Paul's urging to walk worthy very seriously in the last week. I have not done it perfectly; I have not even done it gracefully. I have attempted to do it though and by attempting it every day, I will be better at it tomorrow. I urge you to read this verse again. Meditate on it and let Holy Spirit show you how to live worthy of that calling you have been called to. Strive to do that today. When you fail, decide to strive again. We will never do it perfectly, but we can always do it better.

Jesus said to him, "I am the way the truth and the light. No one comes to the Father except through me."

John 14:6

Salvation through Jesus Christ is the way to the Father. I very often hear that it does not matter if you believe in Buddha, one of the millions of Hindu Gods or Allah. They say it does not matter because all mountains lead to heaven. That is their truth. These statements are so sad to me. First I will get the easy statement out of the way. There is no such thing as my truth or your truth. There is only the Truth. I may interpret things differently but that does not mean that I get to have my own version of the truth. Neither do you. The absolute truth is that salvation is through Jesus Christ, His life, death, burial, and resurrection is the only way to the Great I AM. Being a good person does not get you a free ticket to heaven. Jesus asked in Mark 10:18 "why do you call me good? There is none good except God." Yet society decided somewhere along the line that man could be good enough to just walk into heaven. I would be an irresponsible and deceptive child of God if I let you think this societal thinking of getting to heaven is accurate. It would also be irresponsible if I did not tell you that getting to heaven is a bonus, not the goal. The Kingdom of God, as experienced in relationship is the goal. Walking with God in every moment of your humanity is the gift. This is the truth, salvation comes by being drenched in the blood of Jesus Christ, dying to yourself in Him, being buried in baptism and raised in a new birth with Holy Spirit. This is the only way to God the Father. Salvation does not come in several ways. There is only one way, one truth and one light. Being in the Presence of the Great I AM is the greatest gift and one only obtained by believing in Jesus. Not the type of belief that is simply words. It is putting action behind the words. It is knowing Him and walking in His love. It is having a functional relationship with God and sharing Him with those around you. Do you know Jesus today? Do you believe He is the only true way to God? If not, I earnestly urge you to find someone who knows Him and talk with them, let them pray with you and help you. If you do know Him, are you declaring the way to others, or are you passively letting them believe society can show them the way?

What then? Shall we sin because we are not under the law but under grace? By no means!

Romans 6:15

Before his conversion Paul was Saul. He was a persecutor. Not in the way we think of persecution in the States today. He was not going around making people wear masks or not kneeling for the national anthem. He was hunting down believers and killing them and their entire families. He drug them out of their homes and stoned them to death. He gathered them and beat them. This was not a little roughing up. It was real and bloody persecution. Salvation changed his behavior. He did not continue in the sinful ways because he was covered by grace. I know that is an extreme example. When I was converted I stopped doing drugs and drinking and sleeping around. I did not continue to do those things because I was under grace. Being under grace gave me to desire to stop those behaviors. I know that most people are not that extreme. I imagine that you are reading this thinking that your sin was not that bad, so it is okay since you are under grace. There are a million things that we do that we think are not that bad, so it is alright. We gossip. Of course, we shadow it with believing we are talking about that person out of a concern for them, not out of malice. Still, a sin. We tell white lies, thinking that we could be protecting the person we are lying to. It is not a big sin, so it must be okay. We spend money foolishly, scroll for hours, procrastinate, do things in excess, and make excuses for our poor behavior. After all, these are little things, they do not matter to God. Or do they? Look at how dramatically the lives of the apostles changed. Has your life changed that dramatically? Parts of mine have. There are still areas where I fall very short though. When I do fall short and I sin and then do that sin again, thinking that it isn't so bad, this one is covered under grace, there is a change inside of me. I always know when I am acting outside of the values and character God has planned for me. I feel icky in my spirit. There is a tug, a little voice that is trying to pull me in a different direction. That is how grace works in my life. Holy Spirit whispers in my spirit, "you do not need to do that, there is a different direction." Before salvation, I did not have a choice but to sin. Today, through Holy Spirit, I get to choose. Are the things I am saying and doing glorifying God or me? I do not always answer correctly. Grace does not simply cover my sin; it gives me the option of doing things differently. I do not want to live a life of overt sin today. I want to be a clean temple for Holy Spirit to dwell in. Today I am choosing to not gossip, I am putting away the scrolling and in the midst of temptation I am turning to God, so that in the things I am choosing to do I am bringing glory to Him and not to myself. Is there a sin in your life you know should not be happening? Whether it is secret or out loud, if you are a child of God, Holy Spirit covers you in grace to choose to not do that thing. How are you choosing today?

Elijah was afraid and ran for his life.

1 Kings 19:3a

This verse amazes me. It also allows me to know that the human things I go through are not unique. I am not the only one who doubts and becomes afraid even though I have seen God do great and mighty things. In the passage before this, Elijah called down fire from God to devour an offering. It was not a private thing. There were 450 priests of the idols. Ahab was there. Not only did God hear Elijah and rain fire down on the offering, the offering had been doused in water. Yet it was still completely consumed. Then Elijah had those 450 priests of Baal slaughtered. That was not enough though. Elijah went to the top of Mount Carmel and, while the bible does not specifically say that Elijah prayed for rain, while he was up there with his face between his knees, the rains came, and the famine ended. That was still not the end. He then, overcome by the Spirit of God, ran, and beat a chariot to Jezreel. That is 31 miles that he ran and beat horses there. I imagine he had time to catch his breath and get settled before he got a message from Jezebel that she would avenge the lives of her priests and take his life tomorrow. After all of the amazing things God had just done through Elijah, he was scared of this angry woman. So much so that he ran away to the wilderness. How many times has this happened to me? I have seen God do many great things. I am a walking miracle. I was dying but I live. I was blind, but I see. I have seen people saved and prayers answered. Yet, let my bank account run low, or let me be alone a little too long and I become afraid and I run away. When I read this verse I realize how insane it sounds to run away. When I do run though, my story often takes a turn much like the one Elijah's takes in the next passage. He went into the wilderness where he asked God to let him die, and the Lord met him there. Then Elijah went into a cave. In the cave where Elijah went to hide in darkness with His fear, God also met him there. In His greatest compassion God showed Elijah that He was there with him. He did not coddle Elijah. He did not pat him on his head and tell him everything was going to be alright. God spoke to Elijah in a whisper and asked him why he was there. Elijah told the Lord that they were trying to kill him. In an answer, God gave Elijah a mission, to go back to where he came from. He told him when he got there, it would be okay. Elijah obeyed and the Lord provided the healing for his fear. When I am stuck in my fear, God always lets me know that He is right there with me. He is not only in the cave, but He is in the before, and in the wilderness. His presence comforts me and strengthens me to leave the cave so that He can heal the fear. Have you run away in fear? Did you ask God to let you die in the wilderness? Can you hear the whisper of God from the darkness of your cave? Have you felt His presence in the moments you thought you were alone and forgotten? God is there with you in the fear. He is whispering healing into your spirit. Can you hear Him?

When they kept on questioning Him, He straightened up and said to them, "Let any of you who is without sin be the first to throw the stone at her."

John 8:7

The Pharisees brought a woman to Jesus. She had been caught in adultery and they wanted to test Him in order to see if He would keep to the law of Moses and stone her. I always found it interesting that they left the man at home. That could be because I have been that woman. Judged by men who did the same things I did. I was judged by the people in the church I was raised in as a troubled youth. Parents did not want their kids hanging out with me. Church leaders did not involve me. I was looked down on and cast to the side. There was not much that had changed with the "Pharisees" of the church by that time. The truth is, they did not know how to help me and as cruel as it is, it is easier to appear righteous than to be kind. Jesus never had that problem though. For most of this story, it does not appear as though Jesus even looked at the woman. He focused on the ground. He bent down and wrote in the dirt. He spoke to the men pointedly and challenged them to show grace and mercy to this woman. Then He knelt down and wrote in the dirt again. I always wanted to know what he was writing in the dirt. Some scholars believe he was writing the names of the men and their sins beside it. We will never know though. What we do know is that they left without throwing one stone. I have often imagined this woman. She was facing an extremely brutal and painful death. Then she wasn't. She was shown grace and mercy that she did not deserve. Then Jesus offered her forgiveness. To live the life that she was living and to be caught red handed should have sealed her fate. Having the blessing of meeting Jesus that day changed her fate. When the Pharisees left, Jesus then addressed the woman. I imagine He looked her in the eye and that in that moment of the most intimate contact she would ever have, she not only heard Him not condemn her, she felt forgiven. That is one of the most pure feelings someone could feel. Then He told her to go and leave her sin. We do not know if she did that. I cannot imagine, after having that intimate moment with Jesus that she went back to the same life. She did not seek Him out. She did not ask to be relieved of her sin. However, in that moment of judgment by man, Jesus was there, in kindness, no condemnation, forgiving her. If you are a child of God, you have experienced this moment. Yet so often, we act as the Pharisees did that day. We see then sin in someone else and condemn them. We forget the feeling of forgiveness and in turn we take it from others. Often we do not carry the gratitude for the grace we have been shown and we fail to give that to those whose sin seems worse than our own. We cast them aside and look down on them. I encourage you to step out of judgment. Remember today how much you have been forgiven and share that with those around you. Instead of judging, be kind, show grace, and walk in mercy. Drop the stone that is in your hand. Unless, of course, you are without sin.

Always be prepared to give an answer to everyone who asks you to give the reason for the hope that you have. But do this with gentleness and respect.

1 Peter 3:15 b

In the last day of the last bible study I did, the very last question was, "Who is Jesus?" Seems as though that would be an easy question to answer. I can write out the answer, I think, easily enough. What if someone just walked up to me after a meeting and asked; or if someone I was having coffee with stopped conversation and posed the question? Could I say it as eloquently as I write it? Probably not. That does not matter though. It does not matter if I use fancy words or even if I stumble over them. What matters is that I have an answer. I know who Jesus is. He is the Word. He is Teacher and Master. He is my Refuge and Peace. Jesus is my Healer and my Hope. He is Salvation and Truth. My favorite, Jesus is the Lover of my soul. He is so much more though. Jesus was before the foundation of creation. He is the First and the Last. God wrapped Himself in flesh, stepped out of eternity and into time. He was born and lived a human life. He was a student before He was the Teacher. He was a child, submitted to His parents. He was a brother and a cousin. He was a son and is the Son. He was a carpenter. Jesus was a friend. He walked a life that was perfect on all counts. He was baptized and tempted. He healed bodies and challenged authority. Jesus was a rebel; I am fond of this one too. He was waited for but rejected when He got here. He is Love. Jesus was pure and innocent. He was a man and a lamb. He was unblemished but He was beaten so badly His mother could not recognize Him. Jesus was unbroken yet they nailed Him to the cross. He was ridiculed and scorned, but He forgave. He was without sin, but He chose to take in every single sin committed in time. He bore stripes and sin and anguish and pain so that I would not have to. He chose to die so that you would not have to. He covered the world with His blood, starting with 2 Pharisees who took Him off of the cross. He fought hell and in His victory, He conquered death and rose. He is the fulfillment of every word of scripture. He is the man who saved my life and my God who filled me with His Holy Spirit. He is the air I breathe and without Him I am lost. Jesus is the light in darkness and the wind on my face. He is how I know love. Who is Jesus? He is my everything. I pray, if someone ever stops and asks me why I have hope, these words are my answer. Jesus is my hope, my light, my salvation, and my love. If someone asked you today? What would you say? Would you be prepared with an answer? Could you say it with gentleness and respect? Who is Jesus?

Trust in the Lord with all your heart, and do not lean on your own understanding. In all your ways acknowledge him, and he will make straight your paths.

Proverbs 3:5-6

This is another one of those verses that is often difficult for me to wrap my head around. I mean, am I not the person in my life who makes the decisions and takes care of the things and does the stuff? I am the strong, independent woman that society says I should be. Society is very often wrong though. I find that more often than not, I understand the things that are happening better when I am taking all things to God first and man later. That does not mean that I understand completely, but I understand better. I am usually really bad at doing that though. Instead of trusting God with all my heart, I sometimes wonder if He really sees what is going on in my life. To me the things that are amiss are very blatant. There are times I wonder if God has on blinders when it comes to the things I am desiring in my heart. I forget that my relationship with God is about what I need, not always what I want. This is a season of remembering that though. I notice a definite difference in myself also. When I am in a place where I am trusting the Lord with all of my heart and I seek His understanding instead of my own, I am a much calmer person. My anxiety is super low, I do not anticipate so much and there are more days that I am present with God in this moment. When I intentionally take the time to acknowledge God in my decisions and actions, life is more smooth. Do not think that I am saying life gets easy. I would never say that. There are some days when I tread up hill and through mud and suffer a rocky road. However, when I am seeking and trusting God in all things first and foremost, the path I am on is straight. When I am independent of God and relying on self I still have the hills, the mud and the rocks, and I add in hairpin turns, loops, U-turns and dead ends. If I am trusting in myself, I am getting nowhere. As I trust in the Lord, lean on His understanding, and acknowledge Him, I am moving forward, even on the days that feel as though I am standing still. Are you a strong, independent person? Do you rely on self and draw your own map? I encourage you today to trust God, lean into Him and seek His face in all things. The path does not get easier; however, the straighter God makes your path, the simpler it is to walk.

Jesus wept.

John 11:35

It is easy to forget that Jesus walked the earth just like we do. While He was God, He was also man. He had human relationships and human emotions. When Lazarus died, regardless that Jesus was going to bring him back, He was weeping with the family. I think it is so sweet that in their moments of grief and pain, Jesus was there to be a friend. I know the bible does not say so, but I imagine when He talked to Mary and Martha that He placed a comforting hand on their shoulder. Perhaps when they were standing outside the tomb weeping, He held the hands of His friends, or even held them in His arms. Can you imagine being held in the arms of the Savior as you grieve? It does not need to be grief. Maybe you are just going through something difficult, and you need a friend. Perhaps this is a time of deep breakthrough in your life. The breath that brought Lazarus from the tomb breathes life inside of you. He is calling you out of where you are and inviting you into something completely new. He is not going to call you out and leave you alone. Jesus is constantly near to you. He walks every step with you. His precious Holy Spirit resides inside of your spirit. I know that we do not always feel him. It is difficult when we fear for our children, lose a loved one, or are simply stumped by decisions in life. It is easy to get caught up in the clamor of the world and convince ourselves that we cannot hear God's presence in the midst of our grief. He is here though. He is waiting for you to go to Him, hit your knees and ask Him to join you in this season. He wants to hold your hand and cradle you in His arms as you weep, mourn, and grow. He desires that you know you are not alone. He is there and He is weeping with you. Find time to release yourself to Holy Spirit, let the tears flow, no matter the reason they are flowing. Allow whatever fear, grief, anger, anticipation, or decision you are holding onto to be released into the care and will of God. With that release, know that Jesus is right there beside you, standing in front of the tomb. He is calling a newness to your life in unimaginable ways. Can you feel Him with you? Do you know that Jesus wants to weep with you? Release yourself to Him.

Let such a person understand that what we say by letter when absent, we do when present.

2 Corinthians 10:11

This verse is the definition of integrity for me. Paul very simply stated, what I write about, I walk out. When I read this verse I had to stop and wonder if it applies to me. I want to display the words that I say. So this verse is a challenge for me to look at what I am doing and the things I am saying. It is not always a pretty reflection. I am a human so naturally I fall short of the goal, and I do not hit the target every day. However, each day I do wake up and ask God to walk with me, to guide me in His will and to show me where I am out of step. What I know is that I believe the Word of God. I know that His word is alive and breathes life into me. God causes changes to be effective inside of me so that as I grow I am able to act as I write. Paul had been a follower of Christ 17-20 years before he started to write the Epistles. It is easy for me to forget that he was not a 6 year old Christian when he was teaching people how to behave. I forget that there is a learning process. I lived 36 years with no integrity at all. Today, that just is not true. I value integrity today. I enjoy knowing that people who know me know that I am, mostly doing and getting better at doing the things that I write about doing. I am not saying that I write things that are not true. I will always tell you that I am having a rough time, or I am battling a temptation. What I am learning to be better at are the things that God shows me as I write for you. I am growing in kindness and joy and peace. I am learning discernment and how to lean on God's strength in my weakness. There are things that I am rededicating my life to that I have stepped around and made excuses for so that my actions will better reveal my words. I think we forget that Paul had a process. Just like Peter. I mean, that dude walked right beside Jesus for 3 years and still cut off someone's ear. He still had his prejudices even after he was filled with Holy Spirit. What he did not do was hold onto those. He surrendered himself to God through Christ and Holy Spirit and, like Paul, he changed so that his actions could look like his words. How do you walk today? Do your steps resemble your words? Do you walk like you talk and live in integrity? If not is that something you are trying to grow into or are you talking without walking?

Yet you are holy, enthroned on the praises of Israel.

Psalm 22:3

I love that this verse is encased in this passage. David was not having a good day when he penned these words. He starts the chapter wanting to know why God had forsaken him. He refers to himself as a worm. He talks about being ridiculed and mocked. He had run out of strength and felt as though he was being surrounded by hungry dogs. Can you imagine a day like that? I can. That describes how I felt almost every day of last year. David handled it better than I think that I did. Inside of having a really bad day he penned about thirteen verses about how horrible he was having it and eighteen about praising God and God's goodness. He wrote about the kingship of the Almighty, how those who seek after him will be well. David talks about how God does not despise or abhor the afflicted. David praises God in the moment that he feels as though his world is collapsing. I have to stop and think, do I do that? I definitely do not do it as eloquently. It does not matter if my praise sounds better than David's or even just as good as. Praise God for that because I cannot imagine my words being on that caliber. However, what is the answer to the most important question? When life is falling in on me, do I spend more time praising God or complaining about me? I know that when I praise God He is there with me. I do not just know that because David says so. I know it because I have experienced His presence in my life. You would think that since I do know that and I have experienced that I would naturally turn to praising God as soon as trouble hits. That is not my method though. While I am getting better about it, what I usually do is first freak out then cry then stomp my feet. Once I am exhausted I wonder what God thinks of the situation. Then I will turn on some praise music and release myself to worship and surrender. It is an exhausting process. It is one that I know I am not alone in though. David's first verses of this chapter were whining and moaning about his situation and feelings. Then he acknowledged. Then there was more complaining about him. Ultimately, praising God took over his attitude. It is comforting to know that I do not have to do the process in the perfect order and that I am not alone in doing it backwards. I do have a new goal to work towards though. The next time my world is caving in and I feel the worthlessness creeping in, I am going to be intentional about praising God and inviting Him into that moment with me. Perhaps then the pain will not last as long. What is your process? Do you complain mostly about you, giving God only what is left over? Do you invite Him into your situations through praise? I challenge you today to invite God in first and see if you still want to complain later.

But God shows his love for us in that while we were still sinners, Christ died for us.

Romans 5:8

I love the translation of this verse that says, "He loved me at my darkest." The darkness is different for everyone. For me, the darkest moment was like being curled up in a ball in the deepest, darkest corner of a cellar. That cellar was under the darkest, coldest part of a basement. I did not think I would ever get out of that place. The dark was impenetrable and oppressive. I had no hope, no light, nothing that was even a little bit soothing. I was going mad in that place, a slow loss of mind that is agonizing and brutal. I only knew pain and had totally forgotten what pleasure of any kind was like. I was helpless to make it stop. I would plead for death only to continue to breathe. I despised everything and loved nothing. But God. Jesus ripped through the darkness that I had been helpless to move in. He held me and loved me as I healed. He kissed my forehead, and my mind began again to blossom. When I did not want to breathe for myself, He did that for me until I could hold my own. The light of the Kingdom of the Almighty was shining in my life for the first time and there was no darkness left. It was amazing. I was free and for the first time in my life I fully trusted God. Then tragedy struck. It was not a death, but still the loss of a child. She was here and then with someone else. I prayed for God to intervene and, as always, He gave exactly what was needed, not what was so desperately wanted. The agony of emotions caused a crisis of confusion and the foundation I thought was so strong began to crack and I began to sway. I did not go back to the same darkness. I have been out of the bottom for years. This was something different. I was experiencing a cocktail of grief, loss of control and a diminishing of faith. My decisions became selfish and fell out of alignment with the will of God. For three years I walked in a fog of disappointment and anger. But God. I know that any place without the presence of God is darkness, even if one stage is not quite as deep as the first, dark is still dark. God, again swooped into my life and saved me from myself. I had failed to realize that when scripture says all things work to good for them who love the Lord, that really meant ALL the things, not just the ones that felt good. I also forgot that even when it feels like your heart is being slowly pulled from your chest, even that is possible to heal from with Jesus. Today though, I am grateful that God never leaves me nor forsakes me. It is me who does those things to Him. Since I am His daughter though, He will get my attention. I find it very difficult to ignore Jesus when He walks into my darkness and loves me when I am so unlovable. Today is not dark. The light of the Kingdom of the Great I AM is beaming in my life. Jesus said in Mark 11:22, "Have faith in God." Though the world may shake, my faith will only grow from here on. Whether you are in a time of darkness or having the brightest day of your life, I pray you see Jesus in it and know that He loves you in all times.

You were running well. Who hindered you from obeying the truth?

Galatians 5:7

Do you ever read scripture and feel called out or punched in the gut? I know that is what is supposed to happen, but sometimes it is very uncomfortable when scripture gut punches me like this verse did. Paul was talking to the Galatians about the significant difference of circumcision of law and circumcision of heart. What strikes me is that the Galatians had believed in the difference at the beginning of their conversions and had sunk back into the slavery of the law (v. 1). When reading this passage I had to stop and question things. I know freedom in Christ, but is there somewhere I have gone back into the bondage of slavery of the law or anything else? Yes. For several years I was very legalistic. The outside looked as it was supposed to, modest and pious. My speech was as it should be. I followed the rules and did what I was told. My day became more about doing enough to show Jesus I am His rather than resting in the truth that He already knew that. The truth is, Jesus doesn't care if I wear jeans rather than a skirt. He could care less if I put on mascara or not. When I am swearing in my heart, He hears that louder than if it slips out of my tongue. I had replaced the inward circumcision with the outward. Not that I have a foreskin to cut, but it amounts to the same. The refined outside was covering up the messy inside. I was broken and if I said that would be looked at as if I was doing something wrong. Regardless of the fact that tragedy had struck my heart and the process of grief was rampant. I traded the ability to run into the Throne Room for the guise of making it all look alright on the outside. I shoved everything under an imaginary rug and became a slave to the bondage of unworthiness, disappointment, and inadequacy. In this verse Paul asks a very poignant question. Who hindered you from obeying the truth? The answer is me. I stood in my own way. I listened to the legalistic teachings and put aside what I already believed to be true. I made the decision to do it man's way instead of the way of the God and His Gospel. Such conviction in this short verse. Today I am changing. The process started months ago. I am remembering how to be free in Christ rather than in bondage to my humanity. I am stringing together more days when I am resting rather than working. I run, unabashedly to the Throne Room instead of covering things up so that my inner spirit is more beautifully modest than anything on the outside could ever be. Today, my circumcision is truly of the heart and not just of the flesh. I have stopped hindering myself so that I can again run well. How are you running today? Where has the circumcision happened in you? Do you use the refined outside to cover up the mess on the inside? Are you being hindered from obeying the truth? How can you change that today.

But she answered him, "Yes, Lord; yet even the dogs under the table eat the children's crumbs."

Mark 7:28

I love this passage. This woman was a Gentile. In no uncertain terms Jesus called her a dog. His point was not that she was subhuman. Only that the chosen people of God were to be filled first. This woman took it in great stride. She did not question what the Jews thought of her. She would have known their prejudices and, naturally, would have applied those to Jesus. After all, He was a Jewish Rabbi. Since she knew her place in this house, she agreed with Him as she countered Him. In layman's terms, the verse says, "I am a dog, and I only need a crumb." There is such pure and raw truth in these words. They are also amazing. She said that she only needed the leftovers. She would have heard testimony and perhaps witnessed Jesus performing miracles. She had to have known the power of Christ because everyone was talking about this man who walked all over Israel healing people of all kinds of things. It is even possible that she heard of Legion being sent out of the madman at Gadarenes. This woman believed that her daughter only needed a crumb of the power of God to be okay. This Gentile dog knew that only a little would be sufficient. Can you imagine? Even His own people thought Jesus was a fraud. They accused Him of working for the enemy. Yet, this woman, outside of her religion and territory, came to Him and humbled herself. She owned exactly who she was and asked for the smallest amount, believing, and knowing that it would be enough. And He said yes. It is so easy to get lost in the thinking that we deserve the full meal from God. After all, we are Americans and Christians by nationality and all the ridiculous entitlement bondage. It is easy to forget that if we got what we deserved we would all spend eternity in hell. This story reminds me to come to God in humility of the pure and raw truth of who I am. Though today I know He does not see me as a dog worthy only of the crumbs, there was a day, not so long ago, that this is who I was. It is only by the grace and mercy of God and the cleansing blood of Christ that I belong now to the people of God. Have you forgotten where you came from? Do you get lost in the pride of entitlement of your identity? Or do you go to God in humility, knowing that it is only because of Christ that you are no longer a dog, deserving only of the crumbs?

Yea though I walk through the valley of the shadow of death, I will fear no evil for You are with me.

Psalm 23:4

The valley of death is not my own this time. I find that this valley has different purposes. Sometimes it is my own shadow that is the cause of death and evil and I place myself in the valley. At other times it is simply the natural low cycle of life. This time, however, I have a different purpose inside the valley of the shadow of death. It is to be a beacon. My walk here today is to trudge with the people who are having a hard time getting out of the muck and mire. I am not here alone. Holy Spirit has come here with me and it is the light of Christ that shines through. I am only a vessel, willing to help God as He leads people out. The evil snipping at the heels of the people I love is disguised as a bottle or a pill, a plant or even sex. It presents itself as unbearable sadness, fear, and unworthiness. The evil looks like shame and regret. Today I am not trembling at the evil. I can look around and know that He who is with me is greater than the darkness that surrounds this place. My call at this time is to be a pillar through whose cracks the light of the Great I AM shines. For every step I take with Holy Spirit, He touches someone in the valley. There are those He picks up and carries, allowing me to help them trudge through the darkness until they can walk out. I do not fear this place today because I am trudging with God. I will walk this valley as long as He needs me here so that His light shines on the path of those who are desperate and dying. I will continue to plant His seeds as I walk. Are you stuck in the valley? If you need help, please reach out to the beacons of light that are around you. Is your purpose like mine today? Are you walking in the Light, helping others to trudge? I pray for all of you today. Walk with God. Carry the message, let Holy Spirit shine through you. And when the evil is snipping at your heels, kick it in the teeth. Do not fear, for God is with us.

Come to terms quickly with your accuser.

Matthew 5:25a

I sometimes feel like I live in two different worlds. On one side I have this huge family of people who were once societal outcasts, on the other, I get to walk with some of the most normal people you will ever meet. I love it when my two worlds cross over and everyone is exactly the same, while still being wildly different. It happens when God's word is directing all of us in the same manner. In AA we work the 12 steps of recovery. Part of step 10 says, "when you are wrong, promptly admit it." Jesus says, "come to terms quickly with your accuser." This verse, and countless others, connects the two worlds I walk through. Long before we had the program of AA Jesus taught us how to live. I am particularly fond of quickly coming to terms with others because being able to do so keeps me from walking in anger. The bible says to do it because if I don't, I will be put in prison until the last penny is paid. For me, if I don't come to terms with people, the prison is of my own mind. I sink into "what ifs" and resentment. These things eat at me like poison and cause damage that is self-inflicted and unnecessary. Adversely, if I lay down my pride and ego and humbly go to the person I'm having a problem with, I get to take responsibility for my part, make amends, and walk in freedom. I do not do this perfectly. Often, I do not do it well. However, I do it willingly and with the guidance of Holy Spirit. I pray often and ask God to show me if I have been in a situation I need to address and if so, I ask Him to go back with me and to help me correct it. Do you have something against someone today? Is there someone you are harboring negative feelings against? Do you feel the prison if your mind feeding you poison and trapping you? Go, quickly, and make it right. Walk in freedom today.

Peace I leave with you; my peace I give to you. Not as the world gives do I give to you. Let not your hearts be troubled, neither let them be afraid.

John 14:27

In the last few years I have experienced chaos in several ways. The hardest seasons of chaos have been the ones of grief. The cycle seems to drag on. I think I should be further in healing than where I am and then wake up and feel as though I'm at the beginning again. Inside of grief it is so difficult to feel peace. Jesus said He was leaving peace with us. That does not mean I will always feel it. However, it does mean I always have it. The greatest grief I have ever felt in my life was in the adoption of my granddaughter. While she is not gone from the world, she is gone from my arms. I struggled in denial and anger. I fought through bargaining and depression. Now, most days I am able to rest in acceptance. Grief will have its process though. Even now, years later, I wake up with arms that ache to hold a baby I've never known. What I have known, the whole time is a deep seeded peace. I do not always feel peace around the situation. Sometimes I still get angry and there are days I find myself bargaining with God. Even on the absolute worst days, while my mind is troubled, my heart is not. I know the peace of Jesus. I know Holy Spirit is here and walking with me. I also know that when God sent His Son to die, He felt loss; loss so great the sky went as dark as my loss has felt in me. Knowing that the peace within me comes from God who has felt what I feel and is walking through this with me, helps me to feel His peace. Knowing the peace God has left with me helps me to not live in the grief. He holds my hand and we walk through it, He teaches me to accept it and He helps my heart to not be troubled. I am not afraid of the grief process today because I do not grieve alone.

Wait for the Lord; be strong and let your heart take courage; wait for the Lord!

Psalm 27:14

Waiting is, by far, the hardest thing I have needed to do in my walk with Christ. It ebbs and flows like the seasons. Sometimes it is harder than others. I become impatient and frustrated with the wait. Currently I am in a season of wondering. I wonder about things that are none of my business. I become consumed with "Why them" and "When is it my turn" questions. There is this amazing time of being absolutely thrilled and so happy for the people around me whose wait in this area has completed, while at the same time, feeling this aching agony deep within of continuing in my own wait. Yet, I keep stepping forward in the waiting. I do not lose the courage it takes to walk this path I have chosen. God gave me the choice to live for Him. The choice was not to pick and choose in which seasons to live for Him. The choice is the ultimate vow of in the good times and the bad. In these seasons of wondering if He sees me, does He know, I feel so very weak. Scripture reminds me that God not only sees me, but He has strength for me. God's word beckons me closer to Him in the days when I just do not want to wait. He leads me beside the still waters. He reminds me that He is the Lover of my soul and that He will never leave me, nor forsake me. In the waiting He reminds me that the waiting is not forever. It is okay for me to have days of weakness as long as I am going to God for my strength. I always think that I do not wait well. What I am really learning in this very agonizing season, is that I am not waiting alone. God renews my strength and courage every time I go to Him. He places people on my path who are waiting on the same things and He lets us support and lean on each other. God asks me to wait, but never has He asked me to wait alone. Some days that does not make the waiting easier, however, when the waiting is over, it will have been so very worth it. Are you waiting for something? On those days when you are tired and crying and wondering when it is your turn, in that weakness, go to God. Let Him renew your strength and your courage. Do not give up. Wait on the Lord.

For I know the plans I have for you declares the Lord, plans to prosper you and not to harm you, plans to give you hope and a future.

Jeremiah 29:11

This verse is full of hope and peace in a time when the people it was written for did not feel or know those things. The people of God were in exile, slaves to the Babylonians. In the passage just before this verse Jeremiah told them God wanted them to settle into the life of struggle. He knew it would be a long time before they saw the end of bondage. Through Jeremiah, God told his people to plant, prosper, and pray for the long haul. Then this nugget verse is planted right in the middle of the chaos. It is often amusing to me how I can see that all things do work to good for those who love the Lord and are called to His purpose (Romans 8:28). As God tells his people that they will be captive and bonded in slavery, He also takes the time to remind them that, even when it seems like there is no plan, the best plan is at play. Inside of what had to seem like a never ending chaos, God never stopped giving His people a hope for the future. In the next verses He tells His people that if they will pray, He will hear them. He even promised that if they sought Him, He would be there to be found. How amazing is God? The context of this verse is in no way written to us today. However, the spirit of the verse and the lesson it holds stands the test of time. Everyone, at some point, experiences their own bondage in Babylon, seemingly never-ending chaos, and pain plagues seasons of each of our lives. Though it does not look the same as what the Israelites endured over and again, the oppression feels the same. In the midst of those seasons, though, God does for us what He did for the Israelites so long ago. Even now, His best plan is at play. There is hope inside of all these times. If you are walking in one of these seasons, bound by pain or chaos or oppression, pray and call on God. He does not promise to always deliver you immediately, however, He does promise that He will hear you and He will be found by you. Seek Him and find freedom in His presence. Take hope in His plan for your future.

And after saying this he said to him, "Follow me."

John 21:19b

Amazing things are happening in this entire passage. I really wanted to write about feeding the sheep today, but Holy Spirit kept pulling me here. Jesus has such an amazing encounter with Peter. He asked Peter three times if he loved Him. Each time Peter said yes and each time Jesus gave him the same command - take care of my flock - said three different ways. Then Jesus told Peter how he would die. He did not outright say that he would be crucified upside down. He did make it very clear in the language of the day as to how Peter's life would end. Peter would follow Christ. This is not the first time Jesus said these two simple words to Peter. The first time saying yes altered the course of Peter's life. He left everyone and everything he knew and walked Israel with Jesus. He learned from Him and was in awe of Him. Peter ate with Him and he laughed with Christ. He thought he would have bled for Him, then he denied Jesus three times. Jesus let Peter tell Him three times that he loved Him to cover the three denials. Jesus then gave Peter a job. It was not just any job, but to take care of His children. Jesus does not stop there though. He tells Peter exactly what it will cost him. This time, when Jesus says those two beautiful words to Peter, they have a different weight. Now Peter knows what the end will hold. He understands that when Jesus says "follow me" this time, He means to the cross, not across the desert. His response? He asks Jesus what will happen to John. To answer, Jesus told Peter to stay in his own lane. He said (paraphrase) "What business is it of yours what happens with your neighbor? Follow me." So, Peter did. Can you imagine walking away from that conversation? Peter knew he would die; it is the natural order of things. Now he knew how he would die if this is what he did. He did it anyway. I like to think that I would have said yes too. I even think now that I would want to follow Jesus no matter the outcome. Then I look at the things God has asked me to do so far. For example, writing this book. It has taken a LONG time. I feel unworthy and often defeated. And these are simple words on a page, He isn't asking me to continue a revolution and at the end be crucified. What are you not doing that God has asked of you? Spending less time on social media or putting your phone down? Stopping that bad habit? Leaving that toxic relationship? Communicating with Him more? Opening your bible instead of Netflix? The outcome of the things we are asked to do is so small, yet entirely valid in our walk with Christ. Jesus is not asking you to be crucified, only to follow Him, no matter the outcome. Are you willing to follow Him?

Give thanks in all circumstances; for this is the will of God in Christ Jesus for you.

1 Thessalonians 5:18

This has been a hard verse for me to swallow recently. There for quite a while I did very well praising God in all circumstances. My things were falling apart around me. It was alright though. God knew what was happening and He saw me and heard my cries. He was still Provider and Lover of my soul and all of the things. Then things started to pile up on top of each other. That was good. In the midst of the chaos I had peace beyond understanding and joy in the morning. I was thankful for the things that were still working and that God gave me the ability to help others. After that though, I started to feel the weight of pouring out and not being poured back into. The heaviness of the pile of stuff and the broken things and the giving and the serving was becoming exhausting. (Isn't it funny how we can become worn out even by the good we are doing if we are not taking care of ourselves and doing the good from a place of thankful gratitude?) I was still thankful in the heaviness. I had talked to God and we decided that things would change. Less of this, only some of that, a lot more rest. I am really bad at that though. Then the other day, I encountered the straw that broke the camel's back. I mean, it is a pretty big thing, however, had I experienced that one thing just by itself, I probably could have reacted with a thankful heart for the mass of positive things that surrounded the event. Thanks was not my reaction though. Now, for days really, I have been in a place of being done. I look back and think, I have done this, this, and this and for what? Lies crept in. Fear had become the forefront of my days. I had become so frustrated in the last few days that I told someone I was done with the church, with the program and I would be fine on my own because alone is how I felt anyway. I would dig myself out. I had reached a really ugly place. God has a way of talking to me in irony though. This verse has been stuck in my head for days now. I cannot shake it but I do not want to swallow it. Holy Spirit whispers in my ear, do what you have told countless numbers of people to do in the last several years, Cara. Be thankful. The circumstance is not the will of God for you, the peace in the thankfulness is though. Life sucks right now. Be thankful. You have been crying in public. Be thankful. You are not getting your way. Praise God for that. This morning I know that being inside thankfulness is the will of God for me. If I choose to be there instead of in the junk I have been recently, the junk doesn't matter. I will be able to walk in faith that my Provider and the Lover of my soul will take care of the stuff. I only need to be thankful in all of the ugly and the uncomfortable. That is so hard. However, that is what I am going to do today. If you are in the thick of the junk, I encourage you to be thankful. Change your perspective and focus on the goodness of the Lord. There, in the being thankful for all things, we will find the peace beyond our understanding and that is the will of God in Jesus for us.

For though the righteous fall seven times they rise again.

Proverbs 24:16a

Lately I feel like a weeble-wobble. Those little toys take hit after hit. They bang into the ground, but they stand right back up. It doesn't matter if it is hit from the front, side, or back. It goes down and comes back up. The problem is that I'm not made of plastic. The hits hurt. Recently it seems like I barely get my feet back under me and I'm down again. Sometimes I get hit so hard it's like I bounce back and forth, unable to regain my bearings before the next strike. The constant battle is exhausting and overwhelming. I am in a constant state of emotional hangover while still feeling a bit punch drunk. Strangely enough, I know that this will pass and I'm entering a season of rest. Inside of that knowing, while I'm still getting knocked around, I also know that I'm not alone. God is here and working all of these things to my good. Right now I'm having a hard time seeing the good, but that isn't my business. The constant bashing is also none of my business. My role is to stop trying to regain my balance on my own. I'm not great at that. What is happening though is the longer I am in this part of this struggle, I'm not able to get up by myself as quickly. I'm becoming weak and weakness is turning into a beautiful thing. Inside of this deep weakness, I am understanding that self-reliance avails me nothing. I have no strength left. But God. He is utilizing this time to help me. My faith is blossoming. My reliance on Him is strengthening. Between the two of us a new trust is forming. It is uncomfortable and painful, and I do not like it. However, God is growing me in this time as I weeble-wobble. As each hit gets deeper, His strength gets stronger. Because of the righteousness of Christ who dwells in me, by the Spirit who carries the breath of God into my trial, I will get up seven more times and seven more after that. I encourage you today, if you are in a weeble-wobble season, lean into God to help you up every time you are knocked down. Let Him be your footing and your balance. If you are not in this season, I want to also encourage you to lean into God in preparation for your turn. We can all stand, but when you fall do you rise again.

Then Jesus said, "Come to me, all of you who are weary and carry heavy burdens, and I will give you rest.

Matthew 11:28

In the hustle and bustle of life rest seems to be very elusive. Most days I wake up still tired from the months before. I have a job and then I have life and church and recovery and the gym. I develop relationships and fellowship. Somewhere in there I find time to eat and shower. There are days when I leave my house early in the morning and don't make it back till late at night. Rest is a funny thing though. If I am going on my own steam, giving God the last and rest instead of my first and best, I become weary and the loads I carry seem so much heavier. In the times when I prioritize my relationship with God to come before all of the things that fill my schedule, it doesn't really matter how much sleep I get because my spirit is at rest. Martin Luther said, "I have so much to do today, I must first pray 3 hours." I have found that true rest has very little to do with the amount of time that I sleep. I can sleep enough to rest my body physically, however, if I am not resting in the Lord then my spirit and mind are not rested. When that happens, it matters very little what my body feels. When I am intentional about resting in the Lord though, my life feels lighter and my days longer. How is your rest today? Is it something you focus on only physically, or are you truly resting in the Lord? I pray you rest in Him. If you are weary and have a lot that you carry, lay it down, rest in God and be renewed.

So do not fear, for I am with you; do not be dismayed, for I am your God. I will strengthen you and help you; I will uphold you with my righteous right hand.

Isaiah 41:10

There are times when "do not fear" is the most difficult of all commandments. I have been walking through this weird season. I was taking financial punch after financial punch. It accumulated to the point that I was almost ready to scream. Inside of that time God was urging me to trust Him. Today I know that He was quickly preparing me to trust Him with the small stuff because there was big stuff coming. In my life there is not just a whole lot that makes finances seem like the small stuff. Doctors have become one of those things. I had one of those life altering doctor's appointments. There were tests and more tests. Then there were results. Not terminal, but progressive. Irreversible. Fear. I do very often find God quite funny. All of the financial worry disappeared. As I think about it now, I find that impressive because there is extra financial burden now. I do not think of that much though, because I trust God to provide. I do not know that I have fully processed the news. I feel like a newcomer again, taking first steps into the knowledge of a disease whose sole purpose is to kill me slowly and learning from scratch how to cope with and manage that disease so that I am able to live longer, fuller and as healthy as possible. In the last few weeks I have sunk into this weird despair. I did not think I was being driven by fear, but that is not accurate. I have been consumed by it. I only realized that when I read this verse. It's strange how we can be inside of fear and not realize that we are there. Today I am going to be intentional about trusting God in this very big thing. I am going to rest in His righteous right hand. I am very weak right now, but I will be confident in His strength and His help. As I commit to these things today I can feel His presence grow and the diminishing of fear. While I am tired, I do not feel the dismay that I felt even only moments ago. Are you in the thick of fear? Have you known it was there or are you only now seeing it? Go to God. Be intentional about trusting Him in this time. Do not be dismayed, for He is with you.

384

For this light momentary affliction is preparing for us an eternal weight of glory beyond all comparison.

2 Corinthians 4:17

I always thought Paul was a bit off his rocker when he wrote this verse. Surely he didn't suffer as I do because what I am feeling is not light and nothing about it is momentary. I was partly right. Paul did not suffer as I do. He had it so much worse. Beaten, stoned, shipwrecked, ridiculed, and persecuted. Yet, as he wrote in plain ink, he considered those things light and momentary affliction. Some days I understand, and I feel the same way. Other days, I am crying out to God to remove the irritations and pain of life. Paul did that too. Regardless that he cried out for relief, Paul knew that what he was going through was light and momentary. He understood that glory was coming then his human life was complete. Paul recognized that humanity is but a temporary reality and what is to come is a vast eternity of amazing glory. I know those things also and I know them every day. However, every day I do not live in that. Right now, I am going through a weird time of grief. I am in the time of asking God to remove things instead of having any desire to walk through them. The truth of the situation is that though it seems heavy and burdensome in the present moment, it truly is light and momentary. No matter what happens inside of my humanity, it will not last. This is only a temporary reality and the affliction I feel inside is light and only momentary. The best truth about this temporary reality is what it is preparing me for. The unseen and eternal glory that is coming will diminish this life into dust. That does not mean that humanity hurts less. It just allows a change of perspective. When I am looking at life through the lens of God's time, it makes the pain more bearable. It also makes it simpler to walk in the truth of this verse today even though what I feel is the exact opposite. Are you in the midst of affliction today? Focus on the eternity that is to come instead of today's temporary reality. Regardless that it feels heavy, believe that this is only light and momentary. The glory of eternity with the Lord is to come.

My soul thirsts for God, for the living God.

Psalm 42:2a

I have been in this time of drought. Several times I have thought that the end was on the horizon only to find an oasis in the middle of the desert. That is great, those times nourished and sustained me so that I could continue to walk forward into the desert. It just seems like the desert is so very vast and never ending. I am sure part of it is of my own making. There are things I do to be less lost, but as I said, those things are simply an oasis in the midst of nothingness. I do know that most people go through these times. David certainly went through them. This chapter speaks of David going through a time where his food had been his tears, his soul is cast down and in turmoil within him. David knows the way out though. He felt it in the thirst of his soul. I feel this verse today in the deepest recesses of my spirit. I am thirsty for God. In the chaos of new knowledge and trying desperately to reach a place of acceptance, I have neglected the Living Water. When I do that, the desert grows, and the drought thickens. If I would stop trying desperately, go before the Lord, hope in God, and praise Him (v. 5b), I would again find the oasis. If I would do those things daily, on a regular basis, creating a lifestyle of worship, the oasis would grow, and the desert would shrink. The rains would come, and the drought would end. Yet my soul would still thirst for more of God. That is the nature of our relationship, as deep calls to deep and I spend more time in praise and glory, I only thirst for more. God is always ready to fulfill that thirst and to continue it as well. I see a new oasis on the horizon this morning. I get to choose how long I stay there. Every day that I wake up and satisfy the thirst of my soul with the Living Water of the Lord, the oasis will grow until there is no more desert. Are you in a time of desert and drought? Is your soul cast down and in turmoil? Go before the Lord, hope in God and praise Him. He is salvation not only for the next life, but also for these troubles of this one.

For whatever does not proceed from faith is sin.

Romans 14:23c

There have been times when I have gotten caught up in what is sin and what is not sin. I have read Romans over and again, but I do not recall seeing this verse before. Paul is very clear about what is sin and what is not sin. Anything done outside of faith is a sin. There are some things that are overtly done outside of faith. I cannot smoke in faith. I cannot be a glutton inside of faith. I cannot be immoral in any way and say that I have done those things in faith. Then it gets a little tricky. What if I am ministering and that ministry was self-ordained and did not proceed from faith? There have been times when I was doing so very much. I was running myself into the ground for God. God did not ask me to run myself into the ground. He wants me to serve Him, in the manner that He created me for. There is a distinct calling on my life, as well as yours. When I am walking in the manner that fulfills that purpose and I am being obedient to what the Lord has told me, the things I am doing are proceeding from faith. That does not mean I can't help where there is lack if I am doing so in a manner that is not crowding out God's will in my life. When that happens, I stop doing things out of faith and being acting in self-will. That produces sin - even though that sin appears to be good works. If Paul would have tried to do Peter's job, he would not have been proceeding out of faith. The things that we do amount to the same thing. I want very much to be inside of the will of God for my life. I know that when I am firmly planted in that, life is so very abundant. When the things I am doing are proceeding from faith and not from self, that is where I find peace beyond understanding, joy in the morning and hope that surpasses chaos. Finding God's will for my life is not as hard as it sounds. It only takes a little time and quiet. I find it inside of my relationship with God. When I get alone and nurture our bond, listen to His voice, talk to Him about all the things and choose to be immediately obedient,

I find that I can feel God urging me to go left or right. When I follow that urge the thing I am doing is proceeding from faith. I encourage you today to examine why you are choosing the things you are doing. Have you discussed that thing with the Lord? Is it His will, or are you acting out of self? Does this act proceed from faith, or could it be a sin?

Does not the Lord go out before you?

Judges 4:14c

Some days are rough. There are times when I am disturbed, and I wallow in the disturbance until I begin to feel defeated. Inside of exhaustion it is the worst. Inside of exhaustion is where I have been recently. Test results and more results. I went to the doctor for a solution for one issue and now I have several issues and few solutions. I got stuck in the muck of new information. Everything got heavy. Trudging the road got slower and slower. The battleground of my mind became foggy and hard to maneuver. It feels as though I have been stepping side to side, not moving forward, but wrapped in a weird dance with a partner I cannot see. I have been at war and the exhaustion had been steadily getting deeper and deeper until that is all I could see. The enemy has been standing before me and making it hard to breathe. He is in my face. But God is in my spirit. While this has been a hard time, the victory has already been had. The Lord has been here before I ever stepped foot in this battle. He knew I would struggle to take the next step. He felt the armor getting heavy. God tested the depth of the muck of this field He knew I would need to trudge. While He was here, long before I got here, He declared victory over this place. Not only was He here first, but He is also here again with me now. God did not leave me to this fight by myself. He is with me every step of the way. Holy Spirit breathes into my lungs while I feel as though I am losing my breath. There are people all around me who are holding my arms as we trudge together so that I do not remain stuck in the muck. There are days when I feel defeated and weak. On those days, God is there giving me His strength and whispering reminders of victory over my spirit. Are you in a battle today? Do you feel as though you cannot take another step forward? Have you forgotten that the Lord has already been here, and this battle is already won? I encourage you today to get alone with Him.

Let God whisper His sweet reminders of victory over your situation. Pick up your armor and step into the battle. You are not alone here.

Take every thought captive to obey Christ.

2 Corinthians 10:5c

The past month has been rough. I was just tired. Enough so that I needed to go to the doctor. What happened was hard news on top of hard news on top of waiting and waiting some more. In the process Last week, I hit this weird bottom of myself. I went to my safe place, and I word vomited all over the place. The things I was thinking were pouring out of my mouth. My thoughts were captive to the things of the world and the complications rather than being centered in Christ. When that happened, I did not actually realize it was going on. Very quickly though, the exhaustion increased. My mood shifted to despair. I started to think with the addict part of my make-up rather than the Christ centered being of my identity. I was putting stock in what the humans were saying instead of what my Creator has already said. I had started to walk in disobedience of the defeat of illness. Last week a very dear friend pulled me aside and basically told me to armor up and look to God instead of man. So that is what I have been doing. Amazing things happen when I take every thought captive to obey Christ. I walk in surrender to the victory that He has already given me. Isaiah said that by His stripes we are healed (53:5) and Peter says by His stripes we were healed (1 Peter 2:24). All through the New Testament we read stories of how faith made people whole. Paul said in his second letter to the Corinthians that we are new creations (5:17). These are the thoughts I have not been taking captive to obey in Christ. Today, I am not living inside of the lie of defeat. That does not mean that God will heal me in the manner I deem worthy. It does mean that I know He can, and I walk in the victory of that belief. Today, I bring every thought captive to obey Christ in all things. I obey His victory, His healing, and His ability to make me new. My thoughts today are not captive to the world but to the truth of my identity in Christ. The things that I am thinking today will also come out of my mouth in an effort to edify, encourage and inspire my fellows to lean into Christ. How are your thoughts today? Are you bringing them captive to the things of the world or to obey Christ? I encourage you to bring all thoughts captive today to obey Christ.

In the days when the judges ruled there was a famine in the land, and a man of Bethlehem in Judah went to sojourn in the country of Moab, he, and his wife and his two sons.

Ruth 1:1

Elimelech had hit his breaking point in the famine. There wouldn't have been enough food or enough water. He had had enough. Elimelech knew that if he just crossed the border things would be better than if he stayed. This famine was in the time of the judges of Israel. The people consistently turned their backs on God and did what was most self-serving instead of standing in the promise God had given. For Elimelech to cross the border God had made and walk away from the promised land and the promise of God, was really not so surprising for the times. Regardless, there were consequences. Elimelech did not go alone. He took his family with him. Though the outcome of the story is amazing love and the line of Christ, the story begins with defiance that leads to death. When I read this verse and I understood the implications of Elimelech's decision, I had a visceral reaction. I have been this man. There was a very specific time in my walk with God that I endured famine. It was a time of unbelievable grief and despair. There was a dryness and I cried out in search of God and nourishment, but I felt like I was terribly alone. Instead of remaining in faith and standing on the promises inside the promised land I had already come to, I crossed the border. I again associated with the idolaters and made decisions out of self-serving motives. I remained there as Elimelech did. I also drug my family there with me. Not in such a literal sense. However, my children had experienced the change in my life with God and they also had to experience my decision to cross the borders God had placed in my life. Looking back, I can see the darkness that covered me through that time. While I did not experience the physical deaths this story holds, I did experience death in other ways. What I know today though is that it is possible to leave the lie and go back to the promise. What was waiting when I made my way back to the arms of God was peace. He covered me in grace and mercy. While there was discipline, He offered me the Redeemer in Christ. In coming home to the promised land, I have returned to the greatest love story of my life. Have you ever crossed the borders God has set in your life? Did you think the grass was greener on the other side only to discover death and destruction far beyond what you thought? Are you there today? I encourage you to examine the borders of your life today. Are you firmly planted in the promises of the promised land, or are you flirting with the idols of Moab?

He drew me up from the pit of destruction, out of the miry bog, and set my feet upon a rock, making my steps secure.

Psalm 40:2

I had been bitter. I can look back and see how it slowly took hold. One situation, one emotion, not fully faced and surrendered planted a dark seed. Without realizing it, I watered that seed and visited it quite often. As I went back and visited the bitterness, I walked a rut around it that eventually became a pit. In the process, I made decisions out of frustration and defiance which caused me to sink deeper. Eventually, I couldn't see a way out. It was as though I could only walk in circles causing a bigger rut and a deeper pit. It was miserable. The entire time I could sense God urging me to prayer, to go back to my first love, and to surrender all things to Him. I just could not see how to do that. Until I ran into a different situation. This one knocked me off my feet. I tried everything to control what I was experiencing. But I couldn't. Finally, at the end of myself, I told God I could not do it anymore. Usually, when I'm scared like that, I'm passionately loud. This time was different than anything else I had experienced. All I could do was sit, with hands raised and whisper, "God, I cannot do this." I could almost hear the Great I AM say, "duh" as He reached down and pulled me out of the pit I had dug myself. Like this verse says, God took me out of the pit and set me on a rock. The rock He set me on is not sharp and jagged. It is level and firm. He did not pull me out of the pit to yell at me or condemn me. In His infinite grace, God took me from the despair and mercifully taught me how to again stand stead in Him. He patiently held my hands as I remembered how to put one foot in front of the other and walk in faith. God did not pull me from a miry pit to set me on a shaky foundation. He has set my feet on the solid rock of His foundation. God is ensuring that my steps are secure and guiding me in not again creating a pit that is so very difficult to get out of. Have you dug yourself into a hole?

Can you not see a way out? I encourage you today to stop treading the circle of insanity. Stop and surrender the thing that began the pit, surrender all of the things that have come since then. Reach out to God and let Him pull you out of the mire. What is waiting is His solid rock.

Furthermore, you shall select out of all the people able men who fear God, men of truth, those who hate dishonest gain; and you shall place these over them as leaders of thousands, of hundreds, of fifties and of tens.

Exodus 18:21

While it appeared as though the leaders were chosen by a man, in truth, they were picked by God. He has put you in this spot because He sees your courage and boldness in Him. You are not a leader because you have it all together. You are a leader because you are a cracked vessel. It is through the cracks of your life that His light of truth shines. God will use you as a beacon of hope and love to His children. Leaders are people who should be able to be as broken as they are whole. You are that. You are complete in Christ and broken in humanity. You do not sugar coat and allow the vulnerability in your life to show in order that we may be vulnerable with you. Without even knowing it you guide in healing and harvesting. You teach the fruit of the Spirit by cultivating it in your life and actions. God is going to use you in this season to guide His people into a closeness with Him. It will not be overt and loud, but quietly, by their side. You will walk alongside them as God walks before them. There will be times of grief and victory, blessing and apparent cursing. Through the midst of it all, God will work through you in each of their lives. I pray for wisdom and strength over you in this season. I ask God to anoint your head with oil and prepare you for the greatness of being the least among us. I hope that you walk in the manner of the position to which you have been called. I speak humility, love, and direction over your mind, over your mouth and over your hands. I look forward to walking with you into the Holy of Holies.

After a little while the bystanders came up and said to Peter, "Certainly you too are one of them, for your accent betrays you."

Matthew 26:73

I have been chewing on this verse for weeks. I just cannot fully wrap my mind around it. This was Passover. All of Jerusalem would have been teeming with Jews from all over Israel. It stands to reason that the city should have had a considerable amount of Galileans. All of them would have had very alike accents. So why, in a crowd of people did she know that Peter was of Christ? My mom told me a story about being at a concert once. It was not a Christian concert, however, the woman who sat next to her told my mom that as soon as she saw her and my dad, she knew they were Christian. They were in a room full of people, all of who probably had very similar accents, yet this stranger pegged them for followers of Christ. Mom does not dress any differently than any other woman. Dad does not wear a cross around his neck. Yet still, there was something about them that betrayed them. How awesome is that! I am sure there had to be something else about Peter that betrayed him in that moment. I wonder if there is something about me, or you. When people see us, do they see Christ first? It is my fervent prayer that they do. If not, though, how do I become someone whose accent betrays me for Christ? How do I step out of my own way and begin to look like Christ instead of like Cara? I wonder if it is in spending more time with Christ. If I wake up in communion with God, study His word, talk to Him more, grow and nurture our relationship and seek Him in all things, do I begin to take on the countenance of the Lord? I know that if I do not do those things I can not look like Him, because I do not really know Him. If I am only involved with the Lord on Sunday for an hour, how will anyone ever know that we are even friends. I think the change comes when I truly allow Him to be the Lover of my soul. He begins to feed my spirit and quench the thirst of my flesh. I put on His robe and the world sees the resemblance between the two of us. They begin to see Christ before they see me. Then my accent will betray me in the way that Peter's accent betrayed him. What do people see when you walk into a room? Do they see your flesh and the world? Or do they see the reflection of your deep relationship with Christ? Does the world see you or does your accent betray you as a follower of the Lord?

And he came and took her by the hand and lifted her up, and the fever left her, and she began to serve them.

Mark 1:31

I have read Mark over and again, it is my favorite book. I am pretty sure this verse was not in there until last time I read it though! I love how the bible holds secrets until I am ready to see them. When I read this verse recently, it struck me as a beautiful image of salvation. This is what is supposed to happen, spelled out in the most simple of ways. The woman was sick, Jesus touched and healed her, then she served Him. I will never forget how amazing this was in the beginning for me. I was sick unto death, Jesus touched me and I was healed, and I served Him, without question or delay. Then I faltered. I entered a stage of remarkable grief. I would throw out a fleece instead of simply obeying. I would question what I was hearing. I let anger seep into my decision to obey and choose not to out of spite, like I was hurting God more than myself in those times. I was overcome again by sickness. This time it was of a different source. I was drowned by unforgiveness. It was deep and setting firm like a cement that was blocking everything. Though physically I was fine, spiritually it felt as though I was again on my deathbed, or at least not far from it. I didn't know I could feel like that on this side of salvation. The longer it persisted, and the deeper I felt the despair, the clearer I could see the solution. I went to an elder for prayer. As she prayed over me and spoke words of life into my spirit, I let go. I called out to Christ in the midst of that horrible pain and He took my hand. He forgave me of my spitefulness and anger and unforgiveness and in that moment of healing, I was able to offer full and real forgiveness in return. The thing that caused the grief no longer had the control to continue to cause the sickness of despair. Now, I am able to fully rise and serve Him again. It is beautiful that God does not expect us to come to Him and leave to never falter again. Instead, He wants us to know that, though we fall, He will be there still. He wants to take us by the hand and lift us up, heal us so that we can again rise and serve Him. Were you once well but have become sick again? Has the Lord ever yet taken you by the hand and lifted you up? If not, call to Him, He will be there to remove the fever of life from you.

Peace I leave with you; my peace I give to you. Not as the world gives do I give to you. Let not your hearts be troubled, neither let them be afraid.

John 14:27

Do you ever sit back and think, "What in the world is happening right now!"? It is rarely an actual question and more of a cry for understanding. That is where I am today. I am sitting in this valley of lost control. There is nothing around me that I can direct. However, there are several things that need directing. I only think they need my direction because they are troubling issues and, in truth, I am afraid. At the end of this valley is a very large life change. It will affect every single person in my family and while I know that all will work out exactly the way God's will dictates, my initial reaction is to squeeze harder and take over as director. I know that never works. I always make things so much worse. So, as the trouble and fear hit me today, I decided to take a different approach. I am going to do what the scripture says first instead of waiting until I am a ball of chaos. Crazy, I know. So, the question becomes how do I have peace inside a situation that is going to change my family? As I have said before, the bible does not say this will be easy, but God does not leave me lacking on instruction. As a matter of fact, that is why He sent the Instructor. God told me to go to Him when I am weak and weary and He will give me rest. He promised to send me His Comforter, and He did that. When I remember, when the chaos starts, I get to run to the throne room and I get to talk to God about everything in the valley. I know that when I am in the throne room, there is where I find the peace that God has promised. I don't have to control anything or understand the things. I just get to fall on my face and unload all of the burdens and God gives me His peace. Think of the boldness of that request. I am in this valley, staring at the evolution of my family and I get to ask God for His peace. In response, He gives it! To which I also think, "What is even happening right now!!". When

I stop and ask God for His peace, Holy Spirit, whom God has already given me, fills my being with the peace of the Great I AM. The result is that I am no longer troubled and I am no longer in fear. I may get to repeat this process 20 times before I really am secure in the peace offered in this valley, but God is patient and will answer 20 times. Are you sitting in the middle of the valley? Perhaps you have just entered your valley. Either way, I encourage you today, run to the throne room of our Lord. Let Him comfort you and give you His peace as you lean in to Him to endure this time.

Wait for the Lord; be strong, and let your heart take courage; wait for the Lord!

Psalm 27:14

Waiting is, by far, the hardest thing I have needed to do in my walk with Christ. It ebbs and flows like the seasons. Sometimes it is harder than others. I become impatient and frustrated with the wait. Currently I am in a season of wondering. I wonder about things that are none of my business. I become consumed with "Why them" and "When is it my turn" questions. There is this amazing time of being absolutely thrilled and so happy for the people around me whose wait in this area has completed, while at the same time, feeling this aching agony deep within of continuing in my own wait. Yet, I keep stepping forward in the waiting. I do not lose the courage it takes to walk this path I have chosen. God gave me the choice to live for Him. The choice was not to pick and choose in which seasons to live for Him. The choice is the ultimate vow of in the good times and the bad. In these seasons of wondering if He sees me, does He know, I feel so very weak. Scripture reminds me that God not only sees me, but He has strength for me. God's word beckons me closer to Him in the days when I just do not want to wait. He leads me beside the still waters. He reminds me that He is the Lover of my soul and that He will never leave me, nor forsake me. In the waiting He reminds me that the waiting is not forever. It is okay for me to have days of weakness as long as I am going to God for my strength. I always think that I do not wait well. What I am really learning in this very agonizing season, is that I am not waiting alone. God renews my strength and courage every time I go to Him. He places people on my path who are waiting on the same things and He lets us support and lean on each other. God asks me to wait, but never has He asked me to wait alone. Some days that does not make the waiting easier, however, when the waiting is over, it will have been so very worth it. Are you waiting for something? On those days when you are tired and crying and wondering when it is your turn, in that weakness, go to God. Let Him renew your strength and your courage. Do not give up. Wait on the Lord.

Give thanks in all circumstances; for this is the will of God in Christ Jesus for you.

1 Thessalonians 5:18

My daughter almost died. Not figuratively. She was at the hospital, on the operating table and statistically should not be here today. We do not serve a God of statistics though. Today it is easy to give thanks in this circumstance. I have wondered several times in the last 24 hours if I would still be able to give thanks in the grief. If we were burying her and sending our new grandson to live with his dad, would I be grateful? Could I praise the Lord if we had to tell our granddaughter that her mom was gone? I like to think the answer is yes. Perhaps the thanks would look different though. In reality, the praise looks like smiles and laughter. It resembles joyful prayer and an outpouring of gratitude for the wonder that Jehovah Rapha still heals. Maybe on the other side, thanks would look like weeping. It would be the Body breathing and walking for us while we could only lay on the floor and mourn. We would still be giving thanks; it would look vastly different. Sometimes when I read a verse like this one, I visualize only one way of doing what it says. What I know today is that the doing of the Word appears different per circumstance. Knowing what I know today, I believe that giving thanks in all circumstance will not always look like smiles and laughter. I also believe that whatever way I need to give thanks today is the will of God in Christ Jesus for me. If giving thanks looks like weeping at my child's side that is the will of God. When it looks like joyful dancing, that is also the will of God. If I am hitting my knees and crying out my thanks when I don't understand what is happening, that is the will of God in Christ Jesus for me. No matter what is going on or how it looks, I am giving thanks to God in all circumstances. What is going on in your life today? Is it chaos or peace; is it mourning or celebration. I encourage you to give thanks to God no matter what is happening and no matter how it looks. For that is the will of God in Christ Jesus for you.

And on the seventh day God finished his work that he had done, and he rested on the seventh day from all his work that he had done.

Genesis 2:2

Rest is so hard for me. Even in the night. I go to bed early, but I wake up several times and I am up super early. I am constantly on the go. I am the first in the office and the last to leave. I am horrible at letting anyone help me do things at home. I very much have an "I got this" attitude. I don't need help and I don't need to stop. Lately though, I have found that that simply is not the truth. I have entered into a new time of new habit forming. One of the habits that the Lord has laid on my heart is the habit of resting. He has been talking to me about how leaders show others how to rest in Him. Not a physical Sabbath day of resting in the Lord. Or a once a week resting. Leaders learn to show others how to spiritually rest in the Lord when their child is on the brink of death. They demonstrate rest when they are waiting on a report from the doctor that could alter the course of their life. Leaders show others how to rest in God when life is flowing like a smooth sweet river. We learn to treat every day as the seventh day because God has already finished the work. Jesus said, "It is finished." (John 19:30) For so long life has been mental and spiritual worry and anxiety and go, go, go. I have known for a long time that I am supposed to rest in the Lord. Jesus paved the way, God has already been here, it is finished, and I can rest in Him. Knowing those things and believing them are vastly different. The Word said the Lord rested on the seventh day. Nowhere does it say He went back to work on the eighth. I am not supposed to do that either. We are created to rest in the Lord. He is so sweet that He showed us how to do that at the beginning of time. Are you in the seventh day of rest today, or are you still spiritually striving to work in day six? I encourage you to stop working. The work is finished. Rest your spirit in the Lord today.

You will suffer for a while, but God will make you complete, steady, strong, and firm.

1 Peter 5:10 c

I very often wish that the suffering could just be stubbing my toe, or even something as simple as breaking my arm, or a nice, shattered leg. How wonderful would life be if suffering were only in the physical? That's not how Christ suffered though. Only hours before his physical endurance of suffering -being far worse than what we will ever face - He suffered emotionally, spiritually, and mentally. His internal suffering was so great His sweat became blood. Then came the outrageous beating. That suffering scarred Him, tore the skin from His bone, caused His face to be unrecognizable. That wasn't even the real suffering. What came next, as He hung on the cross, arms wide, willing, and lovingly, every sin for all of creation's time clung to Him. It hung from His already broken body like filth. As the sky reached its deepest darkening and the very last sin was hammered to Christ, He cried out to God. "Why have you forsaken me?" (Matthew 27:46) The deepest, most sorrowful, darkest suffering in all of time was experienced in that moment. But it was only for a while. Jesus did not continue in His suffering. When He walked out of the tomb, Jesus was complete, steady, strong, and firm. God's promises to us are fulfilled first in Christ. He has been where you are. Christ suffered mentally, spiritually, and emotionally so that you would not be the first to go through the suffering and so that you do not go through it alone. We are not promised easy. We are promised suffering. But God also promises He will make you complete, steady, strong, and firm. He did it for Christ, He will not fail to do it for you. I encourage you to suffer boldly and bravely. And remember, this is only for a little while.

And they were filled with the Holy Spirit and began to speak in other tongues as the Spirit gave them utterance.

Acts 2:4

I have said it before, but words are amazing. When you take the time to look up what you think you know, the whole meaning of what you are reading can change. In this verse the word is 'filled'. Since salvation, I have prayed that Holy Spirit fill me. What I envision is me being an empty clay pot, just going through life waiting for God to pour out Holy Spirit into me, kind of like He is being poured from a pitcher into a vessel. In Wuest's commentary of Acts he points out that it really isn't possible for us to be filled like an empty vessel because we are not empty. He says, "our hearts are a symbol of free will, the emotions and the reason of the believer". When you think on that, it is true that we cannot be empty to be filled. That being said, what is the proper translation of the word filled that is also true? In this verse the word is controlled. The verse better ready, "And they were controlled with the Holy Spirit and began to speak in other tongues as the Spirit gave them utterance." Can you imagine having that much faith and hope that when you are filled with Holy Spirit, He takes control? You say what He says, does what He suggests, and step where He says to place your foot. That is what the disciples experienced. In submitting to the control of Holy Spirit they were able to change the world and our lives. When you pray to be filled with Holy Spirit today, are you willing to be submitted to His control, or are you still hoping to be poured into like a pitcher?

For the land commits great whoredom by forsaking God.

Hosea 1:2c

I read Hosea a couple of months ago and this part stayed with me for quite a while. I think it stuck because I thought I understand whoredom. Like most things though, the more I meditated on and studied the word I realize that I really know very little. While it does mean 'to commit fornication,' Charles Stanley says the whoredom spoken of here is spiritual adultery. The people were literally cheating on God. They had left Him and gone to another. God's chosen people became pagan and vile, worshipping the created instead of the Creator (Romans 1:25). I am sure you are super spiritual and have never done something as outrageous as that. Well, I have. When anger became my master it took the place of God. When I stopped praying and reading the Word because I got too busy, life became what I worshipped instead of Him who gives life. I never considered those things as cheating on God. It was just life happening and I was unintentional about forsaking God. In order to absolutely follow Christ, I have to be intentional. I must wake up each morning and before I get out of bed decide who I am going to serve. I get to choose between whoredom by forsaking God or serving the one true King. When I am intentional to choose God, He is a good Father to discipline and remind me of where I am supposed to be aligned. When I awaken in the morning and choose God, life is abundant and full. God meets me where I am and walks with me through all of the things. I have to choose to be a faithful child to God and not act out in spiritual whoredom. What choice have you made today? Have you been walking in whoredom by forsaking God and haven't noticed the change? Are you intentional about your spiritual adultery? Or do you choose God every day with intentionality and purpose to remain faithful to our Creator?

For the Word of God is alive and active.

Hebrews 4:12 a

I understood this verse completely when I read it in 2015. My interaction with scripture had gone to this exquisite level no other book had taken me to. I read a lot. I can imagine faces and places and often get completely lost in a story. Nothing compares to the first time I read the Bible with eyes that see and ears that hear. Reading it with understanding allowed me to experience what was happening. I knew what the fruit tasted like. I saw the Sea part. I heard the army of God go before David. I could hear the Still Small Voice and feel the hunger of famine. I felt the betrayal of captivity and the aloneness in the 400 years of silence. I experienced healing, ate of the body and drank of the blood. I saw the beating, carried the cross and felt the nails. Then I watched the stone roll away and I believed the empty tomb. The scripture breathed each word over my tongue so that I could taste the essence of Truth. It danced in front of me so I could see love. The Word of God whispered the similarities of my life so that I would feel the song of Holy Spirit in my deepest hidden heart. Today I find that the same words I read in the beginning mean different things. God shows me new treasures I did not notice before. I get to experience the story in a different way because I am different. As I mature in my walk, I grow with the Word of God as it grows inside of me. The Word challenges me and inspires me to leave the place where I am at and continue on the journey laid before me. I will constantly be amazed that the thing that is the same yesterday, today and forever seems to be in constant evolution with me. The Word of God is alive and active. Every time I read it I get a new revelation of the character of God. It grows in my heart and directs my life. I do not always follow perfectly but it consistently waits for me. Each time I take a breath I can taste the newness inside of the old and I am encouraged to continue forward into the truth, love and hope that God promises in each letter. I pray, more than anything that the Word breathes in your life today.

Addresses